THE
women OF faith
DAILY DEVOTIONAL

D0167023

WOMEN OF FAITH℠

THE
women of faith
DAILY DEVOTIONAL

patsy clairmont . barbara johnson . marilyn meberg
luci swindoll . sheila walsh . thelma wells

ZONDERVAN®

ZONDERVAN.com/
AUTHORTRACKER
follow your favorite authors

ZONDERVAN

The Women of Faith Daily Devotional
Copyright © 2002 by Women of Faith, Inc.

This title is also available as a Zondervan ebook. Visit www.zondervan.com/ebooks.

Requests for information should be addressed to:
Zondervan, *Grand Rapids, Michigan* 49530

This edition: ISBN 978-0-310-32491-1 (softcover)

Library of Congress Cataloging-in-Publication Data

The women of faith daily devotional : 366 devotions / Patsy Clairmont
... [et al.] .
      p. cm.
   ISBN 978-0-310-24069-3 (hardcover)
    1. Women—Prayer-books and devotions—English. 2. Devotional calendars.
I. Clairmont, Patsy.
BV4527 .W5943   2001
242'.643—dc21   2001007124

Poem "What's a friend good for?" on page 76 is used with permission of the author. Copyright © 2001 by Ann Luna.

"Where Truth and Mercy Meet" (p. 136) by John Hartley and Gary Sadler © 2001 worship together.com songs (ASCAP). Used by permission.

"God has Come to Us" (p. 379) © 2000 Integrity's Hosanna! Music/ASCAP & Little Pilgrim Music (adm by Integrity's Hosanna! Music/ASCAP & worshiptogether.com songs (adm by EMI-Christian Music Publishing)/ASCAP. All Rights Reserved. International Copyright Secured. Used By Permission.

Published in association with the literary agency of Alive Communications, Inc., 7680 Goddard Street, Suite 200, Colorado Springs, CO 80920. www.alivecommunications.com

Interior design by Pam Eicher

Printed in the United States of America

10 11 12 13 14 15 • 24 23 22 21 20 19 18 17 16 15 14 13 12 11 10 9 8 7 6 5 4

CONTENTS

*To the hundreds of thousands
of women of faith
who've walked with us
on this joyful journey
since 1995*

PREFACE

Women of Faith has a longstanding tradition that Sheila explains at the end of every conference. She asks you to imagine that she and each of her porch pals—Patsy, Marilyn, Luci, Thelma, and I—are giving you a little gift to take home, something to remind you of the messages we've shared during the conference. *The Women of Faith Daily Devotional* is an extension of that tradition. It's a book of little daily "gifts" from us to you that will last the whole year through and, we hope, bring you fresh joy and insights as you read it again year after year.

We offer these thoughts to you hoping to lift your mood, ease your worries, make you laugh, and kindle the spark of hope in your heart each day. In these readings you'll be welcomed to join Sheila on a rare, quiet morning in the peace of her Tennessee home. You'll rejoice with Luci as she leads a former atheist in his first prayer. You'll be encouraged to clean your closet with Thelma—and do it *cheerfully*. On another day, you'll spontaneously splash into the surf at Laguna Beach with Marilyn, fully clothed! I know you'll love the lesson Patsy teaches in her "panic-button approach" to housecleaning, and I hope you'll giggle as you read about my ridiculous super-glue nightmare.

Like all gifts of love, these little essays didn't always come easily. *You* just try being profound, uplifting, and memorable in fewer than three hundred words! Those of us who love to talk (and that would certainly include all six of us) have trouble getting our point across within such limits. We usually spend more than three hundred words just saying hello! The struggles we faced in trying to be succinct reminds me of that remark by one ancient writer who said, "If I had had more time, I would have written less."

That's where our editor, Traci Mullins, and her sharp eye (and even sharper editing pencil) came in. She trimmed our rambling thoughts, sharpened our focus, and herded our 366 daily readings into one concise, carefully organized book that flows smoothly through the twelve monthly topics: Hope, Prayer, Friendship, Wonder, Grace, Joy, Freedom, Humor, Vitality, Trust, Gratitude, and Peace.

While we're saying thanks to Traci for helping us put together this gift to you, let's not forget two other people we constantly acknowledge as God's gift to us. Steve Arterburn, the founder of Women of Faith, had the foresight to realize that women all across the continent longed for the kind of nurturing, uplifting, *fun* experience these conferences provide. Mary Graham, the president of Women of Faith, is our coach and our companion, our sounding board when frustrations arise and our soft landing when things go wrong. We're crazy about Mary, not only because she is a gracious leader and a tireless motivator, but also because she slips us candy during the day to keep up our energy! To you, Steve and Mary, we say thank you—not only for being such an essential part of this organization, but also for being our dear friends.

Finally, I hope you'll indulge me in a personal word of thanks to the entire Women of Faith family—and to *you*. As this book was being put together, I had to undergo surgery and subsequent chemotherapy to treat a malignant brain tumor. Throughout this ordeal, thousands of you Women of Faith friends filled my mailbox with get-well wishes and flooded heaven's gates with prayers on my behalf. What a blessing it has been to have you with me during this difficult journey. And what a relief it is now to be nearing a complete recovery. So from the bottom of my heart—and from the empty part of my brain where the tumor used to be—*thank you!*

Barbara Johnson

Hope

May integrity and uprightness protect me,
because my hope is in you. –*PSALM 25:21*

Hope is a beautiful thing. Like a flower that thrives on sunlight and water, hope relies on the daily sustenance of the Word of God, of prayer, and of experience shared with others who have received the gift. Hope is an elusive bird to those who have no relationship with God or reservation in eternity. Hope requires more than simply clicking red shoes or crossing our fingers. It is a sweet and magnificent benefit of walking with Christ. Hope looks at all that is true about the present, lifts the circumstances of life into the tender, loving hands of God—and exhales in trust. Hope makes it possible to live with our feet firmly planted on earth while our hearts and minds are committed to a vision of life that is far bigger than we are.

A new year is like the fresh, crisp page of an untouched journal. We lift our pen to the first day. This year will hold unexpected joys and sorrows, moments of faith and fear, wishes fulfilled and dreams abandoned. There is much we do not know. But there is much we do know with absolute assurance. We know that God is in control and that his heart is good and merciful toward us. We know that we are not alone. We know that everything that happens in our lives and in the lives of those we love has already passed through our Father's hands. And we know that we are loved.

Sheila Walsh

Ripping into the Gift of Another Year

In the morning, O LORD, you hear my voice; in the morning I lay my
requests before you and wait in expectation. —PSALM 5:3

The first of the month has always been my own personal holiday. I just love ripping the old month off all my calendars and starting fresh on a whole new page. How wonderful to look at those clean, fresh, unblemished squares representing days I haven't messed up yet! And if you think I enjoy throwing away the old month, just imagine how much I love celebrating a whole new *year!*

God has given us measurements of time so we have some perspective on our lives. Think how hopeless we would feel if we were stuck in some stressful situation and thought it would never end. But God gives us a new morning—a new month, a new year—to start over again and again. With each new start we lift our voices heavenward, laying out our hopes and prayers. Then we "wait in expectation," as the psalmist said, to receive the gifts and blessings—and, yes, challenges—God has planned for us.

Whatever comes, we know he will be there with us, throughout the day, throughout the night, and as we begin afresh tomorrow. Without him, our lives stretch out to a hopeless end. With him we have the endless hope of a heavenly tomorrow.

Father, thank you for giving me a fresh,
new start every day, every year. Amen.

Barbara Johnson

Anchored

We have this hope as an anchor for the soul, firm and secure. It enters the inner sanctuary behind the curtain. —HEBREWS 6:19

The word *anchor* is used like this only once in the New Testament. The context of Hebrews 6 underscores the impact of each word of verse 19. What is "this hope" that the writer to the Hebrews speaks of? It is the hope that when God gives his word, he cannot lie. In verse 17 we read, "Because God wanted to make the unchanging nature of his purpose clear to the heirs of what was promised, he confirmed it with an oath." When a person swears an oath, the solemn affirmation of the truth of his or her words is anchored loosely in human imperfection. But when God makes an oath on his own name, it is immovable and unshakable. It is firm. It is anchored securely in his flawless character.

The writer goes even further by saying that our hope enters "the inner sanctuary behind the curtain." *The New International Version Bible Commentary* tells us: "That little room symbolized the very presence of God, but people were not allowed to enter it. But hope can. The Christian hope is not exhausted by what it sees of earthly possibilities. It reaches into the very presence of God."

Christian hope has nothing to do with what is going on in this world. Our hope penetrates right into the holiest place, the inner sanctum of God's presence, where it anchors itself to Hope incarnate.

*Almighty God, thank you that you are not like imperfect
human beings who break their promises. As I place my hope
in your solemn word, I can enter the very throne room
of heaven and anchor myself in you. Amen.*

Sheila Walsh

New Year's Commitment

Commit your way to the LORD.
—PSALM 37:5

One of the most reflective times for me is the start of a brand-new year. It wakes up excited anticipation for the days to come.

I don't make New Year's resolutions. No! I have learned that my best intentions collapse into an early grave by January 15. I have been resolving to lose thirty pounds by the end of the year for the past thirty-six years. Baby, *please*. I have resolved to be completely out of debt by the end of the year. Yeah, sure. Every time I make that my goal, I see something else I "need" within twenty-four hours.

But there is one promise I have been able to keep from year to year: My commitment to grow closer to the Lord. A personal reminder of my commitment is under the glass cover on my desk.

Instructions for a New Year

Devotion—

Devote yourself to prayer, being watchful and thankful. —COLOSSIANS 4:2

Wisdom—

Show wisdom by your good life, by deeds done in the humility that comes from wisdom. The wisdom that comes from heaven is first of all pure; then peace-loving, considerate, submissive, full of mercy and good fruit, impartial and sincere. —JAMES 3:13, 17

Blessings—

I will bless the LORD at all times; his praise shall continually be in my mouth. —PSALM 34:1

Bless the LORD, O my soul; and all that is within me, bless his holy name! Bless the LORD, O my soul, and forget not all his benefits. —PSALM 103:1–2

Now those are New Year's resolutions I *want* to make!

Lord, I commit my spirit and my life to you,
in Jesus' name. Amen.

Thelma Wells

The Paste of Hope

Though he slay me, yet will I hope in him.
–JOB 13:15

Job's amazing resolve first attracted my attention many years ago, before I had any experiences in my life that would allow me to fully understand it. Sometimes after years of faithfulness, Christians suddenly find themselves greatly tested and in deep distress, seemingly without reason. We may have terrific battles with doubts, fears, and unbelief, feeling God doesn't care about our problems. I know all about it. My husband was badly maimed in a devastating car crash, two of our sons were killed, and another son was estranged from us for eleven years.

But through it all, I have learned that God has a special purpose in withholding immediate relief. He faithfully uses even our most heart-wrenching experiences to fine-tune us for his glory. I have seen this happen in my own life and in the lives of countless others.

God knew Job's heart. God knew Job would cling to him no matter what. Similarly, we must hold fast to God, allowing our afflictions to not break or embitter us but to push us closer to the Father. I like to say my heart is *wallpapered* to God, never to be separated or torn away. The wallpaper paste that holds me there is hope.

Dear God, my life is in your hands. I will hope in you alone,
no matter what. Amen.

Barbara Johnson

It Is Well with My Soul

May the God of hope fill you with all joy and peace as you trust in him,
so that you may overflow with hope by the power of the Holy Spirit.
—ROMANS 15:13

Horatio Spafford waited a long time for a son. He had four girls before his baby boy was born. His family was complete. He was a successful attorney in Chicago and life was good. But his baby son died, and that tragedy was quickly followed by the Great Fire, which wiped out everything he had.

One of Horatio's friends was the preacher Dwight L. Moody. Moody was holding a crusade in London, and Horatio decided to send his wife and daughters to England for a few weeks to lift their spirits.

It took twelve minutes for the ship they were on to go down. All the girls were lost. His wife sent a two-word telegram: "Saved alone."

Horatio boarded another ship to join his wife. As he reached the point in the ocean where the vessel carrying his daughters went down, the captain joined him. "This is where your daughters lost their lives," he said.

"No," Horatio replied. "This is where their real lives began."

He then took a piece of the ship's stationery down to his cabin and wrote,

When peace like a river attends my way,
When sorrow like sea billows roll
Whatever my lot thou hast taught me to say
It is well; it is well with my soul.

Horatio was a man who had found God so faithful in the past that even as he stared into the cold waters of the North Atlantic, the peace of Christ flooded over him.

Lord, because of you I overflow with hope eternal.
Amen.

Sheila Walsh

What If I Mess Things Up?

My purpose will be established, And I will accomplish all My good pleasure.
—ISAIAH 46:10 NASB

Take a minute and reread those astounding words from the book of Isaiah. Now read the equally astonishing words which follow in verse 11: "I will bring it to pass. I have planned it, surely I will do it" (NASB).

When my friend Judy Hampton was seventeen, she was pregnant and single. In a hastily arranged service she and the baby's father, Orvie, were married. She says in her book, *Under the Circumstances*, "I was convinced our future would be . . . hopeless. We were two teenagers with only ten dollars between us and a baby on the way." From a human viewpoint, the future looked bleak for this young family. But God's purpose was not thwarted by the circumstances they faced. They suffered tremendously as they grew through the hard times, but today both Judy and Orvie are vibrant Christians whom God is using to point the way to Jesus. God certainly accomplished his good pleasure in them.

God doesn't say that he will accomplish his purpose if we go off and get pregnant, take drugs, or get a divorce. He simply says, "I will do it." The "it" he intends is that we come to know him personally, and he can use anything— *anything*—to establish his purpose. His ultimate purpose is that we come to know Jesus so that when we enter the gates of heaven God can say, "See . . . here you are. I have accomplished all my good pleasure."

Lord Jesus, my hope for this life and the next is found only in knowing you. Thank you that I cannot do anything to mess up your perfect plan to bring me into your kingdom. Amen.

Marilyn Meberg

Slathered in the Spirit

Charm is deceptive, and beauty is fleeting; but a woman who fears the LORD
is to be praised. —*PROVERBS 31:30*

Given a choice, we all have something we would change about ourselves—
the length of our nose, the shape of our toes, the width of our hips, the fullness of our lips, the color of our eyes, the tone of our thighs, the style of our
tresses, the size of our dresses. Our culture scurries to accommodate us with
lotions, creams, surgeries, exercise equipment, lenses, and diet plans. We, in
turn, stretch, slather, starve, and subject ourselves to rigorous routines in hopes
of shaping up. Why, today, with the zap of a laser, one can be glassesless, hair-
less, lineless, and chinless (for those of us over our chin limit).

I am afraid if a surgeon started to nip and tuck me, by the time he finished I'd look like I'd been smocked. (Relaxed skin runs in my family.)

I tried to use a tanning bed to add a little color to my life, but I was rejected
at the salon because of my bleachlike complexion. Then I tried to schedule
an appointment for eye surgery so I could eliminate glasses from my wardrobe,
but, alas, I didn't qualify for that either.

To soothe my disappointment I indulged myself with a pedicure ... and
developed an infection. I spent the next two weeks soaking my sore toe.

Maybe Mrs. Proverbs 31 had a point about this beauty business. I think I'll
put my hope in fearing the Lord instead of in "shaping up."

Lord, I want to be beautiful in your sight. Slather me in
your Spirit, soften my heart, and firm up my faith. May I be
taut in my resolve to please you alone. Amen.

Patsy Clairmont

hope

Save the Children

Train a child in the way he should go.
—PROVERBS 22:6

The 'green pastures' are the minds of children," Mr. Phillips said. Now that grabbed my attention. I met this remarkable man when I visited India with the international relief organization World Vision. The three-time president of the YMCA in Kerala, Mr. Phillips believes that if you can reach the open minds of children and teach them moral values, interactive skills, and the knowledge of Jesus Christ, you can change the world. If one child's powerful spirit can persuade his alcoholic father to stop drinking and become a responsible parent, or if one child can convince her mommy that she is loved, such a child can literally change the course of a family, and of the world.

Forty thousand children attend Vacation Moral School in India. The program's theme is "Let us build a new world." Multilingual workbooks teach biblical principles through stories, with Scripture tactfully tucked in to prick the spirits of young students of all religions, sects, and classes.

Mr. Phillips wrote:

We have seen the face of hunger
And have shared a meal
We have felt the anguish of homelessness
And given a roof
We have heard the cry of children
And promised a future
We have seen the darkness of ignorance
And lighted a lamp
We have touched the wounds of the sick
And got them well
We have held the hands of the dying
And instilled strength
We have heard the voice of despair
And provided World Vision.

The results could be the same in America. Think about it!

Father, give me a sense of urgency to teach the children your principles
so they can help arrest the downward spiral of their world. Amen.

Thelma Wells

Thou Shalt Achieve

Whatever your hand finds to do, do it with all your might.
–ECCLESIASTES 9:10

In St. Mary's Church in Rye, England, this poem was found mounted in a dusty old frame in a dark corner:

Upon the wreckage of thy yesterday,
Design the structure of tomorrow.
Lay strong cornerstones of purpose, and prepare
Great blocks of wisdom cut from past despair.
Shape mighty pillars of resolve, to set
Deep in the tear-wet mortar of regret.
Work on with patience, though thy toil be slow,
Yet day-by-day thy edifice shall grow.
Believe in God—in thine own self believe—
All thou hast desired thou shalt achieve.

There are days when achieving seems impossible. We are barely surviving, much less accomplishing anything. Is life really worth it on those days? This poet must have thought so. He determined to plow ahead in spite of the fact that life was hard.

I often wish life weren't hard. In fact, I keep thinking I will run across a Bible verse that reads "...and it'll be easy." Call me collect if you find it!

Although God did not promise us ease, he did promise his presence in the middle of our difficulty. There is great hope in that promise! Knowing that God is near helps me to keep plowing that hard soil—to keep building resolution out of regret, wisdom out of pain, and strength out of sorrow.

Take God at his word. Believe in yourself. Stand tall and embrace hope with all your might. Little by little things will change—and you will achieve the desire of your heart.

Father, my hope is built on your righteousness. In myself I don't
have what it takes to stay strong. Empower me with your strength. Help
me today to continue working with patience. Amen.

Luci Swindoll

It's Up to God

The LORD delights in those who fear him, who put their hope
in his unfailing love. —PSALM 147:11

One hot July afternoon, a friend and I were stuck in traffic on a southern California freeway. We were talking about our children.

"I can't believe how defiant Christian can be at times," I said. "He is such a wonderful boy, but every now and then a malevolent stranger invades my son's clothes."

My friend laughed. "Wait till he becomes a teenager!"

I asked her how her son and daughter were handling life as teens in the new millennium.

"Not well at the moment," she admitted. "My son, in particular, is struggling. He won't come to church or have anything to do with spiritual things."

"How do you cope with that?" I asked.

"Pretty well," she said with a smile. "I believe my children are on God's timetable, not mine. I pray for them and love them. I have instilled the Word of God into their hearts since they were very small. Now it's up to God."

I thought about how happy my friend's response must make our Father. What she exhibits is not a careless attitude toward her children but a simple, pure faith in the only One who can transform a human heart. It is an act of faith to look beyond the what is to the what can be. Today we can place our hope not in what we see, but in the unfailing love of God.

*Father, there are so many things that are uncertain today,
so I place my hope in you alone. Thank you for being in control
of all things. Amen.*

Sheila Walsh

Resurrection Power

Though you have made me see troubles, many and bitter, you will restore my life again. –PSALM 71:20

A story in my hometown newspaper recently reported a glorious resurrection. A church built in 1910 had been near collapse—its facade warped, its walls bowed, and its steeple blown off years before. But after a decade of bake sales and charitable donations, major reconstruction began in 1996. A volunteer crew took off the church roof, hung cables through the structure, and with winches bolted onto the cables, pulled the building back into shape. Today it gleams with new hardwood floors, a fresh pine ceiling, state-of-the-art geothermal heating, and stained-glass windows. Even the hundred-year-old pump organ was restored.

This was the church my father began pastoring in 1946. For me there is a sweet and personal history associated with that church. I was baptized there, and my faith in Jesus was deepened there. And that restored pump organ was the one upon which Mrs. Farr struck many a wrong note as we all pretended not to notice. (I didn't always pretend not to notice.)

I am gratified by the restoration of this dear old church but sobered by the reality that everything and everyone ultimately falls into a state of disrepair. My parents who once faithfully served there experienced the inevitable demise of health and life. Now my own body walls are showing signs of deterioration, and my facade is fading fast. Thus far, however, my steeple hasn't blown off.

There is nothing constant in this life except the God who authored life. He alone restores my soul and pulls my inner life back into place, even as the rest of me begins to buckle.

Lord, my only hope is in your resurrection power.
Amen.

Marilyn Meberg

Choose Your Focus

Many are asking, "Who can show us any good?" Let the light of your face
shine upon us, O LORD. —PSALM 4:6

When I was eighteen years old my sister, Frances, had a principal part in the operatic version of Johann Wolfgang von Goethe's play, *Faust*. I, as a young idealistic evangelical, was horrified that my very own flesh and blood would take part in depicting the story of a man who sells his soul to the Devil for time and youth. I went to the opening night with my mother simply because my filial loyalty was slightly greater than my self-righteous indignation.

I was struck by that presentation. The opening line of the play is a book in itself: "A man sees in the world what he carries in his heart." It reminds me of Paul's admonition to the church at Philippi: "Finally, brothers, whatever is true, whatever is noble, whatever is right, whatever is pure, whatever is lovely, whatever is admirable—if anything is excellent or praiseworthy—think about such things" (Philippians 4:8).

We have a daily choice to fill our mind and heart with the wonder of who God is, or to be pulled down by a fascination with the darker things in life. It is not always easy to recognize a deal with Satan. Our culture has a million subtle ways of leaking lies into our hearts and yanking our allegiance away from the kingdom. But our hope lies in what we carry in our heart. Will we choose to keep our focus on the shadows or turn toward the light of God's face?

*Lord Jesus, let the light of your face shine on me today
so I can see your goodness. Amen.*

Sheila Walsh

Satan Is a Wimp

Your kingdom is an everlasting kingdom, and your dominion endures through all generations. –PSALM *145:13*

There are two forces at war in this world and in our minds: good and evil. Evil expresses itself through pride, arrogance, rebellion, greed, retaliation, devious schemes, hatred, jealousy, manipulation, selfishness, control, blasphemy, addictions, and every act against the perfect will of God. Good expresses itself through love, joy, peace, patience, kindness, goodness, faithfulness, gentleness, and self-control.

Amazingly, we have the power and authority as children of God to deter the forces of evil from working in our lives. Evil will attempt an attack, but God has given us weapons to fight against evil and win!

According to 2 Corinthians 10:3–5, "though we live in the world, we do not wage war as the world does. The weapons we fight with are not the weapons of the world. On the contrary, they have divine power to demolish strongholds. We demolish arguments and every pretension that sets itself up against the knowledge of God, and we take captive every thought to make it obedient to Christ."

Furthermore, we have everything we need to demolish evil when we put on the full armor of God (Ephesians 6:12–20). We need to be clothed every day with:

The Belt of Truth
The Breastplate of Righteousness
The Shoes of Readiness
The Shield of Faith
The Helmet of Salvation
The Sword of the Spirit

Seems to me that Satan is a defeated wimp.

Father, thank you for your absolute victory over the Evil One.
I am more than a conqueror through Christ Jesus,
so I need never lose hope. Amen.

Thelma Wells

Keeping Hope Alive

And the prayer offered in faith will make the sick person well;
the Lord will raise him up. –JAMES 5:15

Ever been to one of those walk-in emergency clinics? I took Mary Graham once when she was nauseated, pale, weak, and beginning to look more like a cadaver than my vibrant friend.

But guess what? Everybody ahead of us was worse off than she. From behind her curtained partition we heard, "Gimme a shot, I'm dying over here!" One of the nurses asked a guy how he got that spike in his cheek. (We parted the curtain on that one.)

Fear. Pain. Cries for help. The cacophony of need was all around us.

The doctor finally came and determined an IV drip would put my little dehydrated Mary back on her feet. But I'll tell you, before we got that simple diagnosis, I was wondering if she'd ever be well again. She was one sick woman!

At times like that, our primary ally is hope. We can't change what is, we don't have answers, and we feel scared and alone. Without hope, the picture is bleak, which is why I love James 5:15. See that part about "the prayer offered *in faith*"? That's the hope part. When our loved one is sick, we keep hope alive by praying and believing the best for that person. God makes the final determination regarding healing, of course, but in the meantime hope gives us courage. Mary needed the healing that day; I needed the courage.

What is your need today? Cry out to the Lord in faith. He will "raise you up" with hope.

Lord, thank you for granting me courage to face
the unknown with hope rather than despair. Amen.

Luci Swindoll

Just the Rehearsal

*If only for this life we have hope in Christ, we are to be pitied
more than all men.* –1 CORINTHIANS 15:19

Late one night as I waited for the elevator in the lobby of my hotel, I saw a friend standing with her back to me. I hadn't seen her in ages and was so glad for the opportunity to say hello. We hugged and chatted about the day. Then she asked me if I had heard her news.

"What news?" I asked, looking into her eyes for some sense of what she was about to tell me.

"I'm pregnant," she said. That kind of news is usually followed by screams of delight—but not if you and your husband carry a rare gene that makes it impossible for your child to reach his or her first birthday.

They had already buried a child. They had taken every precaution to make sure this would never happen again, but they conceived anyway. My friend had already undergone testing, and this baby would be born with the same rare illness that had claimed their first daughter.

We wept together. But even as I saw her anguish, I was struck with the peace and grace that rested on her. "If this life was all we had, I would have no hope at all," she said. "But this is just the rehearsal for our real life."

That is our hope as we stand in hopeless places. We look beyond the pain of this broken world to the place where there will be no more tears. We are not people of a human lifetime, we are people of eternity.

*Father, thank you that though this life is at times streaked
with tears, my eternal hope is in you. Amen.*

Sheila Walsh

It's Dark in Here

There is surely a future hope for you, and your hope will not be cut off.
—PROVERBS 23:18

Jonah rode the vomit wave to shore. What an outlandish story! There are those who believe that the story of Jonah and the whale is a myth, a tall tale, a fable. But Jesus referred to it in all seriousness, implying that we too are to take it seriously. Not only do I take that story seriously, I'm encouraged by it.

Jonah disobeyed God's instruction and ended up in the belly of a whale. It was a terrifying experience: dark, seemingly hopeless. Jonah saw no possible solution for his predicament. But he prayed, repented of his disobedience, and was instantly delivered.

Have you ever had a whale-belly experience? It is dark, terrifying, and you can't imagine how you will survive it. You may have been swallowed unexpectedly, and not only have you not been disobedient, you have prayed and not been delivered. So what do you do? You continue to pray and wait. You don't give in to despair because the God of all victorious outcomes has promised you a future hope—a hope that even a dark whale belly cannot snuff out.

Whether we end up in a whale belly because of poor choices, disobedience, or just swimming in the wrong place at the wrong time, God promises that he will deliver us out of our trouble if we will call on him (Psalm 50:15). Now that is a fact we can swallow.

Lord, strengthen my faith and encourage my spirit.
It's dark in here. Amen.

Marilyn Meberg

Bony People

Do not be wise in your own eyes; fear the LORD and shun evil.
This will bring health to your body and nourishment to your bones.
—PROVERBS 3:7–8

I have osteoporosis, which means my bones are brittle. So don't squeeze the stuffing out of me with a hug or try to shove me out of line at the soft-serve concession stand. I might disintegrate into a pile of bone fragments, and those are hard to sweep up.

And sweeping up was the job God gave Ezekiel. Actually, he shared my problem: dry bones. The difference is Ezekiel had a valleyful while mine would fit in an urn. The prophet's predicament caught my interest as I read Ezekiel 37, since I wanted to know if he found a cure.

The first thing I noted was that the valley of bones portrayed a picture of God's people, the Israelites. They had a dandy case of osteoporosis, leaving them spiritually brittle. The condition came about as they lost their hope. The Israelites believed they would never come together again as a nation or see God's covenants fulfilled, so they began to shrivel in spirit.

My doctor encouraged me to take brisk walks, ingest calcium with vitamin D and magnesium, and do weight-bearing exercises to combat my condition. I'm working diligently to obey, but sometimes my enthusiasm shrivels. It just seems as though fighting this predicament involves more effort than results. My hope for physical agility seeps out as I measure my future by the lack of visible gain.

Oh, wait. I get it. Whether it is physical or spiritual brittleness, hope is the key. No hope, no health.

Talk to you later. I'm going to take a walk!

Lord, I depend on you alone for wisdom, health, and strong bones!
Amen.

Patsy Clairmont

Hope All Day Long

Show me your ways, O LORD, teach me your paths;
guide me in your truth and teach me, for you are God my Savior,
and my hope is in you all day long. —PSALM 25:4–5

I love quiet mornings. They are rare, so I treasure them. We live in the lush green countryside of Tennessee that is still undisturbed by the clamor of life in the twenty-first century. Every now and then I'm the first one up, and I take that first wonderful cup of coffee to the sunroom. I curl up in my favorite chair that knows me so well it has committed my shape to memory, and I let the quiet of a new morning soak into my soul. On days like this I am acutely aware of God's presence. I can sit for an hour without speaking a word, simply enjoying being with him or quietly lifting every concern, every loved one, every task for the day, into his care. I am filled with hope.

Most mornings, however, are not like that. I usually wake to that familiar cry, "Mom!" Some mornings our cat, Lily, saunters in before the sun has begun its ascent. She crawls over my face and settles on my head like an oversized ski cap. Most mornings begin with noise, with rush, with schedules to be kept. This is my life. And probably yours too.

The challenge for us is to hope in God every day—*all day long*. When the noise all around us seems deafening, we *can* find a quiet place inside our soul and remember God. In him our hope is steadfast and sweet.

*Teach me today, Lord, to remember you in all the moments
and the places of this day. You are my hope. Amen.*

Sheila Walsh

No Need to Worry

The Spirit and the bride say, "Come!"
—REVELATION 22:17

In an article in a recent *Jews for Jesus* newsletter, Zola Levitt states, "There's something about the Holy Land, Jerusalem, and especially that empty tomb that shows us that we need not sorrow over anything, even death."

Reading that article reminded me of the time Vikki, my firstborn, and I went to the Holy Land. We stood upon the Mount of Olives where we could recognize Islamic graves on the side of the mountain because they had both a headstone and a footstone to keep out the evil spirits. We thought of the one great stone that was supposed to secure the grave of Jesus. Yet on that Easter morning, when the stone miraculously rolled away, Jesus rose with all power in his hands, showing that he had conquered both evil and death.

With streams of joyful tears running under our chins, Vikki and I looked over to the place of Jesus' ascension and thought about his return to that very place. We rejoiced in the knowledge that one day the trumpet of God shall sound and the dead in Christ shall rise, and those who remain will meet him in the air. The Jerusalem we saw that day will be no more. But the New Jerusalem will exist forever because the Lord promises "a new heaven and a new earth" and a "new Jerusalem" (Revelation 21:1, 2).

Those of us who know him personally will never die. Our hope is eternally secure. There is no need to worry.

Lamb of God, thank you for hope everlasting. Please help me prepare for the day when we will be together without end. Amen.

Thelma Wells

Flying with Angels

Give thanks to the LORD, for he is good; his love endures forever.
—PSALM 107:1

We frequent fliers love to exchange stories about the loudmouthed ogre we sat by on the airplane. Every once in a while, however, a stranger settles into the seat beside us and touches our hearts.

My friend Sue had been accompanying me on the Women of Faith tour and also spending as much time as she could helping her sister, who was battling cancer. The sister, who is single, traveled to medical centers throughout the Southwest seeking treatment, and Sue usually flew to be with her in the hospital. It was an exhausting schedule, and on one of her flights home to Florida Sue dropped into her seat too tired to even acknowledge the woman beside her.

Only as the plane was descending did they speak. Sue was reading one of my books, and the woman commented that someone had given her the same book when her husband was hospitalized. "It got me through a bad, bad time," she said.

Sue answered, "That's where I am now."

The woman told my friend, "Well, don't give up. No matter what." She told Sue the doctors had urged her to hurriedly summon their family when her husband's condition deteriorated. "Three different times the doctors said he couldn't live through the night," she said. "It was awful."

"So . . . what happened?" asked Sue delicately.

"He's picking me up today," the woman said brightly. "That was three years ago."

Sue watched the couple embrace as the passengers deplaned. And she whispered a prayer, thanking God for seating her beside an angel of hope.

Dear God, thank you for sending me ordinary people
as angels of hope and mercy. Amen.

Barbara Johnson

Lights, Camera, Action!

For the LORD is good and his love endures forever; his faithfulness
continues through all generations. —PSALM 100:5

Last night I spoke at a high school honor society induction. I loved watching the students file in, each senior paired with a junior. The seniors carried lit candles on the way in, and the juniors carried them on the way out—the passing of the torch. I wondered as they walked by what great things were in store for these kids. These particular young people had not only done well academically but also were contributors to the community, heading up projects to assist the needy and our environment.

I wondered where the camera crews were to record the next generation's successes for the evening news. I thought, *Let's share this good news; let's tell a hurting world, "Hang on, help is coming."*

Many young folks today are inventive, articulate, caring people in pursuit of a more compassionate world. I'm not saying they have it all together; what generation has? We live in a deeply flawed society. But just when we wonder how things can go on as they are, God shows up, and we see the bright light of a new generation. I guess we shouldn't be surprised when the psalmist tells us God's faithfulness is to *all* generations.

So the next time the evening news tries to convince us that all is bleak, that our children are all criminals and have no values, visit your local schools and find out what the kids are doing. I think you'll be impressed. Hey, try volunteering. Maybe you will be the one to fan the embers of genius and compassion in some young soul.

Holy Lamplighter, may I follow your example and
place my hope in your endless goodness. Amen.

Patsy Clairmont

January 22
A Way Out of the Valley

I . . . will make the Valley of Achor a door of hope.
—HOSEA 2:15

When a gal in Washington started a support group for wives of men who are struggling with homosexuality, she named the group Door of Hope based on God's encouraging promise in the book of Hosea. The Valley of Achor was an isolated region of wilderness where a man named Achan was stoned to death. Achan's name meant "trouble," and that's exactly what he caused for the Israelites. As a result he was killed in that remote and gloomy valley.

The story is harsh, but surely it is recorded in Scripture so that we understand the bigger message: God has promised to transform our troubles into a doorway of hope. Members of that Washington support group gather to help each other remember that promise. Those who have grown through their pain enough to feel the sunlight of hope shining through the clouds reach back to nurture the women who have recently landed in a dark, harsh place.

In life there will be valleys. But we know we grow best there, because that's where the richest soil is. The next time you are stuck neck-deep in "fertilizer," grasp God's hand, feel yourself growing stronger . . . and keep your ear attuned for the sound of a door of hope opening just ahead.

Dear Father, you walk with me through the valleys and hold
me up in my misery. Thank you for promising to lead me ever onward
toward that glorious door of hope! Amen.

Barbara Johnson

Don't Suppose

All a man's ways seem right to him, but the LORD weighs the heart.
—*PROVERBS 21:2*

In the book of Exodus there is an obscure verse that reads, "Moses supposes his toeses are roses, but Moses supposes erroneously." Now if that doesn't make you think, I don't know what will.

All right! I know it is not a real Scripture, but maybe it should be because it suggests an important principle about God's character. When we live out of a supposition as Moses did in this little tongue twister, we are in trouble. Our behavior is based on an assumption, and nothing in God's nature assumes. Everything he is and does and offers is intentional. He never supposes.

For example, today I am having computer problems and I suppose they will last forever. It is like being broke and assuming I will never have money again, or sick and thinking I will never be well again, or discouraged and believing I will never be carefree again. But if I think like that for long, life isn't fun anymore. It feels too hard and I begin believing my erroneous judgment is more reliable than God's Word. I forget that God is always at work on my behalf.

The test in your life today is part of God's plan. You may not like it. You may want to throw in the towel. But God is using it to grow you up. Don't suppose for one minute he doesn't know what he is doing.

*Father, help me this day to remember your ways are better
than my ways, no matter how I feel. Remind me of your truth,
Lord, because sometimes I suppose erroneously. Amen.*

Luci Swindoll

Picture This

God had planned something better for us.
—*Hebrews* 11:40

Today I met a neighbor whose photographs are displayed in area restaurants. I was delighted to make his acquaintance because I love playing photographer, but I know little about cameras. Mine is a point-and-shoot that has adjustments you can choose to use, but I rely on programmed settings. During our visit, I was hoping to learn a few things from an expert. And I did.

He has a point-and-shoot too! And he has only been a photographer since he retired. Once a high school coach, he was amazed to learn while photographing a family vacation that he had an artistic eye. Today folks beat a path to his door, wanting to view and purchase his work.

This photographer was as pleased about the discovery of his gift as a kitten over a warm saucer of milk. And he's not the only one. I was smitten with his framed photograph of pink-and white-striped desert flowers. In his hall hangs a shot of autumn trees graced in a sheer veil of early snow. And his photo of cacti showered in sunlight and shadows is a study in light and dark.

We never know what God has for us. Today a waitress, tomorrow CEO of our own company. Today a schoolteacher, tomorrow a watercolorist with a one-woman show. Today a corporate professional, tomorrow a shepherdess. Don't ever think your story is over until the fluffy lass yodels (or something like that).

Lord, help me to stay focused while you develop the film.
Amen.

Patsy Clairmont

Failing Successfully

My grace is sufficient for you, for my power is made perfect in weakness.
−2 CORINTHIANS 12:9

I find it interesting that many outstanding companies *expect* their employees to experience more failures than successes. The corporate thinking is that talented, energetic, and creative people who continue trying (and failing) will eventually also succeed. The company's leaders want to know who's out there energetically failing and succeeding because those are the people who will prove most valuable to the organization. I have a feeling God may rather like that kind of logic.

The reason I believe that might be God's mind too is because if I were to take that business philosophy and apply it to my spiritual experience, I'd have to admit I learn more from failure than from success. Being crushed and melted in God's refinery has caused me to lean more fully into him than success ever has. And as I look back on my failures I see his loving and healing hand in them all. I also see him lifting me up and prodding me on.

Scripture speaks repeatedly of the failures of many of God's people. Abraham lied in a pinch; David had a wandering eye and a murderously scheming heart. Yet in spite of their failures Abraham was called the friend of God and David was described as a man after God's heart.

Broken persons who fail seem to win the heart of the Father. But that description seems to fit everyone, doesn't it?

Lord, I don't want to live in fear of my inevitable failure but
in anticipation of your expert refining. Thank you that my hope
is not in my performance but in your redemption. Amen.

Marilyn Meberg

Hiding on the Leeward Side of God

We who have fled to take hold of the hope offered to us may be greatly
encouraged. We have this hope as an anchor for the soul, firm and secure.
—HEBREWS 6:18–19

Men and women have gone to sea since ancient times, and sailing vessels
have changed in amazing ways over the centuries. The earliest seagoing boats
were little more than hollowed-out logs, while some of today's ships are gigantic floating cities. Once sailors navigated by the stars; now they position themselves with the aid of satellites. In the beginning, boats moved only by
manpower, then sails harnessed the wind, and next coal and petroleum entered
the picture. Today, some ships move by nuclear power.

An ancient mariner would surely be at a loss with all the high-tech gadgets that allow modern ships to sail the oceans. But there is one nautical necessity that has remained basically unchanged since the first voyagers put to sea.
Thousands of years ago, and still today, no ship sails without an anchor.

Without an anchor, there is no respite from the winds. No way to flee
the waves and hide on the leeward side of an island when storms enrage the
sea. No way to hold firm to a position and stay secure in safe harbor.

The apostle Paul said hope is our anchor that holds us firm and secure to
God and his promises. Hope shields us from the winds of adversity. Hope
anchors us in safe harbor on the leeward side of God.

Dear God, when life's storms threaten to cast me adrift,
I drop anchor in your love, take hold of your promises, and
am greatly encouraged. Amen.

Barbara Johnson

Don't Push the Button

But the pot he was shaping from the clay was marred in his hands;
so the potter formed it into another pot, shaping it as seemed best to him.
—JEREMIAH 18:4

It all started when I named a file in my computer "Patsy." I realize that was a little vain, but I had run out of creative titles for my endless documents. When I finished with the file, I wanted to toss it out, which requires a simple press of a button. But that's when the plot thickened. I told my machine to erase the file, and it inquired, "Are you sure you want to send Patsy to the recycle bin?"

Some days I'd yell, "Yes, send the old girl to the bin; she's getting on my last nerve!" But this wasn't one of those moments, and I found it difficult to push the button that would blast "Patsy" to smithereens—or wherever computers ship their discards.

Had the machine asked, "Are you sure you want to send Patsy to the spa?" I'd have pushed that button. Or, "Are you sure you want to send Patsy to see her grandson, Justin?" Trust me, I'd personally pack her bags. But the discarding permanency of the computer's question troubled me.

Then I remembered a story in the book of Jeremiah when the prophet visited a potter's house. The craftsman had made a pot that was marred, so he decided to remake it (not discard it) into a different pot that pleased him.

I'm marred; how about you? Any cracks in your pot?

I've learned that the pressure in our lives often becomes the reshaping technique God uses to make us more pleasing. And, good news, he doesn't discard his own. Ever.

Lord, in your faithful molding I place my hope forever. Amen.

Patsy Clairmont

Stick with Me, Lord!

My hope is in you.
—PSALM 39:7

What a nightmare I had the other night! In my dream, I was trying to open a little tube of Insty-Stick Super Glue by poking it with a pin. The tube was slick, and I was grasping it tightly when suddenly the end popped open and glue spurted all over my hands!

I quickly grabbed a paper towel—and of course instead of wiping the glue off, the paper towel got stuck to my hands. I wasn't thinking clearly at that point and hurried to the sink to wash off the mess—and promptly got my right hand stuck to the faucet! Wouldn't you know, the phone rang just then. I fumbled as I snatched it off the hook—understandably, since I had to stretch all the way from the sink where my hand was stuck. I guess I got glue all over the phone, because the next thing I knew, my left hand was stuck to the phone, and the phone was stuck to my head! Thank goodness I woke up at that point, before I managed to permanently weld any other kitchen fixtures to my body!

For a long time I've said that *hope* is the glue that plasters my heart to God. My dream reminded me of how intractable that bond must be. Hope is not like the Post-It note adhesive that can be easily pulled away. Hope is the Insty-Stick Super Glue that coats us with God's tenacious presence forever.

Oh, Jesus! I cling to you with all my heart, with
all my mind, with all my strength. Keep me
hopelessly stuck to you today . . . and always. Amen.

Barbara Johnson

Not at Home

Our citizenship is in heaven.
—*Philippians 3:20*

If we feel totally at home on this earth, totally at ease with its atmosphere, we are totally misguided. This earth is not a safe place, and it is not our real home. That doesn't mean there aren't many earthly beauties and pleasures, but in our appreciation of all there is to enjoy here, we must always be wary. Why? C. S. Lewis put it well when he said, "Satan, like a good chess player, is always trying to maneuver you into a position where you can save your castle only by losing your bishop."

There are times when I forget that I live in enemy territory. Sometimes I enjoy my earthly trappings so much that my heavenly hope seems far away and even diminished in its necessity. It often takes pain, injustice, or sickness—in short, my raw human need—to jerk me back into reality. Then I remember that Jesus said, " In the world you have tribulation" (John 16:33 RSV). Oh yeah . . . watch your bishop.

Do I live my life, then, in paranoid dread and fear? Just the opposite. I live my life in hope and confidence. Why? Because he has overcome the world and gone to prepare a place for me. A home. My real home. Forever.

Lord God, remind me daily that my citizenship is in heaven and my hope is in your victory over the enemy of my soul. Amen.

Marilyn Meberg

Sweet Homegoings

If we died with him, we will also live with him.
—2 TIMOTHY 2:11

We have got it all wrong, folks. When a Christian dies, we are supposed to celebrate!

I have attended some sweet homegoings in my life. Family and friends were sad and lonely, of course, but powerfully comforted because they knew the person was not "lost" just because he or she had left this earthly life. We usually say someone has "passed," we have lost them, their life ended. But these words are so final and offer little hope! The Word of God says that those who have died in Christ are absent from the body but *present with the Lord.* Hallelujah!

Many Scriptures refer to death as "sleeping." When Lazarus was dead for four days, Jesus told Mary and Martha that their brother was sleeping. Mary was sure that if Jesus had only come earlier, Lazarus would not have died. But he said to Martha, "I am the resurrection and the life. He who believes in me will live, even though he dies" (John 11:25). And he restored the sisters' hope and proved his power over death by "waking" Lazarus with a single bold command.

Just as Jesus resurrected his friend Lazarus, one day he will call *our* names and we will arise to live forever. When I sleep in death, I insist that my family celebrate because though I'll be absent from my body, I'll be present with my Lord. I know my loved ones will cry because they miss me, but they know I am going home, and my "passing" will be sweet.

God of Resurrection Life, how I marvel at the blessed hope that when I leave this world, I pass from life to life! Amen.

Thelma Wells

Let Your Face Sparkle

Be strong and take heart, all you who hope in the LORD.
—PSALM 31:24

I am not an alien!" my son announced one morning over breakfast.

"I'm so glad, darling. Now eat your eggs."

"Do you want to know how I know I'm not an alien?"

"Absolutely," I replied.

"Well, when E.T. is happy, his heart glows through his skin."

"What happens when you are happy?" I asked.

"Watch," he said. Slowly a mischievous grin spread across his face till his eyes shone. "My face sparkles!" he announced gleefully.

I thought about that all day. I wondered what my face communicates to my son, to others around me. I see a variety of emotions wash across my boy's face every day, bringing shadows or sunlight.

We each have a choice: to be a blank sheet of paper, left to the mercy of the pen of the day's events, or to be settled in heart and mind that God is in control of every moment and to rest in that good news. The latter decision requires faith and resolve. Hope then becomes an action word. It moves from a crossing of the fingers and hoping for the best to a bold stance of reliance on God.

We don't know what this day will hold, but God does. We don't have the strength to face every unexpected heartache, but God does. So let your face sparkle!

Dear Father, today I rest in the fact that you are absolutely sovereign. I thank you that I can find all the hope I need today in you. Amen.

Sheila Walsh

Prayer

God has heard your prayer.
—ACTS 10:31

Have you noticed that the Bible is packed full of prayers? From Hannah's pleadings for a child, to Nehemiah's petitions for a nation, to Jesus' intercession for his people, to John's prayers for the churches, Scripture is crammed with prayers.

Note the different places people pray: mountaintops, altars, roadways, prisons, thrones, pastures, deserts, stables, palaces, sickbeds, ships, and a whale's belly. Isn't it comforting to know that we can pray wherever we are, and God hears us? Whew!

Take Joseph or Paul. Both were thrown unjustly into prison yet emerged wiser. When you add injustice to the inhumane conditions of incarceration, their situations should have been the perfect breeding ground for bitterness. I'm sure what kept Joseph's and Paul's faith fervent was their prayer lives. Prayer softens hearts and makes the impossible possible, the degrading tolerable, the haughty humble, and the future hopeful.

You would think, knowing this, that we would be on our knees from sunrise to eventide. Or at least we would be like Daniel, who conversed with God three times a day. But I confess some days I barely squeeze in grace and goodnight prayers.

How loving that God would hear the content of our hearts, speak individually to us, and give us his mind. And do I ever need his mind! Mine is too little, fragile, and limited to understand how to process life's ups and downs or to know the next step to take. Besides, I need the reminder that somebody way bigger than I am is in charge. Double whew!

Patsy Clairmont

Prayer 101

Lord, teach us to pray.
—LUKE 11:1

If one were graded on one's prayer life, I think I'd nearly flunk. Never have I not believed in prayer, and never have I not wanted to increase as well as enrich my prayer life. I simply don't do it well. The study of Scripture excites me, and I dive into it easily and readily. The discipline of prayer, however, mystifies me and, more often than not, eludes me. What's my problem?

I've asked myself that question numerous times. Perhaps the problem is partially my lack of discipline. To be devoted to prayer requires a willingness to be still, to focus on who God is in all his majesty as well as in all his compassion and love for me—his squirming, easily distracted creation. Focusing on God takes time. For reasons that obviously are not valid, I often don't take time. The result? A woman tearing around tossing prayer balls toward heaven in the erroneous hope she's "praying without ceasing."

In *Into the Depths of God*, Calvin Miller writes, "Those whose prayers are unending monologues make themselves a giant mouth while making God a small ear." How's that for a depressing description of my prayer style?

In Matthew 14:23 we read that Jesus sent the multitudes away and "went up on a mountainside by himself to pray." I guess that's pretty clear, isn't it? Maybe I don't need to flunk Prayer 101 after all.

*Lord God, may I willingly quiet my heart as well as my environment. I
want to hear a voice other than my own. Amen.*

Marilyn Meberg

February 2
"Dear God . . ."

Hear my voice in accordance with your love.
–PSALM 119:149

Many years ago I had occasion to talk about spiritual things with a Ph.D. who was an avowed atheist. Although he had little or no interest in God, he was curious about a person like myself (educated, traveled, happy) whose whole life revolved around personal faith.

"Luci," he asked, "what makes you think there is a God? How do you know he's out there?" Good questions.

"Well, for one thing," I said, "I pray. I talk to him."

We continued to visit for an hour or more as this man genuinely tried to understand the reasoning behind my belief system. A new softness was reflected in his eyes and voice as our conversation deepened. Eventually, I asked if he'd ever prayed. He said he hadn't. Not once in his thirty-seven years had he ever talked to God.

"Would you like to?" I asked.

"Well, I'll try. I'll pray if you pray first." .

It gave me such pleasure to address God as my Father—the One who loves me unconditionally and invites me to call upon him. At the conclusion of my short prayer I heard a contemplative sigh and then these words:

"Dear God . . . I know you are not familiar with the sound of my voice but. . ." My friend went on with one of the sweetest, most sincere prayers I've ever heard. It touched me deeply that this brilliant man admitted he was a stranger to God—yet his awkwardness did not keep him from praying.

Knowing God well is not a prerequisite for communication. The words "Dear God. . ." are only the beginning of knowing him better.

Thank you, Father, that you hear my voice with a heart of love. Amen.

Luci Swindoll

A God Who Listens

As a mother comforts her child, so will I comfort you.
—*ISAIAH 66:13*

I call my mother every Sunday and we catch up with each other's news. One Sunday in February of 2001 stands out. After we had chatted for a while, I asked her what kind of week it had been for her. "This could have been a rough one," she answered.

"Why, Mum?"

"It was the fortieth anniversary of your dad's death."

"I'm sorry, Mum. I should have remembered."

"No, you shouldn't. Anyway, it was a wonderful time."

I asked her what she meant.

"I realized I had a choice to make," she explained. "I could mourn the loss of Frank or I could celebrate the years I've had with the three of you. I decided to celebrate God's goodness to me in my children."

I was moved by my mom's simple act of faith.

When my dad died, my sister was five, I was three, and my brother was a baby. Mom prayed two specific prayers: She asked God to let her live long enough to see us grown and independent, and to woo us into a relationship with Christ when we were young. God honored those prayers. We had little money, yet each of us went to college. We lived in a country where only 2 percent of the population believed in God, and yet all three of us committed our lives to Christ before we were twelve.

Family life is rarely picture-perfect. Things happen that we hadn't counted on. But we can count on the fact that God is a loving parent who comforts us and listens to our prayers.

Father, thank you for "mothering" me as only you can do.
Amen.

Sheila Walsh

What's "Normal"?

But you are a chosen people . . . a people belonging to God.
    −1 PETER 2:9

For years I prayed that the Lord would make me normal. Today that prayer makes me giggle. I wonder if the Lord chuckled too.

Have you ever met anyone "normal"? (Besides yourself, of course.) Most of us like to think we're sane regardless of how frayed our threads might be. We all long to be exceptional yet fear that even on tiptoes we wouldn't measure up to "normal."

C. S. Lewis quipped, "If God had answered all the silly prayers I've made in my life, where should I be now?" I too have prayed a lot of immature prayers, and I thank the Lord he didn't oblige me. I remember when I was housebound with agoraphobia, I told God that if he could just make me normal enough to get to the grocery store and home again, that would be enough. Imagine, I could still be in Piggly Wiggly's searching for sea salt and would have missed the privilege and joy of becoming a seasoning in the world.

In my emotionally wrought twenties, I prayed that God would change my husband's heart, and he did, but not in the way I anticipated. I thought God would convict Les of some of his insensitive ways so he would treat me with greater understanding. Instead the Lord began to work on me! And then an even funnier thing happened. Because Les's behavior was often in response to my poor attitudes, when I changed, he changed as well.

The Lord hears our silly prayers, our self-absorbed prattling, and our disjointed ruminations. Then he answers us in merciful ways.

Thank you, Lord, for hearing past my words and
giving me what I really need. Amen.

Patsy Clairmont

February 5
Prayers of a Passenger

Yet give attention to your servant's prayer and his plea for mercy,
O LORD my God. Hear the cry and the prayer that your servant
is praying in your presence. —2 CHRONICLES 6:19

A lot of folks say they pray most fervently when they're riding with a bad driver! That reminds me of a story I heard about two little old ladies who were out for a drive in a large car. They were both so short their heads were barely visible above the dashboard.

As they were cruising along, they came to a red light, but they just went right on through it. Soon they approached another intersection, and the light there was also red, but the car didn't stop. After the car rolled through a third red light, the old woman in the passenger's seat shrieked to high heaven: "Mildred! Did you know you just ran through three red lights? You could have killed us!"

"Oh, my stars!" Mildred exclaimed. "Am *I* driving?"

We all have times of stress and terror in our lives that send us shrieking to God for comfort and mercy. That's when we need to remember who is "driving" in our life. Thank heaven it's not Mildred!

Lord, help me be constantly aware of your expert and faithful
presence at the wheel of my life. I know you will guide me in the
ways that lead not to fear but to heaven. Amen.

Barbara Johnson

What Fragrance Are You Wearing?

For we are to God the aroma of Christ among those who are being saved
and those who are perishing. —2 CORINTHIANS 2:15

When we opened the closet door in the Ambassador Hotel in Chennai, India, we recognized a familiar smell. It was the same smell that used to be in the closets at my house when I was a little girl. This smell always accompanied spring cleaning. It got in your nostrils as well as your clothes, and it stayed until you aired out the clothes in the fall.

We noticed the same smell in the hotel room bathroom, coming from the drains in the floor and sink. It was such a part of the "ambience" that we soon got accustomed to it.

My curiosity drove me to ask why mothballs were a part of the aesthetics of this hotel. Silly me! I should have known. They were used as deodorizers to camouflage the more uncomfortable odors. Frankly, the mothballs didn't kill the stench; they just made it easier for us to deal with.

It is a wonderful thing that a child of God never has to use anything to camouflage her fragrance. There is a sweet, sweet fragrance that flows from the heart and soul of a Christian who regularly spends time in the company of the Lord. That fragrance never fades in or out of season. Her aroma is always welcoming and calming even in the dankest surroundings. She can walk into a room and fill it with the sweet aroma of Jesus.

What fragrance are you wearing? Refresh your life today with the perfume of the Holy Spirit.

Spirit of God, infuse me with the fragrance of Christ Jesus.
Amen.

Thelma Wells

I Can Fix That!

Be joyful in hope, patient in affliction, faithful in prayer.
–*ROMANS 12:12*

My motto is, "I can fix that!" You name it and I'm pretty sure I can fix it. If your toilet is stopped up or your child has a fever, if your roof is leaking or you sprained your ankle, I'm your woman! I love a challenge. I am the official family "assembler." Whenever something needs assembling, I attack it like a vulture hovering over a carcass. But my apparent competence is constantly fighting with my God-reliance.

My first thought in most situations is not prayer, it is "What could I do?" God is busy with all the incompetent people, I reason, so I'll try to take care of my life first, and if I somehow fail I'll bring the situation to my Father. I am learning to repent over my arrogance! The fact is, there is nothing I can do apart from God. I do know that; I just like to help.

Paul calls us to be faithful in prayer. Faithful means committed, disciplined, constant, and loyal. I wouldn't dream of going out of the house without my clothes on, but I often don't think twice about facing life naked of spiritual armor. Paul was writing to a church in perilous times, encouraging Christ's followers to be joyful, patient, and faithful. It would require a choice. So it is with us. Today we will face situations we believe we can handle and those we know we can't. Whatever we face, may we choose to lift all our moments to God in prayer.

Dear Father, today I offer my life to you. In all the places of my ability and helplessness, I ask you to be present in Christ's name. Amen.

Sheila Walsh

February 8
Desires of the Heart

Ask and it will be given to you.
—MATTHEW 7:7

My husband and I were on our way to a Christmas party at the Ziglar home when I thought, *I sure would like to sing "Sweet Little Jesus Boy" for Zig tonight.* My thought became a little prayer.

Near the end of the evening of great fellowship, food, and festivities, we began to sing Christmas carols. Zig asked, "Thelma, do you know 'Sweet Little Jesus Boy'?" I caught my breath and said, "Yes, I do." Then he asked me to sing it. As I did, tears glistened in Zig's smiling eyes, and when I finished, he said that Christmas was now complete for him.

What a joy to have your heart's desire answered so quickly! God does give us the desires of our hearts—IF those desires are in line with his perfect will for our lives. God is not a bellhop who answers our every whim. He is the sovereign God Almighty who places desires that honor him in our hearts and then opens ways for his perfect will to be done.

So, when you don't immediately get the desires of your heart, remember that God knows exactly what he's doing. He knows your motives; he knows what's best for you; and only he knows his own perfect will and timing. Don't get upset when he doesn't answer the way you want him to. He's the Boss!

Sovereign God, thank you that all the desires you put
in my heart are for your glory. Teach me to discriminate between
your holy will and my own wishes, and to be satisfied when
you answer, whatever the answer is. Amen.

Thelma Wells

No Number Necessary

In the same way, the Spirit helps us in our weakness. We do not
know what we ought to pray for, but the Spirit himself intercedes for
us with groans that words cannot express. —ROMANS 8:26

One of my favorite lines from the delightful movie *The Straight Story* is,
"What's the number for 911?" Sounds like the kind of question I would ask
during one of my brain blips.

The magic number that activates an emergency system first connects the
caller to a dispatcher. If all is working with the computers, there appears on
the dispatcher's screen the telephone number and address from which the call
is coming. The police, fire department, and paramedics are hooked into the
dispatcher's line and are able to hear the caller as well. In the event I should
call 911 in a state of panic and not remember my phone number or address
(I've been known to forget both while not even in a crisis) the dispatcher
will know where I am because the address is right there on his screen. Help
will be sent immediately.

There have been times when I didn't know how to pray. I didn't have the
words; fear and panic were all I knew. But I don't have to know how to pray!
I don't even need to have words to approach the God of the universe. He
knows where I am; he knows my precise condition; and he sends help immediately. Because his Holy Spirit lives in me, I have a direct line to the One
who is always listening for my faintest cry for help.

Thank you, God, that you know where I am,
what I need, and how to help. Amen.

Marilyn Meberg

Swing

Praise the LORD, O my soul.
–*PSALM 104:35*

I love to step out of the rhythm of the world into the rhythm of the wind as I sway back and forth on a porch swing. I say "a" swing because I no longer have one of my own. I swung it into oblivion. *Sob.*

A person is deprived if she doesn't have her own prayer swing. It is a dear place to talk to God because the swinging helps to quiet noisy thoughts and comfort bruised emotions while the rhythmic creaking aids in keeping one focused. A porch swing is downright spiritually medicinal.

Yes, I know we can pray anywhere, but to converse with a backdrop of songbirds is so pleasing. And when the sunlight skips across your face and warms you as you swing, well, it is reassuring.

Sometimes I pray with my eyes open and watch the sunflowers turn their faces toward heaven. I wonder if they are praising him too. I watch the butterflies skitter and imagine them celebrating the new day and the sweet gift of nectar.

I too thank him for my days. I am grateful he has given me many. His generosity makes me want to rise up and join the butterflies in dance! And the nectar of his presence sweetens my soul. It lifts my spirit as I join the psalmist: "I will sing to the LORD all my life; I will sing praise to my God as long as I live. May my meditation be pleasing to him" (Psalm 104:33–34).

Where do you pray? Ever try a swing? (I've requested a new one.) I love to step out of the rhythm of the world and turn my face toward heaven.

I praise you, Lord. I bless your holy name.
Amen.

Patsy Clairmont

Home on the Radio

Ask for whatever you want me to give you.
—2 CHRONICLES 1:7

Lily Tomlin once said, "All my life I wanted to be somebody; I just wish I had been more specific." Don't we all? But, I can tell you where being specific makes all the difference in the world: when talking with God. He invites us to ask for whatever we want!

Before I became a member of the Women of Faith speakers' team, I used to speak solo, traveling around the country to different events. In the summer of 1994 I was invited to a Bible camp overlooking lovely Lake Okoboji, Iowa. I landed in Minneapolis in pouring rain, rented a car, looked out on burgeoning five o'clock traffic, and wondered why I had ever agreed to this. *Oh Lord,* I prayed, *it would be helpful if I felt a bit of homeostasis right now. I'm pretty nervous about the drive ahead of me, with uncertain weather and tricky directions. So would you just give me a "touch of home" . . . something to calm my nerves? Thank you.*

Then I flipped on the radio. Guess what? Right there on KTIS I heard the voice of my brother, Chuck, on his national program *Insight for Living*. He was talking about his childhood—our older brother, Orville, our mom and dad, and me. Wow!

I can't tell you what that did for my spirit. Immediately I felt better and more at peace.

God is so creative and tender in how he answers our individual prayers. Call on him today and find out for yourself.

> *Lord, help me remember that you are always in charge.*
> *Your answers to prayer are specific and personal*
> *and perfectly timed. You don't make mistakes! Amen.*

Luci Swindoll

Prayed into Being

For the eyes of the Lord are on the righteous and his ears are attentive to
their prayer. —1 PETER 3:12

In the 1800s a man known as Pastor Gossner devoted his life to spreading
the gospel to foreign lands. Working untiringly and praying continually, he
gathered resources to send nearly 150 missionaries into the mission field,
directly supporting twenty of those missionaries himself. He was an amazing
prayer warrior who stepped out in faith, always expecting God to make a way
for him to spread the Good News to those who needed to hear it. In an eighty-
six-year-old book, I recently found this inspiring passage from the eulogy
shared at Pastor Gossner's funeral: "He prayed up the walls of a hospital and
the hearts of the nurses; he prayed mission stations into being and missionaries into faith; he prayed open the hearts of the rich, and gold from the distant lands."

Reading those lines, I thought what a thrill it would be to work in a hospital or a school—or anyplace!—that had been *prayed* into being. How com-
pelling it would be to work for God after first having my heart filled with faith
through prayer. What an honor it would be to know that someone somewhere
prayed for help—and *I* showed up!

The very idea that *I* might be an answer to prayer is enough to send me
to my knees! How about you?

Oh, Father, use me! Fill me up and send me out. Put me anyplace where
I can share your promises and restore hope to a hurting heart. Amen.

Barbara Johnson

The Gift

For it is by grace you have been saved, through faith—and this not from yourselves, it is the gift of God—not by works. –*EPHESIANS 2:8–9*

I remember in the fourth grade when Dixie Delmar quit sharing my Almond Joys with me because she "gave up candy for Lent." She didn't seem to have any comprehension of why she was making such a gigantic sacrifice, and stared longingly at my weekly treat.

Sometimes when we're not careful with our reasons behind traditions, sacrificing some personal pleasure is more or less yet another human effort to merit the sacrificial death of Jesus. Scripture is clear that the only appropriate way to respond to Christ's unmerited favor is with prayerful awe and gratitude. Only as we accept his no-strings-attached gift of salvation do we begin to understand that this incomprehensible blessing is based solely upon God's love and not on our faltering self-discipline or, worse, our efforts at self-purification.

I find that celebrating the unmerited love of Jesus by observing the forty-day period of Lent preceding Easter with focused prayer and meditation is soul enriching and spirit inspiring. In so doing, the whole Easter season becomes more personally meaningful.

To that end I have been reading Henri Nouwen's Lenten readings in *Show Me the Way*. As I meditate on Nouwen's reflections, I am moved to a sweet reverie of who Jesus is and what he did for me. To rest in the profound freedom his suffering bought for me without attaching any self-effort is to truly receive what God means to offer: the free gift of himself.

Lord Jesus, I bring you nothing; in return you give me everything. Amen.

Marilyn Meberg

Valentine's Bear

Yet he was merciful; he forgave their iniquities and did not destroy them.
—PSALM 78:38

Lesa, my youngest, thought she had gotten away with forgetting to get her four-year-old daughter a Valentine's Day goodie. On Valentine's morning, Alaya asked Lesa where her gift was. Lesa left the room briefly, rummaged around in her bedroom until she found a little stuffed bear that she'd given her husband the previous year, rearranged the bear's hat and ribbon, blew off the dust, wrote a little card for her daughter, and presented it to her.

"Yeah, Momma," Alaya said, "that's what I'm talking about!"

When Lesa's friend and pastor picked Alaya up from school that day, Alaya reported, "Prophetess, my mama gave me the same bear for Valentine's Day that she gave my daddy last year. But I didn't say nothing, 'cause I didn't want to hurt her feelings."

Can you imagine a four-year-old compassionate and thoughtful enough to not want to hurt her mama's feelings because she knew what her mother did was intended to make her happy? How tender it would be if we responded the same way to people when they are doing their best to help us, care about us, listen to us, and give us advice—even when we haven't asked for it. If we would just accept others' best intentions and respond with tender loving care, there would be more peace in the kingdom of God on earth.

If being compassionate and accepting of others' humanity comes hard for you, spend some extra time in the presence of Jesus today. Ask him to fill you up with his tenderhearted love. That's the kind of prayer he loves to answer.

Father, teach me to have empathy and concern
for the feelings of others. Amen.

Thelma Wells

Rise and Shine

But I cry to you for help, O LORD; in the morning my prayer
comes before you. –PSALM 88:13

I am not a morning person. I'm always amazed to discover that it is time to get up, and I wear that stunned look until lunchtime.

I have, however, become a much more realistic person in my forties than I was in years past. For decades I waited to become so spiritual that I would jump out of bed in the morning with a psalm on my lips and an offering in the pocket of my pajamas. I used to confuse being "used by God" with innate spirituality. I was busy serving God; therefore, I reasoned, I must be close to God. I now know that, for me, that reasoning is obtuse. I can be busy in "God's work" and miles away from him in my heart.

Knowing my very human and sinful heart, I follow the example of the psalmist by crying out to God in the mornings. I am constantly praying for myself, my marriage, my son, and the people I meet across the country who long to know God in a deeper way. I have also learned to come before God in the morning as an act of love and discipline. If I were to wait for the appropriate emotions to bring me to my knees, it would be a long wait. I am busy and distracted, pulled in so many directions. I have never been as aware of my need for God as I am these days. So in the *morning* my first words are to him.

Father, today—this morning—I lift my heart and
my life to you. Guide me in all my ways. Amen.

Sheila Walsh

The Book by My Bed

Those who are wise will instruct many.
–DANIEL 11:33

Whether you are a new Christian or a seasoned believer, it is helpful to find a favorite book on the subject of prayer. We each need a handy reference that teaches us how to establish and maintain a deep prayer life. Since prayer is the lifeline between the children of God and their Creator, it behooves us to get all the counsel we can regarding this intensely personal practice.

The book that has helped me the most is *Prayer—Finding the Heart's True Home* by Richard Foster. Foster examines every kind of prayer imaginable— simple to radical—while sharing a tremendous amount of wisdom. I keep his book beside my bed, and every time I read it I learn something new about how to find the closest relationship possible with the One who hears my prayers.

I encourage you to search for a book that will enhance your own prayer life. Keep it close by; read from it often. Use its instruction to bring you into ever-deeper communion with your heavenly Father. Pray all the time, and make it a habit to listen with all your heart for his voice. Be like Brother Lawrence, who urges us to "make a private chapel of our heart where we can retire from time to time to commune with Him, peacefully, humbly, lovingly."

Take my word for it: Ten minutes spent in prayer will be the most important ten minutes of your entire day.

Blessed Savior, lead me to wise instruction that will help me know you better. Reveal new avenues that lead me into your nourishing presence, and give me ears to hear your voice. Amen.

Luci Swindoll

Your Presence Is Requested

Do not be anxious about anything, but in everything, by prayer and petition, with thanksgiving, present your requests to God. –*PHILIPPIANS 4:6*

Do you have a favorite prayer? My grandmother repeated the same grace at mealtime throughout my growing-up years and probably her own (she lived to be ninety-seven). Her prayer was predictably dear, even stabilizing. She also taught me "Now I lay me down to sleep," when I was a little girl. I still recite that prayer on occasion.

Some prayers (The Lord's Prayer, the Serenity Prayer, Psalm 23) have made lasting impressions on many of us. The Bible teems with prayers; in fact, a best-selling book recently has acquainted countless individuals with Jabez's prayer in 1 Chronicles 4:10, and it has been added to their spiritual arsenals.

Many folks prefer stream-of-consciousness prayers while others are more methodical. I fall somewhere in the middle. I appreciate well-written prayers, especially when they help me articulate my feelings. But I am also grateful for full-heart access to the Lord in which I can stumble and even grumble my way through my prayers. I find it healing to pour out my concerns to the only One who ultimately can do anything about our jagged-edged world.

Whatever your style, whatever your pose (standing, sitting, kneeling), whatever your timing (morning, noon, night, all of the above), may the open invitation to come into the presence of the God of the heavens fill you with relief, awe, and gratitude.

Lord, thank you that you lean close to hear my prayers when
you already know my heart. I can hardly grasp that you would
desire conversation with me. May I remember not
to do all the talking lest I miss your loving responses. Amen.

Patsy Clairmont

Prayer Posture

Pray continually.
—1 THESSALONIANS 5:17

On the way from the hotel to the convention center for a Women of Faith Conference, I asked Braylin to pray with me. She immediately said that we did not have time for her to stop driving so we could pray. I assured her that we could pray while she was driving. She didn't know people could pray while doing anything else! Braylin thought you had to stop, get on your knees, fold your hands, and close your eyes.

Many people may be under the impression that there is a certain posture required for prayer. Well, there is. But it's not a physical posture; it's a condition of the heart. True prayer can only be accomplished when your heart is pure—that is, seeking God's will, and doing so in the name of Jesus. The only reason God hears our prayers is because Jesus is the mediator between God and sinful humankind. If you have placed your trust in Jesus, you can boldly walk into the presence of God and converse with him as your Father and friend! And the "conversation" of prayer is simply your heart's sincere desire, whether expressed or unspoken. So even if you don't say a word, God will hear your prayer. And he will answer you.

What assurance there is in knowing that a living God will come to your rescue, speak peace to your soul, provide for you, heal damaged relationships, comfort you, protect you, heal your spirit, guide you in decisions, and so much more. When you pray, you have got the keys to the kingdom, and your faith unlocks the door.

God, thank you for listening continually so I can
pray anytime, anywhere. Amen.

Thelma Wells

Is That You, Lord?

Speak, LORD, for your servant is listening.
—1 SAMUEL 3:9

Lily Tomlin says prayer is when you talk to God—not to be confused with schizophrenia, which is when he talks back. Now, you probably don't agree any more than I do that "hearing" God categorizes us as schizophrenics. But what does it mean to say God talks to us?

Certainly we know of a few unbalanced persons who have claimed to hear from God and as a result quit their jobs, packed up their belongings, and headed for the hills to avoid the predicted doom due to fall upon all of civilization. Assuming, however, that we are of sound mind, does God really talk to us? Of course. He talks to us clearly through his Word, the Bible—the revelation of himself to all creation. But what about his "still small voice" within? Does he communicate to us that way? Can we really hear him? I say yes.

In addition to hearing from God through Scripture, I experience what I call "holy nudges." He has often nudged me in a direction I had no intention of going, prodded me to talk to a person I would never have noticed, or prompted me to send money to a worthy effort not usually in my "tithe Rolodex." I love this about God because I know when the nudge is unmistakably from him. How? I would never have thought of it myself!

I've come to trust God's nudges (which feel almost like hearing), and my plumb line for that trust is Scripture. When I feel nudged in the direction of anything contrary to God's Word, I figure I've had too much chocolate.

Lord, may I never be deaf to your nudging voice.
Amen.

Marilyn Meberg

WWJD?

*The Spirit of the Lord is on me, because he has anointed me to preach
good news to the poor. He has sent me to proclaim freedom for the prisoners
and recovery of sight for the blind, to release the oppressed,
to proclaim the year of the Lord's favor.* –LUKE 4:18–19

What Would Jesus Do?" Frankly, I'm a bit disconcerted as to why so many
folks seem baffled by this popular contemporary question. WWJD? I've discovered what I believe to be the truth: Jesus would faithfully perform according to God's Word.

We are told that we are judged by every word that comes from the mouth
of God. If that's the case, then when we are trying to figure out what Jesus
would do in a situation, we should go to Jesus for the answer! Jesus is the incarnate Word of God.

The question is not really that complicated when you think about it.
Everywhere you look in Scripture, Jesus was performing God's Word. As we
seek his will in prayer today, he will remind us of the truths from Scripture
we have stored in our hearts. He will point us to himself. And in Jesus' name
we will be enabled to shed light where there is darkness, give good news to
the lost, offer kindness to the brokenhearted, comfort those who mourn, bless
with praise instead of contempt, and love others as we love ourselves.

The next time you want to know "What Would Jesus Do?" pull out the
reference book of God's Word and ask God to help you follow the instructions!

*Teacher, you have made my path so simple I sometimes miss the
point. Help me to depend on the clarity of your Word for answering
my every question. Amen.*

Thelma Wells

Praying at Heaven's Gate

Pray continually; give thanks in all circumstances, for this is God's will for you in Christ Jesus. *—1 THESSALONIANS 5:17–18*

David Livingstone is considered one of history's greatest explorers. Born in Scotland in 1813, he was one of five children in a poor family that resided in two small rooms. His parents were poor in earthly wealth but rich in spirit, and they inspired their son to devote his life to serving God and his fellow-man. Livingstone began working in the cotton mills at age ten and continued there for many years, eventually earning enough money to put himself through college, where he studied medicine and theology.

He spent most of his adult life exploring Africa, bringing "modern" medicine and God's Word to its remotest regions. He was the first person to cross the continent from east to west and the first white man to see Victoria Falls. He planted missions, spread the gospel, and endured incredible hardships. In doing so, it is said that he added a million square miles to what was then considered the known world—and hundreds, maybe thousands, of souls to the heavenly rolls.

He was showered with accolades for his work. But the thing about David Livingstone's life that most touches my heart is the way he died. Early on the morning of May 1, 1873, he was found dead, kneeling beside his bed. While doing God's will, praying alone in a remote African hut, he was lifted up by God's own hand and surrounded by the heavenly host singing a glorious "Amen!"

Lord Jesus, I come to you in prayer because I know
that is your will for me in Christ Jesus. In all circumstances,
I trust you to lift me up by your own hand. Amen.

Barbara Johnson

prayer

Court Favorites

The LORD has heard my cry for mercy; the LORD accepts my prayer.
—PSALM 6:9

Do you suppose God answers the prayers of Prescilla Nitcap more readily than he does yours? (Perhaps Prescilla's piously pursed lips imply a greater depth of spirituality than those lips that tend to run loosely.) Does God have court favorites? Are there some who have more influence at the throne of grace than others?

The answer to Jesus' prayer in Gethsemane can quickly answer those questions. When Jesus, feeling all of his humanity, prayed that his Father spare him from the suffering and death to come, God's refusal clearly had nothing to do with the merit of Jesus. It had everything to do with the preordained role of Jesus and God's intent to redeem the world. Jesus was indeed a "court favorite," but there was a higher purpose intended for Jesus and the world that required a no to his passionate prayer.

Because of Jesus' obedience and death on Calvary, salvation became available to everyone who trusts in Christ. Now all of God's redeemed are court favorites! Therefore, when our prayer is not being answered as we wish, we can be reassured that God has a higher purpose—not that we must practice pursing our lips.

Lord, thank you that you hear and accept my prayers, not because of my "piousness," but because of your passionate, perfect love. Amen.

Marilyn Meberg

Lost Power

For thine is the kingdom, and the power.
–MATTHEW 6:13 KJV

The Super 80 aircraft lifted off from Dallas–Fort Worth, headed for Sacramento, California. Just as it got to the edge of Dallas County, a rattling-shaking noise startled me and the woman sitting beside me. Cabin pressure was diminishing. My seatmate and I agreed that things were not "purdy."

The flight attendants tried to be cool, but when I asked one if we had a problem she was truthful. The captain announced over the loud speaker that we had to return to Dallas immediately.

I started praying, loud enough for my seatmate to know what I was doing. There was no shame in my game. I knew who could get us back to the gate. I also knew that because there were at least twenty other Women of Faith staff on board, plenty of other people on the flight were praying to the same Pilot I was.

Even though the flight attendants had concerned looks on their faces, I believed we would land safely and without incident. I was right.

When we were deplaning to get another flight, one of the other Women of Faith told me that she had confessed all her sins on the way down! She was a former flight attendant and knew that we had lost an engine.

Whether you are on a Super 80 jet or soaring through the circumstances of life, losing connection with the power source can be deadly. Fortunately, there's a way to recharge without returning to home base: Plug into the name of Jesus. Praying through Christ to the Father reconnects you to the Highest Power.

Lord, you are always available when I need to recharge. What a comfort
to know that you are everywhere I am. Amen.

Thelma Wells

Prayer Beads

Listen and hear my voice; pay attention and hear what I say.
—*ISAIAH 28:23*

We all have different ways of remembering for what or for whom we should pray. Some of us make lists, others keep a journal. Some hang notes on the bathroom mirror or refrigerator door. I have beads. Sound unusual? Maybe it is, but it works for me.

Ten years ago Marilyn's daughter, Beth, introduced me to the idea of stringing together beads of different sizes, shapes, colors, and textures—each a reminder to pray for something or someone. During the time I was negotiating to buy my house, I added a little square wooden bead. Beads of different colors and shapes symbolize different people for me. I even have a bead with holes and rough edges . . . for problems I'm praying about.

From time to time I change beads. I remember a beautiful white one, almost like a marble, representing my friend who had a terminal illness. I prayed that the Lord would give her a quiet spirit as she trusted him with the outcome. When she passed away I saved the bead in a small treasure box. It is a sweet and personal remembrance now.

Scripture tells us to pray without ceasing, and in my desire to do that, I take my string of beads with me everywhere—trains, planes, and automobiles! I'm so grateful the Lord has given me this beautiful, creative reminder to hold in my hands as I pray . . . and remember.

Heavenly Father, thank you for reminders to pray for the people and things that matter to you and to me. How grateful I am that you hear my prayers with a tender, attentive heart. Amen.

Luci Swindoll

The Lord's Prayer

Lord, teach us to pray.
—*LUKE 11:1*

The prayer Jesus taught his disciples has been used for centuries in worship, weddings, and wars. We memorize it and teach it to our young. But how often do we fully comprehend the power and significance of this prayer?

The Lord's Prayer fully encompasses the essentials of right communication with God. Each word, so carefully chosen by Jesus in response to one of his followers' requests, penetrates the mind of God and aligns our hearts with his will.

"Our Father who art in heaven, Hallowed be thy name. . ." opens a prayer channel that ushers us into the *presence* of God.

"Thy kingdom come. Thy will be done on earth as it is in heaven. . ." establishes our *priorities*. It acknowledges that God is in charge.

"Give us this day our daily bread. . ." clothes us with God's *provisions*. Jesus is the Bread of Life, the very sustenance and nourishment of God the Provider.

"Forgive us our trespasses as we forgive those who trespass against us. . ." allows us to enhance our relationships by forgiving *people*—and in turn we are pardoned by God.

"Lead us not into temptation, but deliver us from evil. . ." equips us with the full armor of God so that we have *power* over the Devil.

"For Thine is the kingdom, and the power, and the glory, for ever" lavishes God with the continual *praise* he is due.

"Amen" seals the prayer with his promise to fulfill all we have requested in his name and for his glory.

The next time you find yourself saying this powerful prayer, *pay attention* to every word. Jesus taught us all how to pray. Hallelujah!

*Our Father, thank you for showing me exactly
how to talk to you. Amen.*

Thelma Wells

On Our Knees

But when our time was up, we left and continued on our way.
All the disciples and their wives and children accompanied us out of
the city, and there on the beach we knelt to pray. –ACTS 21:5

Paul's life is like a photo album filled with snapshots of the rich life of faith. Imagine this scene.... Paul's ship has docked in the seaport of Tyre to unload cargo. He remained there for seven days to spend time with Christ's disciples there. The picture we have been given is one of strong personal ties and commitment to a common goal. I imagine their time together was full of sharing stories of all that was happening in the early days of the church.

When it was time for Paul to go, they all walked out of the city to the ship together. I can imagine children running on ahead, chasing each other, laughing out loud as Paul and the other men and their wives shared last words of encouragement and love. When they arrived at the beach, the whole group stopped and got down on their knees to pray. I'm sure that wasn't a strange sight to the children. They were living in difficult days. Christianity was under attack. It really cost something to be a follower of Christ.

Today may seem different, but it's really not. It still costs to be sold out to Jesus. Paul's example to us compels us to model to everyone that our very lives depend on God. Before we move on with all the "stuff" of the day, let's stop, get down on our knees, and pray.

*Dear Father, let my life so shine before my children and
others that they will long to know you. Amen.*

Sheila Walsh

The King of Feelers

We do not know what we ought to pray for, but the Spirit himself intercedes for us with groans that words cannot express. —ROMANS 8:26

I was deeply touched by an article in the *Los Angeles Times* about an eighty-three-year-old man from New Jersey who died after an accident on the Angel Flight funicular railway. Mr. Leon Praport and his wife, Lola, were in LA celebrating their fifty-fourth wedding anniversary when they decided to ride the historic cable car. It collided with another car and Mr. Praport was gravely injured. Several hours later he died.

Initially I noticed the article because I have a heart for senior citizens who refuse to let age stop them from living with gusto. The *Times* article told of many things Leon had done that endeared him to his loved ones, and an undated photograph showed his huge smile.

When I finished reading I realized there was a great deal more to this gentleman than his love for having fun. He knew how to cherish his family and friends as well. His granddaughter said of him, "We were extremely close. . . . Every time we saw him he was so excited. My grandfather was the king of feelers. We never had to say anything. He would just know what we were feeling."

Isn't that a tremendous compliment? Longing to be "heard" is one of the deepest cries of the human heart. People who "just know" what we're feeling because they know us so well are priceless gifts.

God knows us better than any human being ever could, and he is always eager for our presence. When we are with the King of Feelers, we don't even have to say anything.

Thank you, Lord, for hearing my heart.
Amen.

Luci Swindoll

Answered Prayers

If we ask anything according to his will, he hears us.
—1 JOHN 5:14

I was asked to speak for a tea one Sunday afternoon, but because I already had been booked for an engagement that evening, I declined. Later that day the evening engagement was canceled, and I was able to speak at the tea.

A few weeks earlier I had gotten a routine mammogram. My doctor was concerned about the "inconclusive" results and scheduled two more tests. I prayed for God to direct me to a trustworthy holistic medicine expert.

During the tea, one of the honorees reported that through herbs and safe alternative therapies, she had recovered from cancer, allergies, and arthritis. She now owns a clinic. When she finished speaking, she walked directly to me, out of all the people in the room, and handed me her business card. We had never seen each other before.

I began treatments the following Monday. When I went back to my doctor for the tests, the results showed that everything was completely benign!

Another prayer was answered at that tea. For three years I had been praying for the right public relations person to hire for my company. Sitting across the table from me was a woman who had worked in PR for a distinguished national personality. As we talked, I discovered that she is not only an expert in her field, but she is also a Christian. After more prayer and a few visits with this woman, I knew she was God's answer to my prayers.

God rearranged my schedule that Sunday because he had heard my prayers and was ready to give me his perfect answers. He organizes and reorganizes for our best good.

Father, give me the flexibility and faith to accept
your order for my life. Amen.

Thelma Wells

Benediction Bonus

*The LORD bless you and keep you; the LORD make his face shine
upon you and be gracious to you; the LORD turn his face toward you
and give you peace. —NUMBERS 6:24–26*

Don't you just love a good benediction? There's something invigorating in those short, encouraging prayers that ask God's blessing as we set off to do his work. The dictionary defines benediction as "the utterance of good wishes" or a "blessing pronounced by an officiating minister," and I, for one, can never get enough good wishes or blessings! (Okay, I admit it. Sometimes I like to hear the benediction because it means I'm about to go home and put on comfortable clothes!)

The apostle Paul was probably the most gifted bestower of biblical benedictions. *Meredith's Book of Bible Lists* cites twelve benedictions in the Bible, and Paul wrote eight of them. Some are short and sweet: "Grace and peace to you from God our Father and from the Lord Jesus Christ" (Romans 1:7). Others are long and flowery: "May the God of peace, who through the blood of the eternal covenant brought back from the dead our Lord Jesus, that great Shepherd of the sheep, equip you with everything good for doing his will, and may he work in us what is pleasing to him, through Jesus Christ, to whom be glory for ever and ever" (Hebrews 13:20–21). Hearing those words prayed over you, wouldn't you feel empowered to rush out the door to do something special on the Lord's behalf?

One of my favorite benedictions came from a pastor who simply exhorted his congregation each week to "Go forth to love and serve the Lord. *Be the church!*"

*Father, whether I'm coming or going, help me
remember to be your church. Amen.*

Barbara Johnson

Friendship

Two are better than one. . . . If one falls down, his friend can help him up.
But pity the man who falls and has no one to help him up!
—*ECCLESIASTES 4:9–10*

When I think of the six of us who are writing this book, I realize time and again that only God could have brought us together. Look at us! Collectively, we represent four decades—one in her seventies, two in their sixties, two in their fifties, and one in her forties. There are four wives, a widow, and a single woman; the mother of a five-year-old and four grandmothers. There is a former college professor and a high school dropout; an opera singer and a talk show host. There is a Scot and five Americans; a shrink and one who suffered from clinical depression. We are tall and short, thin and fluffy, black and white. We are speakers and singers, actors and clowns, connoisseurs and critics, authors and readers, teachers and students, wacky and wise. On and on the list goes, but there is one thing we have completely in common: We're *friends!*

Friendship negates differences. It bonds people together like nothing else. When you make a new friend, you open the door to all kinds of growth because of the additional possibilities that person brings to your life. Friendship is one of God's greatest gifts.

Be encouraged as you read the devotionals this month and thank God every day for your friends. Rejoice with them, be there for them, reach out to them, and feel what they're feeling. Show them the love of the Savior.

I don't know what I would do without these wonderful Women of Faith friends. They are the five sisters I never had, and I am so grateful for them. It can't get any better than this.

Luci Swindoll

Celebrate Friendship

A generous man will prosper; he who refreshes others
will himself be refreshed. –PROVERBS 11:25

Did you know that today is Celebrate Friendship Day? You didn't? Well, maybe that's because I just made it up! I love to celebrate, and I never have to look far for a reason to commemorate *today* as a special occasion. Why, just the other day I celebrated because all the socks came out of my dryer in even pairs!

But on those days when my socks *don't* match up, I still find ways to be happy. The easiest way for me to do this is to call up a friend and share a joke. When I see or hear one I really like, I keep it by the phone so I can remember to tell it to the friends who call. Just yesterday I was delighted to call my friends and share a funny bumper sticker I'd seen that morning. It said: "DRIVER CARRIES NO CASH—(He's married.)"

When you're feeling a little blue, call up a friend and tell her how grateful you are for her. There is nothing like a little gratitude to improve your attitude! Invite her over and make some cookies or fudge or popcorn balls. Wrap them up in a pretty basket and take them to someone in a nursing home or to that new family that moved in down the street. Deliver them with a smile and tell them you're celebrating a special day—and a special friend.

Oh, Father, thank you for the refreshing gift of friendship!
I celebrate your generosity in giving me
a special friend and allowing me to be one. Amen.

Barbara Johnson

More Than Friends

God sets the lonely in families.
−PSALM 68:6

One of my dearest friends is about to turn ninety. We met when he was in his seventies. Wallace Haggarty and his wife, Opal, were regular viewers of *The 700 Club* on the Christian Broadcasting Network while I was the cohost. Wallace wrote me to say that he and his wife had prayed with me during one broadcast and made a fresh commitment to Christ. We became regular correspondents.

Then Opal died. Wallace's world was shattered. He missed her so much. *The 700 Club* became more of a comfort. Then one day I disappeared off the show. Wallace didn't know that I'd been admitted as a patient into the psychiatric unit of a hospital. He told me recently, "I cried and cried when I thought you were gone." Then he contacted a friend of mine who was able to give him my address. I will never forget his letter to me: "You have been there for me when I was sad and lonely, now I will be there for you."

Wallace's love and prayers meant more than I can say. We have never lost contact again. When we talk on the phone we think of heaven and Opal and the day when Wallace and his dearly missed wife will be together again. He has asked that I sing "How Great Thou Art" at his funeral. That is such an appropriate hymn.

Wallace and I have never met, but for more than fourteen years through our common love for God we have been more than friends; we have been family.

Dear Father, thank you that because of your love and
commitment to us, we can truly love one another. Amen.

Sheila Walsh

Take Care

Show me your ways, O LORD, teach me your paths.
—PSALM 25:4

I just came in from a walk. Can you hear me gasping? Trust me, I am.

You can tell I'm a tad out of shape. I've never really taken a shine to walking; seems I have more pressing things to do. Not more important, just more pressing.

Being a friend to oneself isn't easy. I find it a breeze to take care of someone else rather than conscientiously tending to my own affairs. In fact, I love it when a faraway friend comes to visit. I fuss over the guest room, stocking it with goodies: bubbles for the bath, chocolates for the pillow, and books for reading pleasure.

Now, ask me when I last soaked in bubbles, popped Godivas, or lost myself in a dreamy novel. No, don't. I speed through my showers, and if I delve into chocolates, it's affordable M&M's. I do indulge in good books, but rather than luxuriating in a hammock, I read on the run.

What is it about being friendly toward ourselves? Perhaps we feel it is too indulgent. Being a person of extremes, I know I'm capable of overdoing. Proof of that is the last box of cookies that came through my kitchen door. I'd offer you one, but they seem to have disappeared. *Oh, no, wait, there they are, bunched up on my thighs.*

So here is the dilemma: How can we be friendly toward ourselves without being decadent? Hmm . . . maybe two long bubble baths a week, not two a day; two truffles a month, not two an hour; two walks a week, not couch potato-itis. This self-care thing is a job for Jesus.

Lord, I am a capricious dust bunny. Teach me
to be appropriately kind to myself. Amen.

Patsy Clairmont

So What Do You Think?

These are the things you are to do: Speak the truth to each another.
—ZECHARIAH 8:16

Mark Twain said, "When in doubt, tell the truth." I love it when I'm told the truth. There is a security that comes with truth. Even though it may be uncomfortable, I want to know what you think and why you think it.

When it comes to the experience of friendship I feel especially adamant about the truth. The sixteenth-century French playwright Molière said: "The more we love our friends, the less we flatter them; it is by excusing nothing that pure love shows itself."

Now of course I'm not advocating using battering rams and hurling hubcaps as a means of communicating truth; there is a non-abusive way to share my thoughts as well as receive yours. But to remain silent is not love; it is avoidance.

Jesus continually referred to his twelve disciples as his friends. And yet he frequently became exasperated with them because of their inability to believe him. In John 8:25 Jesus responds to yet one more inane question of "Who are you?" with "Just what I have been claiming all along." He didn't mince words. He simply told the truth.

If a friend truly loves me, I'm not left wondering about the status of our relationship; she'll tell me. If a friend truly loves me, I won't wonder if my words were too direct or my behavior troubling; she'll tell me. There is nothing like the truth.

Lord, thank you for giving me the truth in love and in strength.
Help me to be like you in all my interactions. Amen.

Marilyn Meberg

What's a Friend Good For?

> If one falls down, his friend can help him up.
> —*ECCLESIASTES 4:10*

What's a friend good for?
Propping open hearts and airing moldy moods.
Lighting up dark hallways through sad and lonely memories.
Hanging high aspirations and replanting hope.
Hauling heavy worries and pulling stumps of anger.
Shading tender shoots of joy that venture upward through the muck.
Grounding flighty passions during electrical storms of temptation.
Shielding fragile egos from the harsh winds of criticism.
Mending broken dreams and sharing golden moments.
A good friend is a friend for good.

Who needs a friend anyway?
Only those who need someone to laugh with.
Only those who need someone to listen,
someone to love,
someone to care.
Only those who need someone.
Only those who need.
Only all of us.

—ANN LUNA

*Lord, being human means being in need. We are not meant
to walk through this life without caring people by our side.
Thank you so much for giving us each other. Amen.*

Barbara Johnson

March 6
He's Our Friend

The LORD your God is with you, he is mighty to save. He will take great
delight in you, he will quiet you with his love, he will rejoice over you with
singing. *—ZEPHANIAH 3:17*

My granny taught me, "Be nice to everyone, but pick your friends." And,
"If you have three good friends in your life, cherish them."

The other day I decided to count my true friends through the years. I have
thirty! What a blessing.

How do I determine my friends?

True friendship is a relationship of mutual affection and goodwill.

My friends love me in spite of how I act or what I say.

We don't necessarily visit often or talk a lot on the phone, but they care
about me.

When I'm hurting they hurt with me.

When I'm happy they laugh with me.

I can call on them day or night.

They listen to me and give wise counsel.

They don't take sides with me when I'm wrong, but they fight for me when
I'm right.

There is no competition between us.

They rejoice in my successes.

When we disagree, we work things out.

We respect each other's opinions.

We love the same Lord.

The loyalty of my thirty friends reminds me of the loyalty of Jesus toward
his friends.

He accepts us the way we are.

He gives us guidance and clarity.

He's always on the side of righteousness and wants nothing but good for us.

When we disagree with him he waits patiently for us to get the point.

He enjoys us so much that he actually sings over us!

Jesus, you are the model of how to be a friend.
Your friendship has saved me from myself and enables
me to love in your name. Thank you. Amen.

Thelma Wells

March 7
E-mails from Annie

Therefore encourage one another and build each other up.
–1 THESSALONIANS 5:11

In Greek mythology, a muse is a source of creative inspiration, a guiding spirit. On this earth, mine is Anne Lamott—the funniest, dearest, most poignant writer I know. She lives in the *real* world—real time, real life. And I'm so grateful she's in my life. Some people hide their true selves and real feelings, but not Annie. She writes brilliant, vulnerable, authentic prose.

I'd like to be a good author too . . . but I hate to write. I prefer to have written. Writing well is one of the hardest crafts in the world.

In August, 1999, I met Anne Lamott personally and loved her immediately. We began e-mailing back and forth. Annie has been my muse ever since.

When I told her I was discouraged she wrote me this:

Luci, writing is supposed to go poorly. Never forget that. Hang up a clothesline above your computer with bits of paper holding great ideas . . . attached with clothespins, like laundry. When you don't know what to write, pull one down and use it. Write badly with purple prose and evidence of brain damage and terrible character. These are all good things. Almost all good writing begins with bad writing.

Then she added, "I'll help you however I can, every step of the way."

If you are skilled in a particular arena in which someone you love is having trouble, send her an encouraging e-mail. God will honor your kindness, and your friend will feel better. I think of Annie's encouragement every time I take down the laundry.

Lord, how can I encourage someone today?
Show me, then help me do it. Amen.

Luci Swindoll

March 8
Crop Buster

By their fruit you will recognize them.
–MATTHEW 7:16

A few years ago we lived in a house surrounded by flowers and trees. One of my favorites was a pear tree that produced luscious fruit. Our last season in the house the tree was especially productive, and I impatiently waited for the pears to ripen, realizing this would be my farewell banquet. The pears were almost ready when I took a short trip out of town. I knew they would be perfect when I returned.

But when I checked the tree after my weekend jaunt, I found it stripped. And I mean *stripped*. Nary a pear anywhere. I was fit to be tied. How could this be?

I hotfooted into the house and asked—okay, okay, demanded—to know what happened to my pears. My husband proceeded to tell me that an acquaintance had stopped by one day to greet him, and as they chatted the man noted the fruitful boughs and inquired about the pears' future. Could we spare a few? he wondered.

Les, a generous man, knew we had plenty and told the fellow he could have some. The man left, and a short time later Les made a trip to the store. The man returned while Les was away and helped himself. By the time Les arrived home, the once fruit-laden branches sported only leaves.

Beware, my friends, of fruit-nabbers. They usually arrive during seasons of plenty. They appear harmless, and yet they will take all you have and leave you listless.

While we're called to be giving and to joyfully share our bounty, don't be stripped of your strength and left without resources.

Lord, may we be exceedingly generous yet not frivolous.
Amen.

Patsy Clairmont

Marriage of Souls

My loved ones and my friends stand aloof from my plague;
And my kinsman stand afar off. —PSALM 38:11 NASB

An Old Testament prophet gave this pessimistic counsel: "Do not trust in a neighbor; Do not have confidence in a friend" (Micah 7:5 NASB). It sounds as if he and the writer of the psalm had similar experiences. Both were abandoned in a time of extremity and both drew back in disillusionment.

I'm sure every one of us has been disappointed and hurt by persons we considered friends. When a friend lets us down, what should our response be? Voltaire said, "Friendship is the marriage of the soul; and this marriage is subject to divorce." When a friend's behavior is not supportive, loyal, and caring, is it healthy for us to act as if that lack of support was no big deal and we barely noticed? Or, like Voltaire, do we divorce?

Quite frankly, I'm with Voltaire. But before I'd take that step I would first need to have an open discussion with my friend. I'd need to express my heart, my disappointment, and my uncertainty as to the future of the relationship. Depending on my friend's reaction, we would then need to determine whether there is a foundation to build on. If there isn't, then there is no point in expecting from the friendship what has not been there before.

I am blessed with a number of utterly loyal, caring, and supportive friends. They have "come through" for me repeatedly, and I love them dearly. The others, well . . . I introduced them to Job's friends—Eliphaz, Bildad, and Zophar.

Lord, how sweet to experience your spirit of grace in human friendships.
May I be to my friends all that they are to me. Amen.

M a r i l y n   M e b e r g

Help! I Need Somebody

A friend loves at all times
—*PROVERBS 17:7*

Some of the most painful moments of my life are the most treasured because of the gifts they have brought to my soul. In January, all six Women of Faith speakers meet to discuss the year ahead and share our messages with each other. I love these informal times of being together. We laugh and cry, talk till all hours, and go shopping together. There is such safety in our companionship: years of trust, tested friendship, mutual respect, and deep affection.

During one particular trip an issue came up that I felt very strongly about. I became angry and defensive. I thought everyone else was wrong. My words were unkind and unfair. When we adjourned for the day I huffed and puffed back to my hotel room muttering under my breath like a demented street person. Left alone with only my sinful indignation, I knew I was wrong. I knew I had to call every one of my friends and ask her to forgive me.

One of the most valuable gifts I received was from my darling friend, Marilyn. She made it clear to me that my words had wounded her. As we talked I was able to get a much clearer picture of myself. Equipped with the truth, I was then able to bring my whole imperfect self to God and ask for help.

It would have been easier for Marilyn to tell me that what I'd said didn't matter—but she is a friend. She cared enough about me to speak the truth.

Father, give me ears to hear the sometimes painful truth
about my life . . . and the grace to change. Amen.

Sheila Walsh

Pie Pals

Even in laughter the heart may ache.
–PROVERBS 14:13

When you've been knocked to the floor by bad news or splattered on the ceiling by unwelcome surprises, it's hard to believe you'll *ever* laugh again. I know. I've been there! I also know what a blessing it is when someone comes along to lift you to your feet or scrape you off the ceiling and coax a little laughter out of you.

My friend Rose tells how a group of her pals helped her laugh on the unlikeliest of days. Rose's husband had fought a long battle against cancer, and by the end of the ordeal, Rose was devastated by both sorrow and exhaustion. When she returned home after the funeral, her house was filled with the somber conversation of caring friends and loved ones. But as Rose walked to her bedroom she heard an unexpected sound: the muted but unmistakable squeal of giggles. She opened the door to find three of her closest friends sitting on the bed, holding a pie and four forks.

"Oh, Rose, we stopped by Marie Callender's to buy you a pie, and we had the biggest argument over which kind is your favorite," one friend explained. By their faces, Rose could tell it had been a friendly argument. She could also tell they were dying to eat the pie—and didn't want to share it with the rest of the crowd! Rose sat down on the bed with her pals and enjoyed a large piece of pie—and another round of giggles.

Rose has many poignant memories of that sad day. But the gift of laughter her secretive pie pals gave her is surely one of her most cherished.

Thank you, Lord, for friends who help me laugh again.
Amen.

B a r b a r a   J o h n s o n

True Value

Go in peace, for we have sworn friendship with each other
in the name of the LORD. *–1 SAMUEL 20:42*

Not long ago I was visiting with an acquaintance in the gated community where I live. She was remarking on how nice it is that Marilyn and I are friends. (Marilyn lives just a few streets away.) "I think it's wonderful you've known each other for so many years and now you're traveling together all over the country to be with more friends. That's great. I envy that."

I assured her it was indeed a gift that I thanked God for every day. "How often do your friends come out to the desert for a visit?" I innocently asked.

"Oh, I don't have that many friends" she said. "When I was younger I was too busy to develop friendships. But I can tell you now, if I had it to do over I'd do it very differently. I'd give anything to have a close friendship, like yours and Marilyn's." Then she added with a sigh, "But . . . I guess it's too late for that."

As I was walking away from the sadness of that encounter I thought about a line I read once in an Ann Landers column: "Wouldn't it be wonderful if those who bothered us when we were young and busy would come back when we are old and lonely?"

Friendships take time. Nothing of value grows in a vacuum. To have friends we must be friendly. We must carve out time and opportunity for a friendship to take root and blossom.

Put down this book and call a friend . . . now!

Heavenly Father, teach me to value my friends
like you valued your disciples. Help me find time
for meaningful relationships. Amen.

Luci Swindoll

Love Notes

Whatever your hand finds to do, do it with all your might.
—ECCLESIASTES 9:10

I love greeting cards but I must confess that I'm the world's worst correspondent. You can ask my daughter-in-law, Danya, who is one of the most thoughtful note senders alive.

One Christmas Danya couldn't believe I didn't have tags on my gifts. Too much like writing a note, I told her. Instead I designated a wrapping paper for each family member so I didn't have to label the presents.

I love writing books, so how hard could it be to scribble a tag or scrawl a note to someone? Most of my friends have observed my deficiency and put up with me, but unfortunately some have thought it was a sign of how I felt about them. Listen, it took me two years to send out my wedding thank-you cards. Trust me, this is about me. Perhaps I think my books are my gift of correspondence, or maybe by the time I finish a manuscript I'm worded out.

My friend Sally Stewart has sent me a birthday card every year for at least fifteen years. I've sent her one. I'm so pleased she hasn't erased me from her list. Not that I'd blame her. Sally has the gift of cards.

Kay Garrett, my Denver friend, sends me beautiful cards full of sweet sentiments. Her exquisite handwriting is a gift in its own right.

I wish I were more of a letter writer like Danya, Sally, and Kay because it is such a personal way to stay connected. Do you need to drop someone a note of love? Why don't we purpose together to sit down and jot a few lines?

I'll go first. "Dear Sally. . ."

Lord, help me to love others with all my might.
Amen.

Patsy Clairmont

With One Heart

*Behold, how good and how pleasant it is for brothers
to dwell together in unity!* —PSALM *133:1* NSAB

The year 2001 dawned with an unusual urge in my heart to address the necessity of unity in the church. Perhaps it was awakened by the assignment I had to speak to the folks in Blackshear, Georgia, on the topic for their women's conference: "With One Heart." Here is what I discovered from my research:

> It simply is not possible to remain divided if we truly love the Lord.
> God loves everybody and has broken down the walls that separate us.
> Dissension openly contradicts the will of Christ.
> The only way we can effect unity in the church is to realize who we are in Christ.
> We are a peculiar people, a royal priesthood, a holy nation.
> We are sons and daughters of the Most High God.
> We are friends of Christ.
> As Christ's friends we must refuse to play games and "church politics."
> We must love all people just the way they are.
> We must refuse to allow our appearances and human behaviors to be the barometer by which we judge each other.
> We must seek God's divine imprint in every individual.
> We must fall more and more madly in love with Jesus.

Unity can only be attained when people understand that "whoever does not love does not know God, because God is love" (1 John 4:8). Do you know God?

*Father, make me an instrument of your love and peace
so that I may see the best in people and become an agent
of unity in your kingdom. Amen.*

Thelma Wells

Walking in Onesiphorus's Footsteps

May the Lord show mercy to the household of Onesiphorus, because he often refreshed me and was not ashamed of my chains. —2 TIMOTHY 1:16

When someone asked me what Bible character I would like to be like, I quickly answered, "Onesiphorus!"

The man looked a little shocked at my response; after all, Onesiphorus's name *does* sound like some kind of disease, and he was certainly one of the most obscure characters in the Bible. But even though he is only mentioned once in all of Scripture, he has been one of my heroes for a long time.

You see, Onesiphorus was a friend to Paul when he was in prison and nearly everyone else had deserted him. Onesiphorus's visits "refreshed" the weary preacher, and Paul never forgot that thoughtfulness. Onesiphorus encouraged Paul by letting him know someone remembered him and cared for him.

Have you visited someone in prison lately? Maybe you don't know anyone who is locked up behind bars, but remember there are many kinds of prisons. Someone you know may be locked in a prison of despair because a loved one has died or a child is estranged. Others may be imprisoned by depression or illness. Sometimes you have to search out a friend who's dropped from sight, just as Onesiphorus searched for Paul until he found him in prison.

To be a friend today, we can't always wait for an opportunity that's convenient or close to home. It takes some effort to be an encourager to the brokenhearted. Will you make the effort?

> *Lord, you are the great Comforter. Help me to be a friend to someone who needs some refreshment today. Amen.*

Barbara Johnson

Close Proximity

The LORD is near to all who call upon him.
—PSALM 145:18

C. S. Lewis wrote, "If I had to give a piece of advice to a young man about a place to live, I'd say, 'Sacrifice almost everything to live where you can be near your friends.'" I say a hearty amen to that!

Close proximity to my friends allows me to experience the vagrancies of thought and emotion that characterize dailyness. Proximity allows spontaneity of contact and immediacy of expression.

For example, Luci Swindoll, one of my oldest and dearest friends, lives only three blocks from me. She called shortly before noon today and said, "Throw your pen down, flee your desk, and come over for lunch. I've just made a chicken salad and I'm putting it on the table in ten minutes!"

You can bet I dropped my pen and tore over there. I wanted to go to Luci's because I knew that when I sat down at her table I would get more than one of her incomparably well-seasoned, crispy salads. The salad would be served in an atmosphere of nondemanding, accepting warmth that would allow me to be however I was at the moment. I could be profound or a moron, funny or pensive, happy or sad. I could even, perish the thought, be boring.

That's the wonder of our friendship with God. He's right in the neighborhood. We have access to him immediately, and spontaneously sharing our "dailyness" is his delight. There is enormous comfort in close proximity—whether it is with a friend who makes a salad or a God who makes a world.

I thank you, Lord, that you are my ever-present, everyday Friend.
Amen.

M a r i l y n   M e b e r g

Friends for Eternity

A bruised reed he will not break, and a smoldering wick he will not
snuff out. In faithfulness he will bring forth justice. —ISAIAH 42:3

St. Patrick, the patron saint of Ireland, was born in Britain in the fourth
century, the son of a local town councilman. He was raised in a religious home,
but there is no historical indication that he had a relationship with Christ
until he went through an unbelievable trial that transformed him.

When Patrick was sixteen years old he was kidnapped by Irish pirates and
held captive for eight years. He escaped when he was twenty-four and returned
to his family a changed man. He came back with a passion for God, with a
deep commitment to Christ and a sense of divine calling on the rest of his life.
He trained for ministry and spent himself in the cause of Christ. When he
died at about seventy years of age, he left behind a moving account of his
personal journey with God.

History bears witness to the countless ways in which even the harshest trials seem to carve God's initials on our souls and draw us close to his heart. I
have talked to many people who acknowledge that they would never have
chosen the path they found themselves on, but having walked that way they
would never change it now.

God's love seeks out those whose hearts are breaking and whose faces are
tear-streaked, and God our maker and his fragile human creations become
friends for eternity.

*Dear Father, thank you that even in the most painful moments
of my life your love pursues us. Thank you that you know how fragile
and bruised I am, and that you love me so tenderly. Amen.*

S h e i l a   W a l s h

A Friend of Christ

If I speak in the tongues of men and of angels, but have not love,
I am only a resounding gong or a clanging cymbal. *−1 CORINTHIANS 13:1*

The church can be a noisy place, a venue full of resounding gongs and clanging symbols. It can also be a place of quiet rivers. My husband and I discovered that in the cold winter of 1999.

Barry's mother, Eleanor, was in the last days of battling liver cancer. We spent as much time as we could with Eleanor and William. We took turns holding Eleanor's hand through the night, wiping her brow, singing hymns, and praying for mercy from the ravages of a disease that moved in uninvited and refused to leave. Our greatest worry was that when we were not there, William was alone—or so we thought, until we met one of those quiet rivers. Her name is Terri Doucette.

William and Eleanor were members of Martin Luther Church, and Terri was in charge of the ministry of helps. I'm not sure what her job description is, but I'm sure it didn't include everything she quietly did in the name of the Lord. She stopped by every morning to administer Eleanor's medication. She sat for hours holding her hand and praying. She prepared food for William and stayed late at night to share a cup of coffee or a bowl of soup. She had time for all of us. She stayed till the end. When Eleanor took her final breath, Terri was right there in the room, cheering her all the way home.

Her job title introduced us to her, but Terri's spirit sang with the quiet grace of a friend of Christ.

Lord Jesus, may my life reflect my friendship with you.
Amen.

Sheila Walsh

Omelets in the Rain

Put on love, which binds them all together in perfect unity.
–COLOSSIANS 3:14

I love Paris! In the summer of 1995, my dear friend Mary Graham and I were vacationing there. We had a fabulous time filled with museums, shopping, sight-seeing, taxis, trains . . . and miles of walking. From our small hotel room on the Left Bank to extensive sight-seeing, our plans exceeded all our expectations. One of the sweetest memories we share, however, had nothing to do with planning.

One morning we awakened to a thunderous, cold, cloudy, rainy day. Unsure about venturing too far from home base, we decided to forgo our scheduled activity and tackle something more pedestrian: two weeks of dirty laundry! Right around the corner, we found a coin-operated Laundromat. After deciphering the French instructions, we secured the exact coins. *Très magnifique!*

After loading the washer, we spotted a darling little restaurant about a hundred yards away. Dashing through the downpour, we seated ourselves at a table under a big green umbrella and ordered cheese omelets and coffee. Rain was splashing all around us. Our casual conversation soon turned to more meaningful dialogue about life and all we value most in it. Unexpectedly, we had one of our sweetest times *ever* in our long and rich friendship. We laughed and talked and enjoyed the weather as though we'd ordered the rain. We almost forgot to transfer the laundry.

Remembering that occasion of togetherness in the "Paris Wash" always gives us a smile. And it reminds us that it doesn't take expensive plans or places to have a fun friendship. Sometimes its best times are enjoyed spontaneously—in the midst of the mundane.

Lord, help me today to think of something wacky, different,
and completely creative to do with a friend. Amen.

Luci Swindoll

Spring

Flowers appear on the earth; . . .the cooing of doves is heard in our land.
—SONG OF SONGS 2:12

Across the morning sky hope arrived on indigo wings. Spring was near. A bluebird served as significant notification to winter to take its white fury and move on. I danced about in delight.

The winter had been wicked, as it lashed out and lasted far too long. When one endures icy hardships, spring's warmth is an especially welcome friend. Severed tree branches lay strewn about, snapped by an icy, howling wind weeks before. But now nearby shrubs, awakened by the changing landscape, formed small nodes that would grow into buds, then leaves and flowers. Crocuses and snowdrops peeked precariously through clods of cold dirt, flirting with the sun. Their purple-and-white petals were a dress rehearsal for Easter. Two mourning doves cuddled on the corner of our roof and cooed secrets about their nesting site.

Amidst all the signs of a new season stood a small oak shrouded in last year's leaves. The withered, lifeless, parched leaves dangled from the tree's branches like tarnished charms. I wanted to yell, "Little tree, if you'll just let go, God will give you fresh new leaves, and you'll be lovely again."

The words reverberated in my mind. *Patsy, what do you need to let go of? Do you still clutch to parts of the old life?*

Spring is not only a season on the calendar but also a season of the heart. Jesus came that we might let go of the old and burst forth with new life. We can lay aside the shroud of the former (even yesterday's parched behavior) and dance with resurrection vigor.

*Lord Jesus, may fresh sap of faith run through me
as I respond to you. Amen.*

Patsy Clairmont

Closer Than a Sister

*A man of many companions may come to ruin, but there
is a friend who sticks closer than a brother.* —PROVERBS 18:24

How many friends do you have? How many people know your deepest hopes and dreams, your fears and failings?

I realized some time ago that I had many "friends," but no one really knew me at all. It was easier for me to maintain several superficial friendships than to have a few trusted companions who bore witness to the story of my soul. After all, it can feel threatening to be known. It appears easier to live in the shadows. But as this proverb says, it is a dangerous path.

When I ended up in a psychiatric hospital in 1992, all my friends were stunned. No one had any indication of the crumbling inside my head and heart. It was then that I realized how alone I really was. And it was then that I decided I didn't want to live that way anymore.

When we allow a few trusted people inside our walls, along with the inevitable trepidation of being rejected is the joyous safety of being loved and supported. We can have many companions, but if they have no idea of the temptations that pull at us we can indeed come to ruin. But true friends stick closer than flesh and blood. I have found that to be true with my dear sisters on the Women of Faith team. They know my strengths and weaknesses, and they love me just the way I am.

*Dear Father, thank you for true friends. May I be one
who sticks closer than a sister. Amen.*

Sheila Walsh

A Model Friend

A friend loves at all times.
–PROVERBS 17:17

If I were to advertise for a friend, I'd use Carol as a model. Carol and I have been buddies for more than forty years. We attended school together, dated together, and I was on vacation with her family when I met my husband. Carol and I had our first babies within months of each other, both boys. For a time we lived on the same street. But that isn't what makes her a dear friend, although history infuses the years with precious memories.

Carol understands my disjointed road life. As an artist, she too hopscotches around and knows how that lifestyle can affect relationships. Yet as much as her empathy helps, that isn't why we are friends.

Carol and I are different in many ways yet similar in others. She is tall while I am short. She paints pictures with watercolors; I paint with words. Carol is reserved while I'm, uh, verbal. We both enjoy decorating, antiques, and being grandmas. All of that adds to the joy of being girlfriends, but it isn't the most important part of our friendship.

Carol applauds when I do well. She cries when I hurt. She laughs at my antics. She has a child's playfulness and a woman's wisdom. Carol is honest and kind. And she's slightly flawed. These qualities deepen our relationship, but they aren't why we're friends. The most important aspect of our friendship is . . . are you ready?

She loves me. Yep, even when I'm cranky. Carol has seen me without makeup and didn't guffaw. She forgives me when I need it. And she believes in me, even on my worst days.

How is all this possible? Carol loves Jesus. And I'm glad she does.

Lord, teach me to love.
Amen.

Patsy Clairmont

The Priceless Bond

Love and faithfulness meet together;
righteousness and peace kiss each other. −PSALM 85:10

My friend Judy Jacobs has immense energy and diverse interests, which I love. She wins the prize for innovation. We both love photography, music, art, journaling, travel, and much more. When I moved from Dallas twenty-eight years ago we determined to continue our mutual pursuit of happiness. We certainly did not want the miles to come between us.

So for all these years, we have faithfully sent each other gifts on our respective birthdays and at Christmas. We've never missed one. We've met in New York in the winter, Santa Fe in the summer, San Antonio in the spring, Dallas in the fall, and several places in between. We've exchanged cards, letters, phone calls, and e-mails. In short, we have kept sweet fellowship alive. Not only have Judy and I maintained our friendship over the miles, we have watched it grow.

You may have friends you'd love to be with today but it's not convenient. Maybe they live in another city, or even another country. Don't let distance keep you from being close to them. Write a note or give them a call. Better yet, plan a little trip so you can be together. In other words, stay involved with those who remind you that love and faithfulness meet in friendship. Reach out—over the miles and across the years—to keep the priceless bond of friendship strong.

*Heavenly Father, thank you for all the friends you have
given me. I want to find ways to stay close to them no matter
how busy our schedules and how many miles lie between us.
Remind me to reach out. Amen.*

L u c i   S w i n d o l l

Praise and Worship

Rejoice greatly, O Daughter of Zion! . . . See, your king comes to you, righteous and having salvation, gentle and riding on a donkey. —*ZECHARIAH 9:9*

Our church's minister of music hired an accomplished praise and worship leader to assist her. In the first rehearsal I attended I knew we were in for a musical transformation. Minister Taylor is teaching us what the Word of God has to say about praise and worship. Every song he teaches has a scriptural foundation, and he explains it. He has us picture ourselves in God's presence, pouring out our love on him as Scripture instructs us to do.

When Jesus came into Jerusalem on what is now called Palm Sunday, the people joyfully waved palm branches and covered his colt's path with their own coats. When we sing and praise God, Minister Taylor asks us to picture us lying on the ground before Jesus, giving ourselves completely to him.

How awesome it is to imagine yourself in the very presence of God! Giving yourself completely in submission to him. Our heartfelt praise is God's due for his goodness to us. Worshiping him binds us intimately to his heart.

I thank God for the gifts and talents of choir directors and musicians who understand what is involved in praise and worship. I am convinced we can't manipulate or manufacture true worship. It is not just good sounding music; it is the state of the heart that moves God.

Take time every day to imagine how much God loves you. Picture King Jesus coming toward you in humble gentleness, salvation in his hand. Praise him joyfully!

> *I will bless your name, O Lord, for you are righteous.*
> *Amen.*

Thelma Wells

Postcards from the Heart

Like cold water to a weary soul is good news from a distant land.
—PROVERBS 25:25

Charlotte loved to travel. She was an inveterate go-er and do-er. "Have passport, will travel" was her motto. Delighting in adventure, she continued going places even after she was diagnosed with cancer.

However, when this debilitating disease demanded more attention, Charlotte was confined to her home. I asked God for a way to encourage her ... something unique that would lift her spirits on dark days. Very clearly the Lord prompted me to start sending postcards. It was as though he said, *She may not be able to board a plane anymore, but you can take her with you vicariously.*

So in 1997 I began writing to Charlotte. I sent cards from everywhere: all over the USA, Kenya, the Antarctic, Canada, Ireland, England, France, Italy, Argentina, Guatemala—everywhere I went.

Char loved those cards. I visited her home in Dallas and saw them plastered all over her refrigerator, with a shoeboxful nearby. She told me she read them again and again, envisioning all those distant places in her mind. She never threw a single card away!

When Charlotte died last year, the cards were returned to me. I put them in chronological order and reread each one. As I recalled the day I wrote, I thought of my forty-year relationship with Char. There are 104 postcards in all—a visible legacy of a love and friendship that will never die.

Dear Lord, show me a new way today to meet the needs
of my friends. Help me think creatively. Amen.

Luci Swindoll

I Hate "Ministry"

He called you to this through our gospel, that you might share
in the glory of our Lord Jesus Christ. —2 THESSALONIANS 2:14

Ney Bailey got me into this. One day in the mid-1970s Ney and I were chatting when she said, "You should be in ministry."

"I hate the word *ministry*," I replied adamantly. "That means I have to go somewhere and do something, like stand behind a pulpit and pound a Bible. No thanks! I've got two brothers in ministry and that's enough."

At the time I was a happy employee at Mobil Oil Corporation. Ney didn't push. She quietly left the remark in the air and began praying for God's plan to unfold in my life, whatever that turned out to be.

A few months later I wrote Ney a thank-you note for something. She called me and said, "You know, Luci, you should write a book."

"I'm *not* writing a book. Are you kidding? My two brothers are authors and that's enough."

Let me just say here: If you want to enjoy your status quo, don't ever get on Ney's prayer list. Things happen when she's your friend. You wind up changing careers, writing books, and engaged in ministry!

God placed Ney Bailey in my life for many wonderful reasons, not the least of which was to plant a seed. She's never stopped praying for me. And her prayers have continued to change me.

If you have someone in your life who quietly intercedes on your behalf, consider it a gift. Or, if you're praying for someone, don't stop. Persevering prayer pays big dividends. Ask Ney.

Heavenly Father, thank you for friends who know how
to pray for me. Teach me how to pray for them. Amen.

Luci Swindoll

An Invaluable Friend

*If two lie down together, they will keep warm.
But how can one keep warm alone?* –ECCLESIASTES 4:11

Lynda Wigren is the most airheaded person I know. You can't even fathom
the variety of things Lynda has used and lost, found and misplaced again, forgotten and never remembered. Most recently she was stuck in Sacramento
overnight because she lost her car keys and couldn't drive home. Before that
she lost the tickets for an anniversary cruise to Alaska. Then there was the
time she forgot where she was to have an important medical test. Of course
she lost the date of the appointment and the doctor's name too. Keys, tickets, purses, books, phone numbers . . . nothing is safe in Lynda's possession.

Yes, Lynda is an airhead. But more important, she's my friend—my closest pal and most devoted encourager. Somehow, even though she can't remember her own social security number, she never forgets my birthday. Somehow,
even though she can barely find her way home from the mall without getting lost, she always manages to show up on my doorstep whenever my spirits hit rock bottom. She is usually carrying a batch of ridiculous greeting cards
she's discovered somewhere—maybe at the bottom of her enormous, clutter-
filled purse. We laugh out loud, reading the punch lines and thinking up
people to send the cards to. And when I need someone to cry with, Lynda is
there crying with me.

*Father, how blessed I am by the "Lyndas" in my life!
Thank you for all friends everywhere who share laughter,
love, and tears. What a comfort they are to your
world-weary children. Amen.*

Barbara Johnson

Earnest Counsel

The pleasantness of one's friend springs from his earnest counsel.
—PROVERBS 27:9

There is nothing like a friend who brings you dinner when you're swamped, who helps you wallpaper, who applauds your successes, who shares your tears, and, especially, who tells you the truth: "Sweetie, you have a piece of spinach pasted across your front tooth."

Friends don't let friends dangle their pantyhose out their trouser pants as they sashay across town without at least alluding to the dangling participle. Or tell their friend she looks great when her outfit makes her look like a jaundiced camping tent. Or fail to mention the wide swath of magenta lipstick running down their friend's chin.

I have several friends whom I love to shop with because I trust their opinions. They say things like, "That wouldn't be my favorite choice for you," or "It's okay but not great," or "Put it back before it multiplies!"

People help to define us, for they often serve as a second pair of eyes. "Do you think it was inappropriate that I said what I did?" "What would you do?" "See what you think of this."

Life is multidimensional, and we can use every viewpoint we can get lest we miss an angle. Proverbs reminds us that "plans fail for lack of counsel" (15:22).

My five Women of Faith speaking cohorts and I often serve as a mirror for each other before we go onstage. And after we've finished, if any of us is concerned about something in our message, we'll brainstorm together to solve the dilemma. Backstage we frequently solicit each other's counsel to help with personal obstacles we are facing. How pleasant to have earnest counsel!

Lord, thank you for the truth spoken by a friend.
Amen.

Patsy Clairmont

God Broken

For we do not have a high priest who is unable to sympathize
with our weaknesses, but we have one who has been
tempted in every way, just as we are. —HEBREWS 4:15

For much of my Christian life I didn't see the value of paying homage to Good Friday. After all, it was the Resurrection Day that commemorated life over death, salvation over sin, hope over despair, and heaven over hell. Jesus' resurrection marked the establishment of the New Covenant: Humankind no longer lives under the Old Testament law that is impossible to keep, but under grace, which clothes us with cross-earned perfection.

I've come to realize, however, that to overlook Good Friday is to miss the full meaning of Easter. The cross is not only the place upon which my salvation was secured but also the place upon which Jesus experienced the full extent of what it means to be human. It was there he felt shame, agony, torture, abandonment, and murder. As he anticipated that horrendous experience, he knew excruciating fear and dread.

There is nothing in human history—tortuous abuse, misrepresentation, false accusation, or death itself—that God has not felt. We can never say to him, "You don't know what this is like for me"—because he does. Jesus chose to obey his Father's will, to feel all our horrors and suffer all our injustices, so that absolutely no wrenching experience of ours was unknown to him. Why? So he might stand in the middle of our pain with us. Our agony was and continues to be his as well. We are never abandoned. That is good news for Good Friday.

*Lord Jesus, there is no deeper compassion and love than
what you gave to the world from the cross. Amen.*

Marilyn Meberg

March 30
What a Friend!

The Lord knows those who are his.

—2 TIMOTHY 2:19

It is said that the song "What a Friend We Have in Jesus" is often one of the first hymns missionaries teach to new believers. Its easy tune and soothing lyrics have made it a comforting favorite of Christians around the world. What solace there is in these simple but powerful words!

First published in 1869, the hymn began as a poem written by Canadian immigrant Joseph Scriven to encourage his invalid mother in far-off Ireland. In his book *101 Hymn Stories*, Kenneth Osbeck writes that Scriven came from a wealthy family but as an adult "took the Sermon on the Mount literally . . . even sharing the clothing from his own body, if necessary, and never once [refusing] to help anyone who needed it."

Just humming the old, favorite refrain brings peace to my mind on hectic, stress-filled days. Try it sometimes. When the airplane is suddenly tossed around the sky by high-altitude turbulence . . . when your kid is in trouble again . . . when a relationship turns rocky . . . close your eyes and sing the little song to yourself, remembering that Christians have a Friend who will "take and shield" us in his arms, who "knows our ev'ry weakness," who's "still our refuge." What a Friend!

Dear Jesus, my Lord and my Friend, hold me close to you when others turn away. Build me up when life knocks me down. Keep me ever faithful to you. And when my days on earth are done, escort me into heaven to dwell in your presence forever. Amen.

Barbara Johnson

The Unexpected Savior

"Woman," he said, "why are you crying? Who is it you are looking for?"
Thinking he was the gardener, she said, "Sir, if you have carried him away,
tell me where you have put him, and I will get him." –JOHN 20:15

One of my favorite scenes from the Easter story is that moment outside Jesus' tomb when Mary Magdalene mistakenly thought she was talking to the gardener. Perhaps her grief was so deep she couldn't even raise her head to speak directly to the man. Maybe she just couldn't see; after all, John tells us "it was still dark" that morning (20:1). She had seen Jesus die on the cross on Friday. Maybe she just wasn't expecting to find him walking around the cemetery on Sunday!

For whatever reason, Mary Magdalene mistook Jesus for someone else. It was only when he called her by name that she realized who he was.

We have the same "problem" today. We don't expect to find Jesus sitting beside us on an airplane. Or in the bed next to ours in the hospital. Or in line behind us at the grocery store. Sometimes we think we are surrounded by strangers only to realize later that in the midst of the crowd we are accompanied by a Friend like no other. Someone ministers to us with Christ's words, Christ's comfort, Christ's hope. A stranger becomes a friend. And suddenly we realize: Christ is *here!*

*Risen Lord, help me recognize you everywhere I turn. And help
me reflect your Easter lesson in everything I do. Amen.*

Barbara Johnson

APRIL

Wonder

Praise the LORD, O my soul.
O LORD my God, you are very great;
you are clothed with splendor and majesty.
—*PSALM 104:1*

What fills you with wonder? When I saw my newborn grandson for the first time, my breath left me. New life tends to render me speechless, which is why I love the wonder of spring. Tulips, hyacinths, and irises press through hard, cold clumps of earth in resurrection wonder. Baby robins, wide-eyed and hungry, chirp expectantly. Why, even the sun hovers longer, not wanting to miss the unfolding of this lively season.

Our peek-a-boo glimpses of God fill us with a sense of divine reality, like a preview of things to come. We are promised that one day the veil will be lifted from our eyes, and we will see the Lord face-to-face. Imagine that! Try as I might, it is difficult to grasp that kind of holy revelation. But until the day when the mysterious becomes known, God bestows on us encounters in which, for a moment, we are aware we are on holy ground.

Speaking of holy ground, isn't all the earth God's territory? All we know of creation is the Lord's. Therefore, each step we take is on holy land, which means we are on a sacred journey. Sometimes this is hard to remember when we're struggling up a craggy mountain, our shins raw and hands bleeding. Then we thrust our bruised bodies onto the mountaintop, pull ourselves upright, and see the view . . . the wondrous view.

This month let us run, walk, and tiptoe, barefoot and aware that we're on holy ground. Whether we are planting gardens, flipping pancakes, toting our briefcase, or singing in the choir, may we be attuned to the wonder of it all.

Patsy Clairmont

April 1
April Fool

For I know the plans I have for you . . . plans to prosper you and not
to harm you, plans to give you hope and a future. –*JEREMIAH 29:11*

It was during spring break from college, the Saturday before Easter, 1961. I
stayed up all night watching the decorators place the flowers, candelabras, and
lemon leaf plants in the baptistry, in front of the altar, and at the ends of the
pews. All was set for the wedding. The traditional attire awaited the moment
with something old, something new, something borrowed, something blue.

I really didn't think about what day it was until later that afternoon. The
day before had been my birthday, but the only celebrating I'd done was at
the beauty shop.

What if all this preparation was an April Fools' joke? What if the groom
got cold feet and didn't show up for the wedding? What if people thought it
was a joke and none of the guests came? What if the preacher changed his
mind and didn't perform the ceremony? What if the groom forgot to get the
ring?

Fortunately, none of the "what-ifs" happened. George and I have been celebrating April Fools' Day together for forty years.

Life is not an April Fools' joke. We don't have to live thinking about the
"what-ifs." While we can't see the future, we can rest in the Person who holds
our future. We don't have to stay up all night making sure life goes the way
we planned it. Sometimes it will. Sometimes it won't. But in the "won't," it
is always for our good when we trust in the Future Holder.

My future is in your hands, Lord. I marvel at your
perfect plans and your perfect peace. Amen.

Thelma Wells

wonder

A Chronicle of Wonder

Remember the wonders he has done.
—1 CHRONICLES 16:12

Wonder: to be filled with awe; to marvel.

What causes you to marvel? I marvel when I think back on my life's path and see so clearly God's merciful intentions. Isn't hindsight perceptive? Had I known back then what I know today, I would have relaxed more in his care.

I marvel at the Lord's generosity. I'm in awe that he would allow a non-credentialed cracked pot to speak of him across our nation. I marvel at the people he has permitted me to work with and walk with. My heart takes delight in my husband, whom the Lord continues to use in my life in marvelous ways. I'm blessed by our children's intentional involvement with us. And I'm blown away at the wondrous gift of our grandchild.

God instructed the Israelites to speak often of the wonderful ways he had worked on their behalf. They were to recall those ways when they sat at home, when they walked along the road, when they laid down, and when they stood up (Deuteronomy 6:7). In other words, when we are driving on the freeway, working out, debating whether to pick up the remote control, taking a break, or rising in the morning, we are to take a moment to consider our wondrous Lord and his marvelous ways.

Okay, your turn. Make a Chronicle of Wonder. Come on, if we can put together creative scrapbooks, surely we can make a list of spiritual remembrances. It does our hearts good to reminisce. It shores up our faith; it reminds us of what matters; it fans our gratitude; and it helps us to enter our future with a bright flame of hope.

Lord, I acknowledge your wondrous works on my behalf.
Amen.

Patsy Clairmont

Wow!

For great is his love toward us, and the faithfulness
of the LORD endures forever. —PSALM 117:2

Rameses II was a bitter man who determined to eradicate the Israelites, whom he decided produced too many boy babies. He is believed to have had fifty-nine daughters himself! The instruction went out to all the Hebrew women and midwives to kill every baby boy by putting him in the Nile River (Exodus 1:22). The Nile was like the Egyptian freeway. It was the passage for all commerce. It was infested with crocodiles.

The mother of one Hebrew baby wouldn't consider killing her boy when he was born. She hid him for three months, I assume by feeding him every time a tiny cry escaped his mouth! Then when she could no longer hide him she took him to the very place of execution, the Nile, and floated him in a basket near the water's edge while her daughter watched to see what would happen.

The baby was discovered by one of Pharaoh's daughters, who miraculously took pity on him. The baby's sister ran to ask the royal daughter if she should get one of the Hebrew mothers to nurse the child. "'Yes, go,' she answered. And the girl went and got the baby's mother" (Exodus 2:8). Wow! And that was just the beginning of the amazing story of Moses, whom God handpicked to lead his captive people to the Promised Land.

No one, no matter how sinister his heart, can thwart the plans God has for our lives. When we stand back and marvel at the ways of God, they are too wonderful to describe.

Thank you, Father, that your loving hand
has always been on my life. Amen.

Sheila Walsh

April 4
Out the Window

Lift your eyes and look to the heavens: Who created all these?
He who brings out the starry host one by one, and calls them each by name.
—ISAIAH 40:26

I stood at the window last night looking out at the moon. It filled the heavens with the most extraordinary light and my room with luminescence. This morning I watched a bird land in my grapefruit tree, clean its beak, then fly away. Even now the petunias in a window box please my soul.

Have you ever noticed how many artists paint scenes out the window? Ever wondered why? Window paintings capture views far beyond the limits of a studio. They bring beauty into the mundane. Matisse is famous for bringing life indoors. When he was confined to a wheelchair he made cutouts of leaves and stuck them on the wall.

It is hard to stop to enjoy beauty when clothes on the floor need washing, the checkout line is longer than a city block, or the rent is due and you have only ten bucks to your name. I know; I've been there. But, it's at *that time* more than any other when you need a long-distance view. A fresh perspective is in the divine viewpoint, not in our point of view. It may be over the hills and through the woods . . . but it's there.

Every time I stand at a window and take a moment to really look, I dismiss the immediate. Perhaps it is only a few seconds, but those seconds are often what get me through the rest of a long day. Go to your window. Look up. What do you see?

Heavenly Father, lift my eyes and my heart today and give me a point of view that reaches beyond the mundane to the wonderful. Amen.

Luci Swindoll

Transit Wonders

Your eyes will see strange sights and your mind imagine confusing things.
—PROVERBS 23:33

Last year when the Women of Faith tour was in a major East Coast city, my helpers and I decided we wanted to get the real "urban experience," so we rode the transit train from our hotel to the arena. We saw the most amazing variety of characters imaginable on that train: young and old, fat and thin, well-dressed and barely dressed!

The most memorable one was a young man whose face was completely trimmed with jewelry. He had pierced his eyebrows, nose, lip, and tongue. But most striking was the swinging jewelry that dangled from below his mouth. Apparently he had pierced the skin at the very base of his bottom front teeth so that these silvery strands of beads could wave to and fro from his chin. The train was crowded, and he stood over me, hanging on to the pole. As he talked animatedly with his friends, the beads swung back and forth, up and down, in an almost hypnotic way. My mouth dropped open in amazement as I watched those beads bobbing and weaving. My friend, watching me, said I looked like a cat watching a mouse's tail wiggle. She was terrified I would reach up and swat at the beads!

In my ministry, I work with parents struggling to cope with all kinds of shocking situations involving their children. As the boy with the chin jewelry exited the train, I thought of his mother and whispered a little prayer for her. I whispered a little prayer for myself too: "Thank you, God, for keeping me from swatting at those beads!"

Lord, thank you that you are never too "shocked" to love me.
Amen.

Barbara Johnson

April 6
True Love

The LORD does not look at the things man looks at.
—1 SAMUEL 16:7

Alec is in love. He is so sure of his love, he's talking marriage. Alec is three years old; so too is his fiancée. They met in preschool. They place their little chairs next to each other during story time, swing together on the playground, and share the chocolate chips plucked from their cookies during snack time.

Since there appears to be an enduring passion, I asked if I could sing at his wedding. (Alec is my grandson; it seems only reasonable I should participate in the ceremony.) He looked puzzled when I asked him that, but after thinking for a moment he responded with a flat no.

"Why not?" I asked.

"Well, Maungya, you're just too old."

"Well, how old do you have to be?"

Again he thought for a minute. "You gotta be three!"

Last week I picked up Alec at preschool so we could go get an ice-cream cone before I took him home. I was eager to meet the potential little bride so I asked Alec to point her out to me. Just as she was climbing into her mother's minivan, she turned, grinned at Alec, and called a warm "See ya."

I must admit to being a trifle stunned to see that this dear little girl was exceedingly cross-eyed and wore very thick glasses. As we drove away Alec commented dreamily, "Isn't she beautiful, Maungya?"

So like God, I thought. We often say love is blind, but God's love sees all our imperfections and, like Alec, says, "Isn't she beautiful?"

Lord Jesus, the fact that you see me as beautiful when I am not is too wonderful for words. I humbly say, "Thank you." Amen.

Marilyn Meberg

Off the Wall

May God be gracious to us and bless us and make his face shine upon us,
that your ways may be known on earth. —PSALM 67:1–2

Just when I thought I had signed every accessory and article of respectable clothing I could at speaking engagements, I was asked to sign something stranger than the infamous 48D-cup, white lace bra that I signed in Arkansas several years ago. A lady at a Women of Faith conference had the gall to ask me to autograph a pair of pink cotton, queen-size panties. What do you write on panties? (I wrote on the bra, "My cup runneth over.") Well, on the panties I wrote something like, "Bee blessed with a BIG hug."

The lady said she was having them signed by all the speakers as a gift for one of her friends who, at the last minute, could not attend the conference. We welcome everyone to the conferences regardless of their physical, mental, or spiritual condition. But I just hope I'm not asked to sign any other intimate articles of clothing. No nighties, please. That's too off-the-wall.

God uses off-the-wall activities to get our attention. Jesus spit on the ground to make the mud pack that restored a blind man's sight. He opened a fish's mouth and got income tax money. He fed over 5,000 people with a fish sandwich. And all because he loves us. Who says God can't use autographed pink panties to encourage a sister who missed an anticipated event!

Hug your friends with an off-the-wall gesture, just for the love of it.

Father, your expressions of love to me are sometimes
a bit, um, bizarre. But I praise you for your wondrous love
that will go to any lengths to bless me. Amen.

Thelma Wells

Through a Child's Eyes

*Anyone who will not receive the kingdom of God like
a little child will never enter it. –MARK 10:15*

We filed onto the plane road-weary and dulled by an hour's delay at the gate. Most of the other passengers were equally blasé. Shuffling down the aisle, people bumped and twisted carry-on bags and looked at the row numbers. Then, just as everyone was getting settled, two tiny youngsters came dancing through the plane, excitedly chattering nonstop as their parents tried to steer them toward the correct row.

"Is this the plane, Daddy? Is this plane going up in the air?" "Mommy, are we gonna fly? Are we gonna go up, up, up?" The kids obviously were delighted to be off on this grand new adventure. Their parents had arranged things so that each child sat by a window, one in front of the other, with a parent beside them. They bounced on their seats until their parents buckled their seatbelts.

As the plane taxied down the runway, the kids shrieked with glee. "Mommy? Are we flying? Is this flying? Are we flying right now? Brittany, we're flying! This is flying! Do you like it! Look! We're going up! Whoa! We are HIGH!" one of them exclaimed. "AWE-some!" It was impossible not to smile at this running commentary. Suddenly I realized just how amazing air travel really is.

The experience reminded me of the simple, childlike openness Jesus expects when we enter into his presence. Next time you settle into the church pew with a road-weary attitude, let the enthusiasm of the service wash over you. And when your spirits soar, let your childlike self revel in the wonder of God's love. AWE-some!

Father, I long to dance into your kingdom with childlike glee.
Amen.

Barbara Johnson

April 9
Alpha and Omega

"I am the Alpha and the Omega," says the Lord God, "who is, and who was,
and who is to come, the Almighty." –REVELATION 1:8

I don't think that's very nice, Mommy!"

"What's not very nice, darling?" I asked.

"Well, that man on television called God an elephant."

I was fascinated. I stopped what I was doing and tuned in to see what Christian was talking about.

"There! He did it again."

"No, darling. He called him the Alpha and the Omega, not the Elephant and the Omega."

"Well, what's that?"

What a question. Where do we as human beings even begin to wrap our minds around the total wonder of God. One thing we do know is that whatever we have gone through or will go through, God will be there. It is reported that those who have gone through a trauma together have a close-knit bond for life. There is the empathy of presence, of having "been there."

We have that with our Father. There has never been a moment in your life that almighty God has missed. There will never be a crisis in your life that God will be absent from. They say elephants never forget, but these keen creatures have nothing on the wonder of our God.

Father God, you are Alpha and Omega, with me before
the beginning and long after the end. Incomprehensible!
Thank you that you have been and always will be present
in all the moments of my existence. Amen.

Sheila Walsh

April 10
Anything's Possible

For nothing is impossible with God.
–LUKE 1:37

I saw the most beautiful oil paintings when I was in Nairobi. They were lining the walls of the Norfolk Hotel. Everywhere I looked, there they were: scenes of natives in fez hats, English women wearing long dresses, wild animals on the Serengeti . . . and more. Every one of them was beautiful and signed by the same artist—Timothy Brooke. I simply had to have one, but how?

I inquired at the front desk if anyone knew this Mr. Brooke. "Oh yes, madam. Timothy Brooke lives in Nairobi. Would you like his telephone number?"

"Indeed I would."

I left a message on Mr. Brooke's answering machine that I'd like to talk with him about buying a watercolor or oil; but before we were able to make contact, I left Africa for the States.

Months passed. I could not forget those wonderful paintings! Through friends who live in Nairobi, I got Mr. Brooke's e-mail address and, believe it or not, he and I began corresponding.

Over the course of eight months not only did I buy paintings, but I also learned that Tim was in the movie *Out of Africa*, was married with two daughters, and was taught to paint by his father. We never met. Never heard each other's voice. Never knew if the other would keep their word. But across thousands of miles we maintained an honest business relationship and became friends. Anything's possible!

I firmly believe we can do what we set our mind to. It takes time and commitment and faith, but God is in the business of miracles. Don't give up. You have no idea what's ahead for you.

Help me, Lord, to believe anything is possible . . . with you.
Amen.

Luci Swindoll

April 11
You've Got to Be Kidding

They saw the works of the LORD, his wonderful deeds in the deep.
—PSALM 107:24

People say surely a "great fish" did not swallow a guy named Jonah and surely he could not have survived! The Bible says both facts are so. And the *Encyclopedia Britannica* states that the structure of the sperm whale and its habits make it perfectly plausible for a man to be swallowed alive and vomited up after an interval. Sperm whale studies reported in the encyclopedia also show that it would be possible for the guy to remain alive for two or three days within the whale, though certainly with great discomfort.

You've got to be kidding. Nope. Inside the whale's belly is air to breathe because it's needed to keep the mammal afloat. The heat is intense (104–108 degrees), and it would be most unpleasant to be in contact with the gastric juices, which may affect the skin. However, the juices don't digest living matter; if they did, they would digest the walls of the creature's own stomach!

The encyclopedia goes on to recount the swallowing of a sailor off the whaling ship *Star of the East.* His shipmates had lost sight of him and only found him when they opened the belly of the whale they had harpooned two days earlier. The sailor was unconscious but was revived and ultimately resumed his duties on board the vessel.

I am thrilled when I read this kind of secular substantiation of biblical happenings. God has made it perfectly clear to us that his ways are not our ways, and I'm so glad. My ways are not nearly as inventive or exciting as his.

Lord, enlarge my mind that I may embrace wonders
that are larger than my mind. Amen.

M a r i l y n   M e b e r g

April 12
Water Bottle Wonder

Before they call I will answer.
—*ISAIAH 65:24*

Helen Roseveare is an English missionary doctor in Zaire, Africa. When she was in America recently she told this amazing story:

"One night I had worked hard to help a mother in the labor ward; but in spite of all we could do she died, leaving us with a tiny premature baby. We would have difficulty keeping the baby alive, as we had no incubator. A student midwife went to stoke up the fire and fill a hot-water bottle. She came back shortly in distress to tell me that in filling the bottle, it had burst. Rubber perishes easily in tropical climates. 'And it is our last hot-water bottle!' she lamented.

"The following noon, as I did most days, I went to pray with any of the orphanage children who chose to gather with me. I told them about the tiny baby. One ten-year-old girl, Ruth, prayed with her usual blunt conciseness. 'Please, God,' she prayed, 'send us a water bottle. It'll be no good tomorrow, God, as the baby will be dead, so please send it this afternoon.'

"Halfway through the afternoon, I got a message that there was a car at my front door. By the time I reached home from where I'd been teaching the nurses, the car had gone, but there, on the veranda, was a parcel. I felt tears pricking my eyes. I could not open the parcel alone, so I sent for the orphanage children. Inside the package was a brand-new water bottle. That parcel had been on the way for five whole months."

Faithful Father, you are an awesome God who delights to answer our prayers even before they are on our lips. Thank you! Amen.

Sheila Walsh

April 13
Divine Handiwork

In the beginning God created the heavens and the earth.
—*GENESIS 1:1*

God fills me with wonder at his creation. During a bike ride today, I saw a roadrunner dash across my path, his head low, tail feathers high, speeding toward a pressing appointment. This evening I watched low clouds slather over mountain peaks and drizzle down the crags. Then, after sunset, I heard a coyote croon the desert blues. Or perhaps he was serenading the bazillion stars in the velvet sky and I just don't know the difference between his sadness and his sense of wonder.

I know I'm exhilarated with what I see when I lift my eyes to the heavens or peer into the endless sea, as I did on a recent Women of Faith cruise to the Caribbean. I watched with awe as dolphins danced, turtles waltzed, and schools of silver fish darted about like liquid lightning. Water the color of paradise caressed the white, sandy shores, and seabirds skimmed the water's surface. The visual pleasure replays in my mind even now.

But I don't have to go on a cruise to applaud God's handiwork; I can just step out my door and wander through my flowers. From the upturned, sanguine pansies' faces to a dazzling rose, the flowers press a song into my heart: "When I in awesome wonder, consider all the worlds thy hands hath made . . . then sings my soul. . ."

Yet the most breathtaking of God's creations is new life—whether that takes the form of a newborn baby or a heart of stone transformed into a heart of flesh. From a baby's tiny gurgles to a change of direction in a once wasted life, I stand—no, I kneel—in awe.

Lord, your creative work amazes me.
Amen.

Patsy Clairmont

Nets Full of Wonder

He called out to them, "Friends, haven't you any fish?"
"No," they answered. He said, "Throw your net on the right side
of the boat and you will find some." *–JOHN 21:5–6*

Jesus was dead and buried. And like men and women still do today, his friends fled from their grief. They had been fishermen in their old lives, and in their anguish they returned to the sea. They fished all night, but their nets came up empty.

Early that morning a man called to them from shore. They did not realize that it was Jesus (John 21:4). But surely there was something about the man, something about his voice as he called out the ridiculous advice: Throw your net on the other side of the boat. Sure! Like there would be fish on one side of the boat and not the other. But the Bible doesn't say the fishermen rolled their eyes or shouted back smart remarks. They just did what he said, and they were unable to haul the net in because of the large number of fish.

Can't you just see them, straining at those nets, staring at the harvest of fish, and gasping in wonder. Can't you just see John gaping one long second at those flipping, flopping, squirming fish and then hear him say to Peter, "It is the Lord!"

It is the Lord! He is risen! And today he walks along the shores of our lives, calling out ridiculous instructions to us: Love your enemy. Forgive those who wrong you. Believe in me, and even though you die, you too shall live!

Dear Jesus, I believe. I marvel at the way you fill the nets
of my life with love and mercy. Amen.

Barbara Johnson

April 15
For the Birds

Look at the birds of the air; they do not sow or reap or store away in barns,
and yet your heavenly Father feeds them. –MATTHEW 6:26

I'm so glad Jesus encouraged us to be bird-watchers. You talk about an interesting pastime! I live in the desert of southern California, and we have the most fascinating birds. That wily ol' Roadrunner was made for comic relief. The other day I watched one climb a tree. Yes ... *climb!* He took off running and in no time was several branches high, after scaling an eight-foot trunk. I could hear in my head strains of "The William Tell Overture" as this Lone Ranger raced along on cue.

Then there are those delightful hummingbirds. As I was watering flowers one summer evening a beautiful green one flew right into the stream from my hose, fluttering his wings. He then sat on the grass, turned over, and *took a bath*. Two days later I watched another hummingbird completely dismantle a spiderweb piece by piece, carry bits of it in his mouth to a fruit tree in my backyard, and construct a nest. Mesmerizing!

I've drawn pictures of birds in my journals, observed them as I've traveled, made notes about their habits, and captured them on film. Yet I continually find myself mystified and thrilled by the wonder of them all. But here is what's really astonishing to consider: In spite of all their cunning devices, it is God who takes care of those little birds. They are so tiny—but he remembers to feed them!

If he does that for them, how much more will he do for you and me?

Heavenly Father, remind me today that it is you who
meets my needs ... and that you are enough. Amen.

Luci Swindoll

wonder

Dancing Daughters

Delight yourself in the LORD and he will give you the desires of your heart.
—PSALM 37:4

Vikki, my firstborn, told me she had prayed at the beginning of 1999 that God would give her a chance to dance for him. Twelve months later when one of the dancers in the Christmas pageant at church could not dance, Vikki substituted. That started a snowball effect. People began to ask her to dance for their worship services.

Lesa, my youngest, told me several times over a three-year period that she wanted to learn to dance in sign language. On December 2, 2000, my daughters surprised me at my ministry's twentieth anniversary celebration with an interpretive dance to my new album recording, "Jesus Loves Me This I Know." Little did we know that that surprise dance would open a door for my daughters to dance for God all over America.

Mary Graham, president of Women of Faith, was in attendance that night, and she asked Vikki and Lesa to dance at each conference the following year. *Impossible!* I thought at first. I knew Vikki's hectic schedule, and Lesa has a husband, two little girls, and a business. But Vikki's reply was, "Momma, I'll do it. Only what you do for Christ will last." Lesa's immediate reply was, "Yeah, sure. I'll do it." Her husband, Patrick, immediately replied, "Oh yeah, I'm down for that."

I shouted, "Thank you, Jesus!"

When God gives you a talent and you are willing to use it for his glory, he opens doors for you to use it. His timing is perfect, and his plan is wonderful.

Lord, remind me today that you have marvelous ways to fulfill
all the holy desires you have planted in my heart. Amen.

T h e l m a   W e l l s

Now What Was Your Name?

We ourselves, who have the firstfruits of the Spirit, groan inwardly
as we wait eagerly for our adoption as sons, the redemption of our bodies.
—ROMANS 8:23

I milled about a palatial home staring myopically at name tags. Looking from tag to face I struggled not to blurt out, "What in the world happened to you?"

I was attending Seattle Pacific University's reunion for the graduating class of '61, of which I am a muddled member. It makes sense to me that I should have a thirty-seven-year-old son, but surely perky little Jonna Beth who played the piano couldn't be old enough to have a child that age. And what about Clarita Bridges? She has as many wrinkles as I do. What brought that on, and should she be doing something about it? And then of course there was John Malcolm's hip replacement. Mercy!

But as the evening wore on and my whiplash toned down I recognized the familiar and ageless twinkle in Barry Solem's eyes; the droll, subtle wit of Alan Goodmanson; and the irrepressible exuberance of Joyce Olsen. We were strolling around in bodies that showed signs of wear and tear, but our spirits were still youthful, still fun-loving, still hopeful, and still recognizable.

What is it about the human spirit that appears to be ageless in spite of its physical container? It is that divinely placed essence that defines us and distinguishes us from one another, setting us apart as unique creations. That spirit does not have wrinkles or need hip replacements.

Nevertheless, in spite of the wonder of that laudable human spirit, it is not divine; it was created to receive redemption, to become the container of the Holy Spirit. If that's not wonder-full, I don't know what is!

Lord, thank you for your awesome plan of redemption.
Amen.

Marilyn Meberg

God Doesn't Need Your Business Card

I know you by name.
—*Exodus 33:17*

I keep boxes of old business cards. A little weird, I know, but I carry them around as scratch paper. For instance, when I meet someone I try to put special information about her on the back of a card so I can remember her more easily. But as time passes and the cards pile up, I usually don't have a clue who she is.

Isn't it amazing to realize that of all the bazillion people in the world, God doesn't need our business card? We never have to worry about God losing or confusing our identity. Like he told one of his prophets, "Before I formed you in the womb I knew you" (Jeremiah 1:5).

He knows us so well that he always knows where we are, what we're talking about, what we're listening to, what we're eating, what we're wearing, and what we're thinking. He never has to write down anything about us to remind him of who we are.

I want to get to know him that well. His business card is written in sixty-six books of the Bible. His signature is on every page, with emergency phone numbers listed for easy access. When you're in trouble, call John 14. When you worry, call Matthew 6. When you're lonely and fearful, call Psalm 23. When you feel down and out, call Romans 8. When your pocketbook is empty, call Psalm 37. When your attitude toward others needs some tweaking, call 1 Corinthians 13. He wants you to know his mind as well as he knows yours.

All-knowing God, thank you for the wonderful truth that when I call on you, you will never get me confused with anyone else. Amen.

Thelma Wells

Take Off Your Shoes

For in six days the LORD made the heavens and the earth,
the sea, and all that is in them. *–EXODUS 20:11*

Ever felt God gave you more than you could bear? I have. On those days my long-term goal is to have the anxiety go away. My short-term goal is to find a moment's peace. Since only God can provide the former, I try to work on the latter.

One thing that helps me is to go outside barefoot and mess around in my garden. As I put my hands in the dirt, prune flowers, weed plants, and water the lawn, my perspective often changes. There is something about touching real estate that reminds me God is on his throne. The beauty of the earth turns my thoughts toward heaven. Elizabeth Barrett Browning captures the idea:

Earth's crammed with Heaven and every common bush afire with God;
and only he who sees, takes off his shoes.

A few months ago I was burdened about a situation that began to sap my energy and emotional well-being. I struggled with it mentally throughout the day—praying, worrying, and trying to solve it. Couldn't do it. About 5:00 P.M. I thought, *This is ridiculous . . . I've had enough*. So I put on my grubby clothes, took off my shoes, walked outside, and began weeding my flower bed. I worked for more than an hour in the dirt. As the sun was setting, I realized I was humming, and before long . . . singing. The situation had not changed a bit, but I'd found a moment's peace.

Take off your shoes, step outside, and rejoice in the simple wonders of your surroundings.

Lord, help me see that the beauty of earth is crammed
with heaven. Put a new song in my heart. Amen.

Luci Swindoll

"I Wonder ..."

The whole earth is full of his glory.
—*ISAIAH 6:3*

I wonder sometimes if God dreamed up certain creatures just for a laugh. For instance, there is a fish that sucks in air and then hiccups. Its hiccup can be heard by other fish a mile away. Wonder why God did that? I wonder if he laughs over it.

Then of course I wonder about the duck-billed platypus. When the first specimen was brought to England from Tasmania in 1880 the zoologists were mystified by the creature. Its two-foot-long body was covered with thick gray-brown hair (mammal?) but it had a flat tail (beaver?), webbed feet and a wide rubbery bill (duck?), and two spurs behind its rear ankles that secreted poison (snake?). The fact that this bizarre creature laid eggs caused the scientist to finally conclude that it must be a hoax. That theory was discarded, however, when a team of scientists discovered a whole pondful of platypuses in New South Wales. Those creatures could growl like dogs, lived most of their lives in the water, but were also capable of climbing trees. Wonder what God was thinking? I wonder if platypuses make him laugh.

A little-known fact is that bedbugs bark when they smell human flesh. U. S. Army scientists came up with a scheme to use the bugs in Vietnam. The plan was to pack bedbugs in capsules rigged with miniature radio transmitters. The capsules were to be dropped on suspected Viet Cong hideouts. If a radio man overheard their hungry barks, jets and artillery would be called in. The war ended before the bugs saw active duty.

God is a wonder. I think he's also funny.

God Almighty, may I never cease to revel in your uniqueness.
Amen.

Marilyn Meberg

Figuring It Out

And we know that in all things God works for the good
of those who love him. —*ROMANS 8:28*

My husband, Bill, is a stickler for having everything in its place, especially
his stuff—and most especially his tools and workbench things. But it turned
out his four sons enjoyed tinkering with tools as much as he did—they just
didn't enjoy putting things back. It got so bad that by the time Barney, our
youngest son, started his mechanical pursuits, Bill had started padlocking the
tool cabinet! He had learned the hard way that teenage boys couldn't always
be trusted to return things to Bill's neat-and-tidy toolbox.

But Barney outsmarted Bill! He loved to work on his motorcycles and
other projects, and he couldn't afford his own tools. So one summer, as soon
as Bill left for work, Barney would disassemble the tool chest (except for the
padlock through the clasp), use the tools to do whatever it was he needed to
do, then return them to their exact spot inside, and put the toolbox back
together! I can't remember exactly how Bill finally figured out what was going
on, but when he did, he had mixed emotions—frustration that his beloved
tools had been used without his permission and awe at his mechanically talented son!

Sometimes we don't trust God to use us and "put us back" in the right
place. But God outsmarts us! He takes us apart, uses us, and puts us back
together. And when it's all over, we stand in awe of all God did with us.

*Lord, make me a tool of your love to do your work in
the world. Take me apart, use me for your glory, and put
me back together stronger than before. Amen.*

Barbara Johnson

Changed for Good

Therefore, if anyone is in Christ, he is a new creation;
the old has gone, the new has come! –2 CORINTHIANS 5:17

I can imagine what people would have said about Rahab after the walls of Jericho fell and they discovered who had hidden the Israeli spies. I'll bet it really blew their minds when they found out that only Rahab and her family survived the battle. *How in the world did that woman get saved?* everyone probably wondered. *Who is she anyway? I thought she was a lady of the evening. I wonder if that was God or the Devil using her. She's not even good enough for God to save like that.* Can't you just hear it?

Consider people you know who have lived sinful lives, doing everything and anything they wanted. But one day, they heard the good news of Christ and received him into their lives, never to be the same! They began to live out their commitment to Christ, but their reputation preceded them. The grumbling seemed almost inevitable: "I knew them when they were. . . . They're not good enough for the blessings God's giving them. There's something wrong with this picture. People just don't change like that."

Rahab did. She recognized the truth when she heard it. She sacrificed her business for what she believed. She was skillful in transferring her benefits to the people who mattered most to her. This "bad girl" believed in the God of the Israelites and her life changed for good . . . forever.

Savior, the cross was the battleground of my salvation. Because of the blood you shed there, I am not the same. Praise your holy name! Amen.

Thelma Wells

The Divine Engineer

I provide water in the desert and streams in the wasteland,
to give drink to my people. —ISAIAH 43:20

Habitat for Humanity could probably publish an encyclopedia of stories about how their organization has demonstrated the power of trust as it has built homes—sometimes whole neighborhoods—with folks who otherwise could not afford one. In their book *The Excitement Is Building,* Habitat founders Millard and Linda Fuller tell how an all-volunteer crew was struggling one day to assemble prefabricated roof trusses that "simply would not fit. With half of the trusses already incorrectly in place, it was soon determined that no manner of recalculation or relocation would solve the problem."

They barely noticed a passerby who had stopped to watch. When he asked to take a closer look, they were so intent on solving the mess they were in that they just nodded and returned to their challenge. "Because everyone was so frustrated by this time, the man was hardly noticed as he scurried nimbly up the framework and examined the layout. He soon came down and gave all the dejected volunteers a jolt. He explained a detailed but basic solution to the seemingly insoluble problem. The volunteers quickly set about doing just as he suggested, and his plan worked to perfection."

The workers were so busy—and so relieved—that they never noticed when the man left. They had never seen him before, and they never saw him again. But they had no doubt who sent him. They called him their "divine engineer."

Oh, Father, you are the Divine Engineer who makes all things work
together for good. Help me put my trust in you and you alone. Amen.

Barbara Johnson

Around the Next Bend

The desert and parched land will be glad;
the wilderness will rejoice and blossom. —ISAIAH 35:1

I was riding my bike down a street when I turned a corner. An endless, gray pavement that stretched out to meet the drab curb and dingy sidewalk greeted me. Running alongside the walk was a dusty patch of earth that piled up against a beige wall. Then, into this colorless picture an absurd addition intruded itself. Atop the wall and spilling down its side was a vibrant swath of fuchsia flowers.

Suddenly the boring became breathtaking. The dismal became dynamic. The mundane became magnificent. Like a cup of cool water in a desert, a sudden breeze on a stifling night, a rainbow as the storm clouds part, the unexpected appearance of something grand caused my heart to skip a beat.

Isn't life often like that? Think about it.

You're experiencing one of those days when you're tired of yourself, and then someone steps into your landscape and plants words of encouragement. The person values you, and you begin to bloom. Or your work has become a drag, and you think if you have to file one more useless paper, change one more messy diaper, or listen to one more grumbling client, you're going to scream. Then you receive a promotion, the baby asks to go potty, and the client becomes your husband.

God tends to use blah settings to display marvels. We mustn't give up when we experience a succession of gray days and beige encounters. Some stunning surprise awaits us around the next bend.

Lord, thank you for adorning the world with your dazzling touches.
Amen.

P a t s y   C l a i r m o n t

Wonderfully Faithful

Give thanks to the LORD, call on his name; make known among
the nations what he has done. Sing to him, sing praise to him;
tell of all his wonderful acts. —1 CHRONICLES 16:8–9

Most biblical scholars are not specific as to who wrote 1 and 2 Chronicles. Jewish tradition has it that Ezra, the priest and scribe, was the author. These two books are a historical record of the time of creation to the return of God's people from exile in the sixth century. This particular verse calls on God's chosen people to remember all the wonderful things God has done. The writer pulls directly from Psalm 105.

> Give thanks to the LORD, call on his name; make known among the nations what he has done. Sing to him, sing praise to him; tell of all his wonderful acts. Glory in his holy name; let the hearts of those who seek the LORD rejoice. Look to the LORD and his strength; seek his face always. Remember the wonders he has done, his miracles, and the judgments he pronounced (vv. 1–5).

"*Remember. . . ,*" the writer of the psalm says. There is a life-changing principle here. The people of God had a written record of God's faithfulness to them. When days were dark they could return to this record and recall the wonders and miracles of their amazing God.

I have begun a journal for my son that I plan to give to him when he leaves home. It is a record of God's faithfulness to him that I as his mother have observed. Wouldn't it be a worthy tradition if every Christian family had its own book of the faithful ways of God?

Father, you are faithful to every generation.
Thank you for your wondrous ways. Amen.

S h e i l a   W a l s h

Sweet Fragrance

His lips are lilies dripping with myrrh.
—*SONG OF SONGS 5:13*

Every lady I know enjoys getting a gift of fresh flowers. I guess my Women of Faith speaker pals felt either pity or disgust for me because they know I plant artificial flowers in my yard. At my anniversary celebration of my ministry's twentieth year, Luci Swindoll presented me with a gift of fragrant, colorful flowers, to be delivered once a month for a year.

When I received my first amaryllis, I watched it bud to red—its lily-like blossoms attached to tall, green stalks. Soon the flowers faded but the stalks remained sturdy.

The next month I received daffodil buds that I watched bloom. The graceful flowers faded but the tall, green stems remained intact.

Watching, watering, and waiting to plant my monthly perennials in the ground reminded me of the fragrant, multiplying, life-giving attributes of two names given to Jesus: the Rose of Sharon and the Lily of the Valley. The Rose of Sharon is known for its low, bushing flowers and sweet fragrance. The Lily of the Valley is known for spreading and wrapping itself around objects.

Our Rose of Sharon lowered himself from the Incarnate God and died for you and me to make sure the fragrance of his love could blossom in us. Our Lily of the Valley wraps himself around us to protect us from harm.

We have the wondrous privilege to bloom and spread the fragrance of Christ in our world. The Rose lives eternally in the soil of our hearts. What better gift to give or receive than the sweet fragrance of our wonderful Lord.

Jesus, help me spread your sweet fragrance throughout
the world to everyone I meet. Amen.

T h e l m a   W e l l s

April 27
Celebrating Sadness

Sorrow is better than laughter, because a sad face is good for the heart.
—ECCLESIASTES 7:3

I grew up in a happy family. In fact, as a child I wasn't permitted to be sad. When I felt sad, I tried to hide it from my mother. She never said, "Put on a happy face," but I got the message. Since childhood, sadness has produced feelings of guilt in me. To be sad was unacceptable and un-Christian.

Then, Pat Wenger came along.

Pat works in the mental health profession. One day when she and I were chatting, I found myself apologizing for feeling low. I didn't like myself when I was sad and I couldn't imagine she liked me either. She listened attentively, then said, "Luci, don't run from your sadness, and don't feel bad about being sad. *Enjoy* it because it connects you to your childhood where it all began. Your sadness can serve you."

I was amazed. She added, "Some of your best work will be produced out of your sadness."

That made so much sense. Of course! Sadness is often better than laughter. It gives me deepening moments of creativity, contemplation, and wonder. And that's true for anyone. Many of the most thoughtful, creative, and well-respected projects in the world were produced from a person's sadness or pain.

If you feel sad today, lean into it. Don't fight it or try to put on a happy face. Feel whatever you feel. You are in a good place. Tell the Lord about it and ask him to connect with you right where you are. Then see what surprising things happen.

Dear Lord, I bring you all my feelings today—every one of them! You made them, and I celebrate the wonder of them all. Amen.

Luci Swindoll

A Splash of Answered Prayer

In my alarm I said, "I am cut off from your sight!"
Yet you heard my cry for mercy when I called to you for help. –PSALM 31:22

The concourse was packed with women eagerly trying to get to their seats at the Women of Faith conference. Through this throng of bodies, a snakelike chain of ladies, holding hands, worked its way toward the appropriate gate into the arena. As the chain bent toward my book table, my daughter-in-love, Shannon, held out a shiny flat marble, a little gift we were giving out that evening. Shannon's eyes met those of a young woman in the chain. "Do you need a splash of joy?" she asked with her brightest, warmest smile. The young woman released the hand of the woman in front of her, accepted the marble, dropped it in her pocket, then grasped her friend's hand once more and moved on through the crowd.

The next day a woman from that group told Shannon this story: "Of our entire busload of women, that young mother is the one who is really hurting," she said. "Her heart is broken, because her baby died a few weeks ago. On the bus we all prayed that something would happen here to ease her pain, and somehow that little splash of joy has been like a spiritual vitamin for her. Showing it to us, she laughed for the first time in ages. We just wanted you to know: That silly little marble was an answer to prayer."

Lord, thank you for those precious moments when you use me
as a conduit of your love to someone who is hurting. Never let me forget
what a wondrous privilege it is to be your servant. Amen.

Barbara Johnson

I'm Booked

Jesus, the author and perfecter of our faith.
–HEBREWS 12:2

When a friend asked me what I wanted for my birthday, I responded promptly: "A book." I love books—books on all topics (well, perhaps not all) and books of all sizes. I especially appreciate little books with big messages and big books with great art. I display books in stacks, baskets, and on bookshelves. The older the books the better, although many new releases catch my interest and charm me with their presentations.

Recently my husband surprised me with a twenty-four-volume set of Robert Louis Stevenson's works. What a great gift (as much for decorating as for reading) because of their petite size, leather covers, and gilded lettering. Books warm up an environment and are friendly since they invite inspection.

Sometimes I purchase a book because of its author; other times the topic draws me in or the artwork or the clever design. I have a growing collection of children's books, including the hilarious adventures of Junie B. Jones by Barbara Park.

By far my most treasured book is the Bible. It's the Author that draws me into this one. I've found the book to be moving, mysterious, devotional, biographical, prophetic, poetic, romantic, dramatic, historic, and more.

In search of a good read? Allow this book-aholic to influence your choice: view Joseph in prison for a crime he didn't commit; help Deborah to fight a war without weapons—and win; go from a cry of anguish to an aria of praise with Hannah; visit with Lydia, a successful businesswoman, and watch her faith at work.

The Scriptures are more than just a good read; they give your life greater definition. Trust me; I know.

Lord, write your words on my heart.
Amen.

Patsy Clairmont

Open Your Eyes

Though your sins are like scarlet, they shall be as white as snow; though they are red as crimson, they shall be like wool. –ISAIAH 1:18

Close your eyes. Picture a sunset . . . a flower garden . . . a clown . . . a butterfly . . . a stained-glass window . . . a carnival. What does every one of these have in common? Color—vivid, intense color. The world is a spinning color wheel and we are its fortunate inhabitants.

Henri Matisse said, "Color has its own existence; it possesses a beauty of its own." The color of things is one of life's added attractions, incidental to whatever makes the world go round. Knowing we would have dark days, maybe God just threw in color to give our lives sparkle and joy. Like in Genesis 1:16 where it says, "He also made the stars"—as though such magnificence were an afterthought! Perhaps color is like that: a treasure, flung out there by his almighty hand.

Have you ever noticed how often Scripture speaks of color? There's *blue* yarn, *green* pastures, *purple* clothing, *yellow* breastplates, *brown* horses, a *white* throne . . . and more. In the Scripture for today, Isaiah paints a picture of redemption in living color—brushing away the red stain of sin to reveal the pure white of atonement. The Bible is an artist's palette.

Don't permit yourself to be trapped in a drab, flat, colorless life that lacks luster and brightness. Christ's death on the cross enables you to live in the light. Color *is* light. It is manifested in a blue sky, a golden dawn, and an iridescent rainbow. God's wondrous handiwork is all around you. It's a masterpiece. Open your eyes.

Heavenly Father, open my eyes and my heart to the beauty that's around me. Help me think of ways to create a more colorful life. Amen.

L u c i   S w i n d o l l

MAY

Grace

I do not set aside the grace of God, for if righteousness could be gained through the law, Christ died for nothing! –*GALATIANS 2:21*

What would you think if my son Jeff called me today with the suggestion of what he considers a good installment plan? That plan is a series of payments for the Titleist golf club I gave him for Christmas. He claims it has so improved his game he feels guilty about not paying for it, and he also fears I may have gone beyond my budget with its purchase.

Feeling a little hurt, I explain that the club was a personally selected gift I wanted him to have. If he set up a series of payments, it would no longer be a gift; it would be a loan. He concludes the conversation by saying I can call the club anything I choose, but he plans to pay for it in spite of my protest.

"Well," you say, "what's wrong with your son, Marilyn? What did you do to him during those formative years that made him think he is not worthy of a generous Christmas present?" Sighing, I might answer your question with, "I'm not sure what went wrong, but I've failed somewhere. I can't imagine why he feels he has to do payback on everything. He's thirty-seven years old and still making payments to me for his orthodontia."

God offers us an extravagant gift: his grace. It cost him everything; it costs us nothing. The only payback God asks is that we reach out and take the gift and then rest in it with guilt-free comfort.

As you read this section on God's grace, fight the impulse to call God and suggest an installment plan. It will hurt his feelings.

Marilyn Meberg

Spanning the Chasm

To God's elect, strangers in the world. . . . Grace and peace
be yours in abundance. *–1 PETER 1:1–2*

When fire broke out in a packed theater in Chicago on December 30, 1903, an eighteen-year-old college student, Will McLaughlin, was one of the first to respond. The theater was filled with nineteen hundred women and children who had flocked to see a popular holiday matinee. When Will heard the cries for help, he scrambled up the steel fire escape to perch precariously from a third-floor exit as the fire swept unabated through the theater. A board was laid between the high-level exit and the adjoining building, and Will assisted several mothers and their children across the harrowing escape route.

Will McLaughlin died as the result of injuries he suffered when bodies and debris fell on him during the Iroquois Theater fire. Six hundred others perished as well. But at least seventeen mothers and their children lived because he handed them across that wobbly plank to be rescued. Afterward, the board was engraved with his name and the date of the fire and sent to his parents as a token of gratitude.

None of the rescued women and children had known Will McLaughlin before the fire. When they set out so merrily for the theater that morning, none of them could have dreamed that a stranger would give his life for them before the day ended. They received a gift that afternoon that they could never imagine receiving and never begin to repay. It's a lot like the marvelous gift we Christians enjoy every day of our lives: God's rescuing grace!

God, thank you for your grace that hands me across the chasm
of sin and saves my life anew each day. Amen.

Barbara Johnson

Where Truth and Mercy Meet

The Word became flesh and made his dwelling among us.
We have seen his glory, the glory of the One and Only,
who came from the Father, full of grace and truth. –JOHN 1:14

Lord, you see me through your mercy
I am guilty, still you love me
In your kindness there is justice
Through your goodness you have brought me here
Where truth and mercy meet
You triumph over me
Your love has won my heart again
And still I am so amazed, my guilt is washed away
Upon your cross of peace
Where truth and mercy meet

–JOHN HARTLEY & GARRY SADLER

A multitude of miracles took place on the gallows of Golgotha. Sinful men and women are now able to come into the presence of our Holy God through the blood of his own slain Lamb. At the cross, all that is true about us came face-to-face with the mercy of God. That is grace. It is not that God ignores our sin or pretends it never happened, but because of his great love for us he declares us worthy through Christ. There is no need anymore to hide in the shadows. We can be known and we can be free.

Truth and mercy are strange companions. Often it is the truth about our lives that separates us from one another. We are disappointed in each other and exchange mercy for miles, putting distance between us. God is not like that. Knowing all that is true about us, he reaches out and pulls us close.

Father, this love and grace you extend is overwhelming.
Your love has won my heart forever. Amen.

Sheila Walsh

May 3
You Can't Pay for It

Not that I am looking for a gift, but I am looking for what may be credited
to your account. —PHILIPPIANS 4:17

For months I saved to buy a car. When I saw the new Chrysler PT Cruiser,
I thought, *That's for me.* But it was impossible to find one. Dealers set up
appointments but sold the car before I arrived. Hoping to just sit in one, I'd
search them out in malls; but when I got there, the door was locked. After
months of trying, I gave up.

I decided to check out the ol' Oldsmobile. I told the Lord on the way to
the dealership, "You know I want to pay cash for the car, but I'd rather not
spend the money today. Guide me, Lord, and help me trust you."

There was a model I drove, loved, and decided to buy as soon as possible. Then the dealer shocked me. He said, "Oh, by the way, you can't pay for
this car."

"Huh?"

He laughed. "Oldsmobile is offering an incentive to whoever buys today.
You wait one year to actually pay for it, interest free."

"Really?" I stammered. "When did this go into effect?"

"Last night."

"And how long does the offer last?"

"I don't know. You're the first customer I've presented it to. I guess it's your
lucky day."

That deal had nothing to do with luck. It was grace through and through.
I didn't even pray for something so outlandish. It was God's idea. I just asked
him to guide me, and he did.

Now when I see a PT Cruiser I smile, pat my dashboard, and sail on down
the road.

> *Lord, when I don't get my way, help me
> believe you have a better plan. Amen.*

Luci Swindoll

May 4
Santa Blew It for Us

Yet what is due me is in the LORD's hand, and my reward is with my God.
—ISAIAH 49:4

I have a theory about one of the reasons it may be so hard for us to grasp the concept of grace. I suggest the fault lies with Santa Claus.

Many children are raised with the theologically unsound notion that there is an omniscient fat guy who lives at the North Pole feverishly working along with his elves to reward good behavior with gifts at Christmas. Children are reminded throughout the year that Santa knows who is naughty and nice, and the day of reckoning will occur on Christmas Eve.

Some children try to give Santa a testimony of their worthiness by writing to tell him how good they've been all year. Santa then weighs their fine deeds according his performance grid. Think of the tension for the child who misbehaves in July and has to wait five agonizing months to know whether or not all gifts for her will be expunged from Santa's sleigh!

I was walking behind a little boy and his mother in the mall this past Christmas. The boy had just climbed off Mall Santa's lap, and Mom and son were talking about the experience. The little boy remarked, "Santa doesn't seem to remember about my cheating in spelling." The mother's response was to assure her son that just because Santa didn't mention it didn't mean he didn't remember it. "I guess you'll find out in a few weeks," she said.

I couldn't stand to listen to one more word so I ducked into the local pie shop where grace abounds.

Lord Jesus, thank you that your continual love and acceptance
does not depend on my performance. Amen.

M a r i l y n   M e b e r g

Grace in Action

God opposes the proud but gives grace to the humble.
—JAMES 4:6

I enjoy watching figure skaters move across the ice with the grace of twirling snowflakes. They make it look easy, natural. Most of us realize the countless hours of practice necessary to achieve that appearance of ease. Years of rigorous training, including exercise programs, diets, and dance instructions, mixed with athletic giftedness to prepare the skaters to glide, jump, and spin so effortlessly. Yet during a perfect performance we forget the cost and find ourselves wishing we were that fluid and graceful.

I've witnessed folks like that—people who, through the rigors of hardships, disappointments, and even tragedies, amaze us by living their lives with seeming ease. Joni Eareckson Tada is one of those people.

Joni has been a guest speaker at Women of Faith conferences many times. She was paralyzed from the neck down by a diving accident when she was seventeen. But Joni enters our group with gentle strength, directing us to Jesus with her words, her songs, and her heart. And has this woman got heart! Joni does more in her disabilities than most of us do with our abilities. She speaks, writes, paints (with a brush between her teeth), and travels, distributing wheelchairs to Third World countries to help disabled people.

Don't you think she would be more comfortable and secure at home? Instead, she skates out on what would seem like, for many of us, thin ice, and she does so with generosity and ease. She makes grace seem effortless. Her performances on and off the stage leave one breathless. Yet I know Joni has paid and continues to pay a tremendous price.

Grace isn't cheap.

Lord, may I never forget the price you paid to give me grace.
Amen.

Patsy Clairmont

Never Off Duty

Let no debt remain outstanding, except the continuing debt to love one another, for he who loves his fellowman has fulfilled the law. –ROMANS 13:8

Will you scratch my back, honey?" my husband asked one evening.

"Barry, I'm tired. My back's sore too, you know," I replied.

"You know, Sheila, sometimes I think I would get more of your time if I stood in one of your book lines."

He didn't say it with any venom. It wasn't a low blow, just a simple statement of what seemed real to him.

I thought about that for a long time. He was right. It is easy to be loving and kind for twenty-four hours to thousands of complete strangers knowing that I'll fly home shortly. But my lifelong commitment is to my husband. Our son, Christian, will one day head off and make his own life, but Barry and I have chosen to be together until God takes one of us home. We have accepted the call to love as Christ loved.

Jesus loved expecting nothing in return. That's hardest to do with our families and closest friends. We feel like they know us so well that they should anticipate our needs and feelings and, perhaps, not expect too much. But that is not the gospel. Christ calls us to give out of full, grateful hearts with no thought for ourselves. We are never off duty as believers. We have an outstanding debt to love and love and love.

So, if you come to a conference and I'm not at my book table, I'm off somewhere scratching my husband's back!

Heavenly Father, teach me to love as you love, to give as you give, to live as you lived amongst us. Amen.

Sheila Walsh

Cramped Quarters

*Let's make a small room on the roof and put in it a bed and a table, a chair
and a lamp for him. Then he can stay there whenever he comes to us.*
—2 KINGS 4:10

I love small rooms. Homes. Nooks. In this place on the roof, the prophet
Elisha brought a woman's son back to life. It was a miracle designed by God,
but I'm impressed that something so astounding happened in such a small
space. No big crowds. No cheering section. No onlookers. In fact, Scripture
says when Elisha learned the boy was lying dead on the bed, he went in the
room and *shut the door.*

I think of my brothers, both in international public Christian ministry,
who shared a tiny bedroom while they were growing up. I can still remember
them down the hall at bedtime, quoting aloud the Scriptures they were mem-
orizing or singing hymns together in harmony. The walls of that room housed
the first spiritual words and music of these two dynamic leaders.

Did you know that on May 7, 1945, the document of surrender between
Germany and the Allies was signed inside a little red schoolhouse at Reims,
France? This unassuming building had been the headquarters for General
Eisenhower while he was leading the American Armed Forces. Think of the
difficult, major decisions that were made during those eventful days. And it
all happened in that tiny room.

If you find yourself in a small space, God knows you're there. He's with
you, and he can do something mighty big. Trust his amazing grace.

*Father, give me a sense of your presence right now. Remind me that
your grace reaches into the most cramped quarters. Amen.*

Luci Swindoll

Standing in Grace

Remember not the sins of my youth and my rebellious ways; according
to your love remember me, for you are good, O LORD. —PSALM 25:7

Once there was a young man who had great skill and potential. He bragged
obnoxiously about how good he was. He tried to demand people's respect. But
one day his cockiness caught up with him: He lost his job and could not find
another one for months.

Almost a year passed and nothing good happened, he thought. Nobody
would hire him. He tried to start his own business, but he failed. He got so
depressed and ashamed that thoughts of ending it all played in his head. It was
difficult for him to believe that in spite of these demoralizing circumstances,
God was still at work in his life. But he'd accepted Jesus at an early age, and
at the very moment of salvation, the Holy Spirit had come to live within him.
Even though he didn't feel secure in his current circumstances, he tried to
bank on the truth in Scripture: "Therefore, since we have been justified
through faith, we have peace with God through our Lord Jesus Christ, through
whom we have gained access by faith into this grace in which we now stand"
(Romans 5:1–2).

We *stand*, even when life beats us down.

One day the young man got a life-changing phone call, offering him the
opportunity to interview for the job of a lifetime. He got the job! The grace
of God was imputed to him even though he didn't believe he deserved it. He
learned that bad behavior does not stop God from lavishing us with his unmerited favor.

Lord, thank you that your grace is greater than all my sins.
Amen.

T h e l m a   W e l l s

Hourly Dependence

We believe it is through the grace of our Lord Jesus that we are saved.
–ACTS 15:11

Obviously, I wasn't thinking clearly in 1975 when I promised God that, if I survived my family's latest crisis, I would start a ministry to help other parents cope with the problems we were facing. Frankly, I couldn't imagine how I could survive the estrangement of our homosexual son, Larry, after also losing two sons in five years—Steve in Vietnam and Tim in a crash with a drunk driver. No, I thought for sure I was going to die; otherwise I never would have made that promise!

But today, Spatula Ministries is the result of that anguished vow. It is an outreach that scrapes parents off the ceiling with a spatula of love when they have landed there due to problems with their children. And in the year 2000, the 100th Spatula group was organized when a group of parents of homosexuals got together to support each other in, of all places, a little town called Cut and Shoot, Texas! I could not have imagined, twenty-six years ago, that something good would actually come from the agony I felt. Back then I wasn't even surviving day to day; it was more like breath to breath.

"If God wants you to do something, he'll make it possible for you to do it," said Louis Cassels, "but the grace he provides comes only with the task and cannot be stockpiled beforehand. We are dependent on him from hour to hour, and the greater our awareness of this fact, the less likely we are to faint or fail in a crisis."

God of love, Father of mercy, thank you for your sustaining, empowering, and energizing grace. With you, all things are possible! Amen.

Barbara Johnson

Used by God

The stone the builders rejected has become the capstone.
–PSALM 118:22

Lloyd Ogilvie, now chaplain of the U.S. Senate, was the commencement speaker at our son Larry's junior-college graduation. After hearing the honors Larry had earned, Dr. Ogilvie told Bill and me, "God has his hand on this boy and will use him in a wonderful way."

The very next day I found homosexual magazines and letters in Larry's room. We argued bitterly, and shortly afterward, Larry disappeared for eleven years. Often during that anguished time of estrangement, I remembered Dr. Ogilvie's words and thought, *If you only knew...*

Eventually God brought restoration to our family. Larry came home, and although his sexual orientation didn't change, his heart changed, and he assured us he stood clean before the Lord. A few months later, Dr. James Dobson invited Larry to comment during a radio program he did with me for the national broadcast, *Focus on the Family*. Larry said, in part, "If we as Christians can purpose in our hearts to be kind and loving ... and put away a condemning spirit ..., then surely the light of Christ will be able to shine in our disbelieving world and restoration and revival will take root in the lives of those we touch on a daily basis."

For years since then I've played a tape recording of Larry's words to audiences around the country, and today, more than a million people have heard his message of hope and grace. Spatula Ministries is an outgrowth of what I've learned from having a gay son. God has, indeed, used Larry—and me—in a wonderful way.

*Father, by your grace the weak become strong and the
rejected come home. Thank you, Lord. Amen.*

Barbara Johnson

Agents of Grace

Each one should use whatever gift he has received to serve others, faithfully administering God's grace in its various forms. —1 PETER 4:10

The apostle Peter makes it clear that no matter what personal and spiritual gifts each of us in the body of Christ has been given, we are all called to administer God's grace to each other.

We tend to categorize service in the church. Those in so-called full-time ministry are looked on as the "real" administrators of God's grace and love. I remember a family of four in our church when I was growing up in Scotland. The father had a good job, but the mother had a restlessness for full-time ministry. She believed that the only way to prove to God that she loved him was through evangelism. Several nights a week she would go door-to-door in our town with tracts and invitations to church. More often than not her two sons came home from school to an empty house. Many nights they put themselves to bed while their mother was off "serving God."

When I look into the eyes of my son, I am convinced that one of the greatest callings on this earth is to share the grace of God with our own families. How sad it would be if Christian grew up resenting a God who took his mother away from him to serve God when he was a child!

Whatever you put your hands to today, use your gifts to administer grace to those around you. And start at home with those who need your presence the most.

Father, thank you that you do not categorize worthwhile service,
but that you receive all things done in your name.
Make me an agent of your grace. Amen.

Sheila Walsh

Momma's Sword

Take ... the sword of the Spirit, which is the word of God.
—EPHESIANS 6:17

When I think of the thing for which I am most grateful in life, it would have to be God's Word. From childhood, I heard Scripture from my mother day after day. And she encouraged her children to learn and study as well. *Thank you, Momma.*

In the front of her own well-worn Bible she wrote,

> Once I settle it for good that there is nothing in the Bible that is trivial and meaningless, once I am assured that *everything* in Scripture has significance and value, then I shall prayerfully ponder every section and expect to find "hidden treasures" (Proverbs 2:4). And according to my faith, so it will be unto me.

Momma taped Scripture verses all over the house, muttering them to herself as she went about her work. One evening she said to me, "I want to quote for you what I've just memorized, okay?"

"Great, Mom. What is it?"

"First Peter."

I waited a second, then asked, "First Peter? First Peter *what?*"

"Oh ... the book. I memorized the whole book. Wanna hear it?"

Without hesitating she started in and quoted every single verse. I was amazed. My sixty-three-year-old mother was a whiz. She never missed a beat as Daddy and I listened, mesmerized. I was the witness of Momma's love of God's Word throughout my childhood, and I'm the richer for it.

If you are a mother and discouraged about your children, don't lose hope. Spend time in God's Book. Hidden treasures will be found and passed on. And your children will be grateful someday. According to your faith, you will see things change.

> *Give encouragement to my heart, Lord, through your Word.*
> *Amen.*

Luci Swindoll

Customer Delight

So in everything, do to others what you would have them do to you.
—MATTHEW 7:12

Doing business in this fast-paced world can easily become impersonal. Yet, if we are to maintain complete customer satisfaction, we must do more than simply meet demand, we must offer delight.

I saw customer delight demonstrated after deplaning at an airport and watching a lady discover that the rental car company she'd contracted with had moved. A representative from another rental company offered to help the perplexed customer. This is some of what I heard her say: "May I assist you? What is your name, please? Ms. Johnson, they have moved to another location, so let me help you. Because it's Sunday, they do not have a driver. But I'll call a taxi for you, let them know you're coming, and give you a voucher so you can pay the taxi driver. Do you have any bags I can get for you? Is there anything I can do for you to assure you that we are glad you're in our city?"

Do you think that customer was delighted or what?! The representative called the customer by name, solved the problem, and offered additional courtesies that were out of the ordinary.

Many in the business world seem to forget that they are in the business of *servicing* their customers, clients, patients, passengers, students, and staff. It is our responsibility as Christians in business to demonstrate to others how to treat people with grace and abundance. Therefore, let us be reminded that customer satisfaction is not enough. Customer delight is in demand.

Holy Spirit, prompt me to give my best to people I serve.
Help me to treat them as Very Important People—because you
say they are. Amen.

Thelma Wells

So What's a Buzzard Like You Doing Here?

And be kind to one another, tender-hearted.
—*EPHESIANS 4:32 NASB*

Perhaps you have heard about the time-honored tradition of swallows returning to San Juan Capistrano. But what you may not know is that on the same day the swallows return, so too do hundreds of buzzards flap back from their winter homes to the dead, twisted trees of Hinckley, Ohio. And every March 15, the townspeople of Hinckley sponsor a buzzard festival that attracts thousands of tourists from miles around.

There is something wonderfully encouraging about the warmhearted receptivity of the Hinckley people who welcome those unattractive scavengers into their midst. After all, there is nothing even remotely appealing about a buzzard. They have that way of perching in a tree, staring motionlessly at the ground waiting for lunch to walk by. With lightning speed the buzzard swoops down to seize the unsuspecting mammal with its talons and then gobbles it down. I find that unsettling; I'd rather spend the summer with swallows.

We'd probably all rather spend the summer with swallows rather than buzzards in our trees. We are not comfortable with ways that unsettle us or appearances that repel us. We want our environment to look good ... feel good. In fact, the swallow voice in us might say in defense of the environment, "Isn't that halfway house being considered for our community a threat to the wellbeing of our families? And certainly the home for unwed mothers should not be located near our neighborhood. Then of course there's that group of alcoholics who use our church basement for their support group meetings; is that really necessary?"

Hard to believe God created buzzards, isn't it?

> *Lord, your grace is kind and tenderhearted. Help me to*
> *extend your grace to everyone around me. Amen.*

Marilyn Meberg

May 15
Fervor

Those who are wise will shine.
–*DANIEL 12:3*

I was at a hospital visiting a dear friend when I saw a framed statement that, like a spark, ignited my interest: "By their very existence people have the right to be treated with dignity, to be heard, to have their beliefs respected, and to participate in decisions which affect their lives."

Hear, hear! I thought that statement should be displayed in every home and office in the land. I could benefit from that piece of advice. Actually, it's more than a piece; it's almost a whole pie.

Imagine if we put those words into effect in our daily lives. Why, no one would call us names like "Stupid," "Dummy," or "You idiot!" Wouldn't that be refreshing?

We wouldn't have to hear salesclerks abuse customers, or customers demean salesclerks, or one driver's rage against another. We would give each other the benefit of the doubt and extend courtesy. We would draw people in instead of closing them out. And by listening to each other, we would develop greater understanding.

I'll bet we would even have fewer divorces if we really heard each other. And what about our children? Wouldn't they be floored if we went out of our way to show them respect and to look—past their inexperience and tattoos—right into their hearts?

I'm thinking about having the above statement done in calligraphy and made into a brochure. Then I'll distribute them door-to-door. Why, I could put them on car windshields at the mall and bus stations and send some to the United Nations.

Hmm . . . on second thought, maybe I'd better start the kindling of grace at my own house before I try to ignite a world flame.

Lord, light my candle.
Amen.

Patsy Clairmont

Shame-Free

The man and his wife were both naked, and they felt no shame.
—GENESIS 2:25

I wonder what it was like to feel no shame. Adam and Eve are the only two human beings who ever tasted a shame-free existence. Even Christ as he walked amongst us was witness to the depth of the well of shame we mercilessly cast each other into. He wrote in the sand as some religious people put on display a woman who had been caught with a man who was not her husband. Did they catch her in the act and drag her naked through the streets? They just brought her—not the man. She was alone and shamed . . . until Jesus set everyone straight (John 8:1–11).

Or think of the woman who broke the jar of expensive perfume and poured it over Jesus' head, only to experience the ridicule of the onlookers. "'Why this waste of perfume? It could have been sold for more than a year's wages and the money given to the poor.' And they rebuked her harshly" (Mark 14:4–5).

We are and always will be imperfect. In one moment we will be guilty of breaking God's law; in the next we will cruelly cast stones at another who has done the same. But when Christ was crucified he took on himself all the shame and self-righteousness of our sick and twisted hearts. The one who had never tasted sin was made to clean the plate. Shame was the order of the day.

Through the veil torn by the wounds of Christ we can stand before God and feel no shame. God's amazing grace allows us to trade our overcoats of shame for garments of praise.

Thank you, Father, for your amazing grace
that saves a wretch like me. Amen.

Sheila Walsh

Too Good to Be True?

If God is for us, who can be against us?
—ROMANS 8:31

One of the greatest gifts God wishes to lavish upon his human creation is high self-esteem. The foundation for self-esteem is not within the self, but in Christ alone. We experience a deep sense of worth and value only as we realize God's unconditional love for us. We could say then that healthy self-esteem is seeing ourselves through God's eyes and then loving ourselves as he does.

His decision to love us was not based on our ability to stay out of trouble and avoid mistakes. Romans 5:8 assures us, "But God demonstrates his own love for us in this: While we were still sinners, Christ died for us." Nothing can defeat us because the God of the universe is on our side . . . always!

Such esteem-producing truths can seem too good to be true because they don't reflect the human system. The human system tells us we must *earn* esteem; it has to be worked for and established by our own efforts. God says it is already established and our efforts have nothing to do with it.

"Well, surely there is something I must do to receive it," you might say. Yes, there is something you must do: believe it! By faith in the truth of God's gracious and boundless love for you, you can relish being adored, esteemed, valued, and cherished beyond measure.

God, thank you for loving me just as I am. Help me, Lord,
to simply receive your gracious gift deep into my heart
so I can hold myself in the same high esteem you do. Amen.

Marilyn Meberg

Cheap, Cheap!

For everyone who has will be given more, and he will have an abundance.
−MATTHEW 25:29

Men are so funny. I wanted my husband to have a designer tie from Paris. When we were visiting that gorgeous city, we went into a shop and picked out a sumptuous tie. When the salesman quoted the price, George nearly had a stroke and refused to pay "that much" for a tie.

I was determined that whether he wanted one or not, he was going to get a tie from Paris. The understanding salesman, speaking compassionately in his beautiful French accent, said, "Monsieur, this is the top of the line. Perhaps we can interest you in one that is very fine but a bit more to your taste."

So the salesman went through a number of boxes of ties to satisfy the apparently cheap American who was trying to get out of buying one at all. There was something wrong with every tie, either the color or the pattern. Nothing seemed to satisfy George. But the salesman searched patiently until, finally, George said, "I kinda like that one. How much is it?" We knew we had him then. The salesman announced a price that was cheap enough to interest my husband. (In other words, the clerk wore him down.) We walked away with a fashionable tie from Paris that George enjoys wearing.

Have you ever been offered the best of something but were unwilling to invest because you thought the price was too high? Jesus paid the highest price ever to invest in you and me so we could have the finest mansion in glory. He died so we could live forever.

Savior, I will never forget the price you paid to set me free.
Thank you! Amen.

Thelma Wells

Grace in Service

From the fullness of his grace we have all received
one blessing after another. —JOHN 1:16

Before we went to Paris, we were warned that the French merchants give bad service. We expected to be treated unkindly and even ignored.

Not at all! We were treated with the utmost respect and kindness everywhere we went. Some of the merchants even gave us gifts and trinkets from their stores. Others offered us drinks and pastries. Each experience was charming. It made me wonder what other travelers had taken with them into the stores to make people treat them so badly!

I really believe that the way people treat us is usually a direct result of how we treat them. I've watched it. When I go into a store looking preoccupied and unfriendly, I get that same treatment from the workers. If I smile, speak to them, and treat them with respect, I usually get the same treatment. It's called reciprocal response.

How do people treat you when you are shopping or needing service? If you are getting poor service, maybe you are bringing with you an appearance or action that causes others to back off from you or to treat you with a long-handled spoon.

A good attitude and warm smile, a friendly handshake, or a sincere compliment wins half the battle in all our relationships. When service is shoddy, you can change the atmosphere with kindness. Do not reciprocate negatively! Two wrongs don't make a right. Grace is what God gives us when our attitudes are bad. And grace we should freely give.

Master Grace Giver, thank you for giving me grace when
I give you bad service. Help me to become an extender
of grace to others even when they don't deserve it. Amen.

Thelma Wells

The Wisdom of Os

Let your conversation be always full of grace.
—COLOSSIANS 4:6

I always record in the back of my journal the name of my favorite person I met that year. In 2000 it was Nicole Johnson, the dramatist on our Women of Faith conference team. Little did I know through our sweet friendship that I would meet Dr. Os Guinness. Nicole and Os were close friends for many years, and she introduced Os to the team.

I first heard of Os in the early seventies when he was working at L'Abri with Francis Schaeffer. More recently I knew of his affiliation with the Trinity Forum in Washington, D.C., and I've read a couple of his books. He was born in China, educated in England, graduated from Oxford, and lives in the States. He's one of the most brilliant persons I know.

In January 2001, Os was invited to spend a day with the Women of Faith speakers. Never referring to a single note, he mesmerized us with history, wisdom, eloquence, and charm. He reeled off dates, people, places, and facts from the time of the Greeks to the present day, establishing the premise upon which America's freedoms were built. Then he reduced all of that historical and biblical perspective down to how it affects us . . . six wacky women.

I love all this brainy stuff about Os. He's my favorite "new person" so far in 2001. But the most noteworthy thing about Os is his love for God and his genuine warmth. He is friendly, funny, and fabulous.

People like Os are God's gift to the whole world. Someone said we become like those we spend time with. Obviously Os has spent a lot of time with the Savior. That's why he's full of grace.

Bless our leaders, Lord. Give them the grace
to be warm and wise with everyone. Amen.

Luci Swindoll

May 21
Amazing Grace!

O LORD, you have searched me and you know me. You know when I sit and
when I rise; you perceive my thoughts from afar. You discern my going out
and my lying down, you are familiar with all my ways. . . . Such knowledge is
too wonderful for me, too lofty for me to attain. —PSALM 139:1–3, 6

The legendary British Prime Minister, Sir Winston Churchill, was once asked,
"Are you ready to meet your Maker?" In typical pithy response he replied, "I
am ready to meet my Maker. Whether he is ready for the ordeal of meeting
me is another matter entirely."

But that is the wonder of the gospel. God knows us thoroughly and loves
us completely. I think the reason it is so hard for us to embrace this truth is
because we have never experienced that kind of love in human flesh. All
human love is conditional. We hide from one another, believing (at times
rightly so) that if we were fully known we would not be accepted. But that is
not true of our heavenly Father's love. He knows all our shadowed places and
longs to fill them with his light.

The psalmist proclaims the wonder of the fact that God is familiar with
all our ways. David was a man who knew shadows well. His choices resulted
in the death of a man as he seduced the man's wife and arranged for him to
be lost on the field of battle. Yet here he is able to sing praise to God. He
does so not because he takes his sin lightly but because he is confident that
his God knows completely, loves totally, and forgives utterly.

Gracious God, thank you that you know
all my ways and love me still. Amen.

Sheila Walsh

Scales of Justice

Give thanks to the LORD, for he is good; his love endures forever.
—PSALM 107:1

During one of my pregnancies I found a way to outsmart my doctor. That was back in the time when doctors ordered their patients to watch their weight religiously, but of course when you're pregnant, everything tastes sooo good. So the only thing I watched my weight do was climb!

Fortunately for me, the scales in my doctor's office were next to a windowsill. So each time I'd go in for a checkup, the nurse would have me step on the scale, and I would secretly press down against the windowsill, taking some of my weight off the scale so it didn't really show how much I'd gained.

My plan worked fine until the day I went into the office and saw that the walls were being freshly painted and all the furniture and fixtures had been pulled out into the middle of the floor—including the scales! I had no way to continue my charade, and the doctor nearly fainted when he saw how much I weighed. I had no choice but to confess my little game and hope for the best.

The doctor gave me quite a lecture after that, and I did my best to control my appetite. Even though I didn't quite follow *all* the rules of a healthy pregnancy, God blessed us with another healthy son. How thankful we were for that beautiful baby! How gracious God is to understand our weaknesses and not give us our just due!

*Thank you, Father, for loving me despite my faults and
weaknesses. Thank you for balancing the "scales" of
my misdeeds with your perfect, gracious love. Amen.*

Barbara Johnson

Shorty

The LORD looks at the heart.
−1 SAMUEL 16:7

When my doctor announced I had osteoporosis, I thought, *I'm five feet tall; I can't afford to get any closer to the sidewalk!* Then my ricocheting reasoning took me to this thought: *Golly, I'm not going to die; one day I'm just going to fold up on myself and disappear.* Poof! Perhaps someone will crochet me a grave blanket that reads, "Short, shorter, shortest."

I know, I know, I have a strange way of dealing with reality, but then life is often caustic, and we all seek ways to survive. I think we tend to misunderstand each other's behavior during stressful times because another person's response is foreign to our own. We then pass judgment. *That person doesn't hurt as much as I do . . . or love as deeply as I do . . . or just plain ol' isn't as spiritual as I am.*

Those assessments drive wedges in our relationships and make us haughty. Or, as my kin quipped, "Young lady, your head's too big for your shoulders."

Some folks under pressure lose their appetites. I find that mystifying. When I'm stressed, I gnaw on doorjambs in between massive meals.

Can we tell if someone is suffering more than we are by watching her survival tactics? I think not. The folks who can't eat and those who down their weight in M&M's every thirty minutes might be experiencing equal amounts of pain. They just have different methods of surviving it.

In my household we use humor, which could cause others to think we don't take things seriously. Actually it's our way of swallowing the truth with as little indigestion as possible.

Let's keep the door of mercy ajar.

Gracious Lord, help my heart to be bigger than my head.
Amen.

Patsy Clairmont

A Transforming Gift

And we, who with unveiled faces all reflect the Lord's glory,
are being transformed into his likeness with ever-increasing glory.
–2 CORINTHIANS 3:18

Isak Dinesen is best known for her book *Out of Africa*, but her short story, "Babette's Feast," richly portrays the transforming power of grace.

The story is set on the desolate coast of Denmark. The local pastor has two beautiful daughters, Martina and Philippa, whose youth and dreams are sacrificed to their father's understanding of piety. He believes that the greatest way to show God that you love him is through harsh self-denial. Their lives are gray. Even after their father's death the young women cannot shake off the heavy cloak of duty.

There is no laugher and no joy until a stranger enters the picture. Her name is Babette. She is a refugee from the French civil war. Babette becomes their maidservant until a letter arrives from Paris. Babette has been left a large sum of money, enough to keep her for some time. But Babette decides to spend it all on one feast. She imports the finest food of every imaginable type from France and throws a banquet for the village.

At first the meal is a somber affair. Then the warmth of the gracious feast begins to thaw the lifelong chill in cold bones and someone laughs, then another and another. By the end of the evening people who haven't spoken to each other in years are wishing one another well.

Grace is a transforming gift. Without speaking a word, Babette's kindness danced across dark faces and brought light and love. Grace calls us to lavish our lives on one another.

Lord Jesus, as you lavished yourself on me,
help me to lavish my life on others. Amen.

Sheila Walsh

Chocolate-Covered Grace

But he gives us more grace.
—JAMES 4:6

One of my favorite things is Godiva Chocolate. Once there was a piece missing out of a gift box I received so I promptly reported it, thinking they'd send me a free pound. No such luck! All I got was a little Godiva patch, which I saved as a reminder to boycott the company. (Don't worry, that didn't last long.)

A young friend of mine, on the other hand, received $6,000 worth of Godiva by mistake! It was delivered to his place of business by an American Airlines truck. Not knowing what it was, Paul signed for the delivery. When he opened one of the boxes, he realized the mistake and immediately called AA to come back. They refused. Can you believe it? So, being an upstanding citizen he called Godiva. They also refused and said to Paul, "It's too difficult to pick up; just keep it and enjoy it."

Now, folks, that is what I call an incredible expression of grace. Boxes and boxes of chocolate-covered grace! Paul didn't expect it, didn't earn it, didn't deserve it, and he couldn't return it. So he simply enjoyed it. Six thousand dollars' worth of enjoyment dropped right in his lap! Godiva owed me one measly piece and they wouldn't pay up. Nothing was owed to Paul and he got the whole truckload.

So like God's grace, isn't it? God doesn't operate out of what we think he owes us. He operates out of his own index of generosity. When we least expect it, here he comes, driving a truck.

O Lord, how excellent is your expression of love for me.
Thank you over and over. Amen.

Luci Swindoll

May 26
Click!

Their sins and lawless acts I will remember no more.
—HEBREWS 10:17

Wouldn't it be way cool to have a portable delete button? We could clip it on our belts and head out the door with confidence. Just think of all the benefits if we could point, click, and delete things that got on our nerves.

Take, for instance, the line of traffic in the left-hand turn lane when we're in a rush. *Click.* Or how about the grocery clerk's cranky attitude? *Click.* Hey, as long as we're out, let's delete all the grocery carts with wobbly wheels. And those product stickers that won't peel off! *Click! Click!* Now, ladies, this is fun!

A store in town accosts you with raucous music when you enter. *Click.* Grin. Then a car deliberately slips into the parking spot you were headed for. *Click.* Tee-hee!

I wish I had thought of this sooner, say, when I was sixteen. That's the year my mom gave me a three-dimensional globe for Christmas. C'mon, a globe? Tickets to Europe, yes. A globe, no. *Click* (the globe, not my mom).

About twenty years ago I was given a purse made out of, ah-ah-choo, horsehair. *Click.* Then my husband and I moved into a house with bright orange cupboards; a tiny, dark red bathroom; and living-room windows with moons painted on them. *Triple click!*

Deleting would be a great way to deal with bad hair days, bad mood days, and just plain old bad days. Of course, then with whom would I identify?

Lord, thank you for providing me with the "delete"
of your blood to deal with my sin-sick, self-absorbed heart.
Amen.

Patsy Clairmont

Understanding the Cost

For God so loved the word that he gave his one and only Son,
that whoever believes in him shall not perish but have eternal life.
–JOHN 3:16

My husband, Bill, is a pretty tough fellow. He has been my rock, a constant, solid presence I could always lean on when the storms of adversity threatened to wreck our lives.

During World War II Bill was a lieutenant commander in the navy, an ace pilot who made the military's first nighttime landing on a Jeep aircraft carrier. He's an unpretentious, meat-and-potatoes (or, more accurately, popcorn-and-hot dogs) guy who doesn't get emotional about sentimental things that quickly bring tears to my eyes.

But there's one thing that obviously touches Bill's heart. During national holidays when America honors the men and women who fought to keep it free, I sometimes see Bill wiping away a tear or two. Parades and ceremonies bring to mind his own dangerous wartime experiences, the buddies he served with—and the friends he lost. For a long time, freedom probably meant more to Bill than it did to me, because he had paid a higher price for it. Then our son Steve died in Vietnam, and suddenly I understood.

Sometimes freedom comes at an awful price. God sacrificed his Son, Jesus, to set us free from sin's bondage. Whenever I feel myself taking that fact for granted, I imagine one of *my* sons hanging on that cross. The very thought makes me weep, but the exercise helps me realize the terrible price that was paid.

Loving Father, thank you for your great gift of grace
that frees me from sin's grip. Help me never forget the price
that was paid for my salvation. Amen.

B a r b a r a   J o h n s o n

Claiming Someone Else's Prize

The share of the man who stayed with the supplies is to be the same as that of him who went down to the battle. All will share alike. –1 SAMUEL 30:24

When David and his six hundred men returned to camp to find it burned to the ground and their wives and children taken captive, they were so distraught they "wept aloud until they had no strength left to weep" (1 Samuel 30:4). They pursued the Amalekite raiders to the edge of the Besor Ravine, "where some stayed behind, for two hundred men were too exhausted to cross the ravine" (vv. 9–10).

David and the remaining four hundred warriors continued on, eventually overtaking the raiders. The two armies fought "from dusk until the evening of the next day" (v.17), and eventually David and his men defeated the Amalekites, recovered their families and possessions, and took all the Amalekites' belongings and livestock as well.

When they returned to the Besor Ravine, the men they had left behind came out to greet them. "Forget it!" some of David's men shouted. "You didn't fight for it. You didn't risk your lives like we did. You deserve nothing!"

That's when David interrupted. "All will share alike," he said.

Today God extends to us the same outrageous grace. We share in an incredible bounty—eternal life—even though we didn't fight for it, don't deserve it, and can never even begin to pay for it. All we can do is accept it and pass it on to others.

Dear Father, I am not worthy to touch the hem of your garment,
yet you promise me a crown of glory. Thank you!

Barbara Johnson

A Spacious Place

*I will be glad and rejoice in your love, for you saw my affliction
and knew the anguish of my soul. You have not handed me over to the
enemy but have set my feet in a spacious place. —PSALM 31:7*

Psalm 31 is one of my favorite psalms of David. I love it because I have lived it. God is not stingy in his rescue missions but lavish and outrageous. Devastation never seems like a gift at the time, but in retrospect we can see the gracious hand of God lovingly weaving his pearls of mercy through our brokenness.

When I was little my grandmother used to say, "I need to be rubbed out and drawn back in again." I feel as if that is what God did with me. Those who share my tendency to clinical depression will understand that there are overwhelming moments when you feel as if life will never be all right again. When I had my first major bout with the illness, I had never felt so hopeless or helpless in my life. It seemed as if I had fallen into a deep well and would never be able to climb out. I was crying out inside, but so quietly that no one else could hear. No one but the Lord.

Even though my cries to him were faint, God is so merciful. He is a joyful deliverer who not only rescues his children from bottomless pits but also sets their feet in spacious places. God does not box us in to squeeze a reluctant assent to his will. Rather, he sets us free in wide-open spaces with the wind of his Spirit at our backs.

*Father God, thank you for delivering me.
I rejoice in your gracious love. Amen.*

Sheila Walsh

Heaven Came Down

There is no condemnation for those who are in Christ Jesus.
–ROMANS 8:1

Geronimo, the American Apache chief, said, "I want to live well. I know I have to die sometime, but even if the heavens were to fall on me, I want to do what is right."

There is something touchingly admirable about the heart's desire expressed in that statement. By the same token there is something hopelessly futile in wanting to live well, above reproach, always doing the right thing. Why futile? Because we can't do it. No matter how well intentioned we are, we will on occasion fudge the truth, put ourselves first, respond jealously instead of generously, and hate instead of love. That is, of course, the short list.

I want to do what is right too. If I want to, why don't I? It is that cursed thing called sin that throws everything out of balance. Wanting to be a good person, trying in every way possible to do the right thing, is an admirable goal; but it is also an unattainable goal.

So what's the solution? The solution is Jesus. Jesus took on himself at the cross all the sin that separates me from God. The Almighty's demand for perfection was met solely in his sinless Son. My most sincere efforts could never be good enough. God's grace allows me to live my life without guilt or condemnation. Amazingly, in God's eyes, it is as if I didn't go off track, make mistakes, or fall short. That's the miracle of grace.

The heavens did fall on us, Geronimo. In a little town called Bethlehem.

Thank you, Father, that you see me through Jesus—the
ever-secure lens of complete forgiveness. Amen.

Marilyn Meberg

A Feast for Sinners

But the tax collector stood at a distance. He would not even look up to
heaven, but beat his breast and said, "God, have mercy on me, a sinner." I
tell you that this man, rather than the other, went home justified before
God. For everyone who exalts himself will be humbled, and he who humbles
himself will be exalted. –LUKE 18:13

One Sunday evening in London, the Archbishop of Canterbury was delivering a sermon at Westminster Chapel. At the end of the message all who
believed in Christ Jesus were invited to come up to the altar and partake of
communion.

The Archbishop noticed that the only one who did not come to the rail
was a shabby-looking man who sat in the last row of the church, hiding in
the dim light. The clergyman carried the elements of bread and wine to this
man and asked him if he knew Christ as his Savior. The man said he did.

"Then take and eat, my son," he said.

"I'm not worthy, sir."

"Then this feast is for you," he replied. "This is a feast for sinners."

God's grace provides a Lamb for sin and a feast for sinners.

Father God, your grace to sinners is overwhelming.
Thank you that you receive me as I am, not as I wish I were.
May I extend that grace to others with humble joy.
Amen.

Sheila Walsh

JUNE

Joy

You turned my wailing into dancing; you removed
my sackcloth and clothed me with joy. —PSALM 30:11

Many years ago when I thought I'd reached the bottom of the barrel, God
touched my heart and replaced the black, gooey cesspool of grief and
anger with a wellspring of joy that has bubbled exuberantly ever since. As
someone once put it in computer terms, joy became my "default setting." Now,
that was a miracle!

Having a joyful attitude doesn't mean I haven't shed a tear since that day
when God put the joy in me. Oh, no! I've shed *many* tears since then, most
recently when I was diagnosed with a malignant brain tumor. But after the
bad news has been delivered, God's gift of joy enables me to move on, to get
past the trauma, and to return to that miraculous default setting.

For example, when the doctor told me that all my hair would fall out due
to the chemo, I shuddered to think of being bald. But when he mused that
my hair might be curly when it grows back in, I was delighted. Just imagine!
I'll have a brand-new head of hair! And it might be *curly!*

Over the years I've learned to look for splashes of joy in unexpected places
(like in hair follicles that suddenly sprout curls), and now I make it one of
my regular goals: seeing just how many "joy gems" I can discover in each day.
(I think of it as a great way to kill time between disasters.)

I have been blessed with the gift of joy—and so have you! As you meditate on my favorite topic this month, I pray you will experience the joy of having the God of miracles living in the marrow of your bones.

Barbara Johnson

June 1
Good, but Not Wonderful

But may the righteous be glad and rejoice before God;
may they be happy and joyful. –PSALM 68:3

Happiness and joy are two different things. Happiness has to do with a circumstance; joy has to do with an assurance. That's why this verse says the righteous will be made *both* happy and joyful, rejoicing not only in the moment but in their standing before God.

During the days I sang with the Dallas Opera, I met a delightful woman from Italy with whom I became close friends. She had the most unique expression that clarifies my thoughts on the difference between happiness and joy. If I asked her whether or not she enjoyed something she'd often say, "Well . . . it was good but not wonderful."

I finally asked her, "What does that mean exactly?"

"Often I feel very fortunate about something that happens," she explained. "But that feeling doesn't last. It's fleeting. There are other times when I feel completely satisfied—almost triumphant. The first is *good,* but the second is *wonderful.* It's kind of hard to explain."

I knew exactly what she meant. One is happiness; the other joy.

The next time a butterfly sits on your shoulder or you enjoy a great dinner, that's happiness. But when a friend comes to know the Savior, or you internalize the fact that God's love is based on his character and not your behavior, that's joy.

To me, the powerful truth of Psalm 68:3 is that we as believers are the only ones who can truly know both happiness and joy. That's not just good news—that's wonderful!

Lord, the assurance of your abiding love for me makes me
not just happy . . . but overjoyed! I thank you with all my heart.
Amen.

Luci Swindoll

June 2
The Everyday Sounds of Joy

He will yet fill your mouth with laughter and your lips with shouts of joy.
—JOB 8:21

How thankful I am for a keen sense of hearing. My ears are like radio receivers that detect joyful sounds. Each morning I awaken early and lie in bed, waiting for the sound of the newspaper landing on my doorstep. As I wait I enjoy the chiming clock in the hallway, imagining it as God's rhythmic reminder saying, "I-love-you-Barb, so-very-much!" Next, while I crunch my breakfast cereal, I hear the laughter of children as they pass through our park on their way to school. Then I notice the twittering, boisterous songs of the birds outside my window. Above them, a jet comes in for a landing at nearby Los Angeles International Airport. Gradually, my day fills with the sounds of activity. I'd recognize the sound of the UPS truck anywhere, and throughout the day, bells and gongs and goofy gadgets ding and ring, clatter and clang in my Joy Room, where I keep my collection of "laugh-nudgers" and "joy-jigglers."

Throughout the day, I'm cheered by the voices of loved ones. One friend calls to share a joke: "Yes, I have flabby thighs. Fortunately, my stomach covers them!" Another calls to report a great bumper sticker: "Oh, no! Not another learning experience!" In the evening Bill and I laugh together, watching reruns of a favorite comedy on TV, then head for bed. Lying again in the darkness, I listen for the chiming clock and the quiet sounds of the night.

Many folks complain about the very noises I've enjoyed today. They notice and feel annoyed; I hear and feel encouraged. One of us needs a new receiver!

Lord, I strain to hear your joyful noise everywhere.
Amen.

Barbara Johnson

Laundromat Rock

Let them praise his name with dancing and make music
to him with tambourine and harp. —PSALM 149:3

On Sunset Boulevard in Hollywood there used to be a Laundromat that could have passed for The Pantages Theater. One summer afternoon when I walked by, the place was filled with music, laughter, and dancing. Some kids had turned up their boom box and were putting on a show. And they were *good*. A smiling crowd gathered to watch them through the big windows.

The guys were throwing girls over their shoulders, a cute couple was beating out rhythm on Tide boxes, and a little kid was tap dancing on top of a dryer. Joy was in the air and we had front-row seats. The show lasted about ten minutes, then everybody went on their way—happier for having taken a few minutes for jubilation.

Almost every day I dance around my bedroom or down the hallway. I learned that from my mother, whom I often saw waltzing with the kitchen broom. Music would start, she'd grab the broom, and off she'd go. I loved that. Mother was demonstrating a deep sense of joy that could only be expressed by dancing.

There is something about rejoicing that makes us want to dance. The rhythm of joy gets under our skin and before we know it, our feet are tapping!

Today, while you're working in your kitchen, imagine you're Ginger Rogers. Fred Astaire is leaning against the wall over there. See him? Ask him to dance.

May your presence fill me with joy, Lord—so much
so that I find myself kicking up my heels! Amen.

Luci Swindoll

Zeb

Rejoice in the Lord always.
—PHILIPPIANS 4:4

I feel as though I know the lad, but we haven't been formally introduced. He appears to be fifteen, and he hangs out at the corner of Fred Waring and Deep Canyon. Well, hangs out doesn't quite capture his demeanor—it's more like he jives there. Yes, jives. You see, this teenager hip-hops on the corner to draw attention to the large arrow-sign he holds (pointing passersby to new homes). He is a living advertisement for the nearby real estate.

Les and I always look for him on weekends. He has no idea we're scrutinizing him or that we look forward to seeing him. Since we don't know his name, we've tagged him Zeb, the Zealous One. I mean, Zeb knows how to boogie. Headphones plastered to his head, his neck sways, his feet jump, and his shoulders oscillate. Every once in a while, in grand showmanship, he sets the huge arrow spinning dramatically. Zeb's cool.

Les and I think that whatever Zeb is being paid isn't enough. I mean, young Zeb works hard. We see other young people with his type of job but without his enthusiasm. The others often sit under the shade of nearby trees with their signs propped against rocks. These kids sip sodas while our boy wears out the sidewalk with his footwork.

I want to be a Zeb, don't you? The type of person who's so exuberant about her life that others notice. Our diligence and our passion would be obvious by our behavior, and so impressive that folks would be drawn to the One we're "advertising."

No doubt others take notes on our lives. I wonder what their read is?

Jesus, give me zeal for you!
Amen.

Patsy Clairmont

June 5
If You're Happy and You Know It ...

Is anyone happy? Let him sing songs of praise.
—JAMES 5:13

Singing lifts our spirits—even if we can't carry a tune in a bucket! I learned that fact when the Billy Graham Crusade came to our area a few years ago. Because I'd been to other crusades, I knew that volunteer choir members were guaranteed good seats, so I signed up right away. But Bill and I wanted to go together, so I signed him up too, even though he can't sing at all!

As gently as I could during our rehearsals, I suggested to Bill that he just mouth the words silently so our little secret wouldn't be discovered. After all, I pointed out to him, lip-synching is a common thing among big record-ing stars! All went well through the rehearsals, but when the crusade itself began, Bill got caught up in the joyful exuberance of the soul-stirring music, and he belted out the hymns for all he was worth.

Now, there were hundreds of talented singers in that huge, majestic choir, and I doubt that anyone would have known about Bill's ear-numbing rendi-tions except for one little thing. He had carried a tiny little tape recorder in his shirt pocket to tape the program. So he recorded himself loudest of all, and believe me, under normal circumstances, it would *not* be something you'd want to listen to more than once! But Bill's voice was so joyful that night, I can't help but love listening to that tape, even if his singing was a mile off-key and sometimes you can't tell if he's singing or in pain.

Lord, thank you for hearing all my joyful noises as praise to you!
Amen.

Barbara Johnson

Tailor-made Joy

As for God, his way is perfect.
—2 SAMUEL 22:31

This morning I was having tea and toast with the *Today* show. On the program was the most captivating interview with a darling first-grade girl named Madison. She had won a naming contest for a baby elephant from Thailand, which is now living in a Seattle zoo. The child's prize was two tickets to Thailand, but she had given the tickets to her teacher.

This action caused the city of Seattle to want to reward Madison's generosity. So on the show the mayor of Seattle presented two more tickets to Madison so that she could indeed go on the trip and take her mother with her. Contrary to all expectations, Madison's live television response was, "No . . . no . . . I don't want the tickets. I don't even want to go to Thailand. I never wanted to go to Thailand."

I laughed so hard over her authentic and unpretentious response I choked on my tea. As the camera pulled away she could be heard saying, "I just wanted the elephant to have a name so it wouldn't be called 'Baby' all its life." Madison's joy came simply from giving the baby elephant name identification. She had no desire to cloud her pure pleasure with the well-intentioned actions of the adult world.

Sometimes that's the way with joy. It comes to us in ways not always understood or appreciated by others. Joy can be a tailor-made, just-for-us kind of experience. That's how it came to Madison, and that was good enough for her.

Lord, thank you that everything you give me is personal and
tailor-made because I am your beloved, one-of-a-kind creation.
Amen.

Marilyn Meberg

When a Child Comes Home

*There is rejoicing in the presence of the angels of God
over one sinner who repents.* —LUKE 15:10

There is a small church in Glasgow, Scotland, where you can find a wall plaque in honor of John Harper, the minister there before he went down with the Titanic. He was heading to America for an evangelistic crusade.

It took over two hours for the ship to sink after it hit the giant iceberg. The captain cried, "Women and children first!" But one survivor claimed that John Harper cried, "Women, children, and the unsaved first!"

When the ship disappeared into the inky water John found a piece of wood and held on as long as he could. Hypothermia began to set in, and his breathing became labored. He saw a man float past him and, fighting for breath, asked, "Are you saved?" The man said no and floated off a ways. Then once more he passed John, and with his last breath John Harper proclaimed, "Believe in the Lord Jesus Christ and you will be saved." Then the minister's hands slipped off the wood and he was gone, gone into the presence of Christ amidst the rejoicing of angels.

The man John spoke to survived, and some time later he stood in a pulpit in Canada and announced, "I am John Harper's last convert."

There is nothing more important than a personal relationship with Christ. It is what everyone is looking for whether he knows it or not. We belong to God our Father. And when one of his children comes home, there is joy!

*Father of life, today I rejoice because I am yours. Shine the
light of your life through me to those who are in deep waters.
Amen.*

Sheila Walsh

Identify Yourself

Do not grieve, for the joy of the LORD is your strength.
—NEHEMIAH 8:10

A guy and two young women came into a restaurant where we were eating, and the guy insisted on getting a seat in a reserved area. I was sitting where I could see him and noticed his insistent and somewhat strange behavior. The waiter attempted to seat the party at a table on the upper floor, but the guy refused. Finally, to the dismay of the staff the guy told the two girls to sit down at a table in the front of the dining area. Almost as soon as he told them to sit down, he ordered them to leave. A lady sitting at the table next to them happened to reach down on the floor for her purse, but it was gone—stolen by one of the ladies that left so quickly.

A waiter, cook, and a couple of other people went in hot pursuit of the gangsters. The victim was in disbelief. I started praying that the lady's purse would be found and her ID would be left intact.

After about forty-five minutes, one of the waiters who chased the threesome on a motorbike walked back into the restaurant holding the stolen purse. Of course all the money was gone, but the lady's driver's license and other ID was recovered.

When we least expect it and are having a great time in life, there are people who might try to steal our joy. But if we identify ourselves with the Lord and make the pursuit of his joy our aim, our emotional and spiritual identity will remain intact no matter what happens.

Jesus, help me to look to you alone as my source of joy and strength.
Amen.

Thelma Wells

Treasures That Last

My fruit is better than fine gold; what I yield surpasses choice silver. I walk
in the way of righteousness, along the paths of justice, bestowing wealth on
those who love me and making their treasuries full. *–PROVERBS 8:19–21*

When I moved from Texas to California, seven friends got together and gave
me a pair of sterling silver napkin rings. Their initials are engraved inside
one of the rings. I often use them at dinner parties with my mother's silver
place settings and the goblets Daddy won for being the best insurance salesman in the company. These are among my most prized possessions, more so
now that my parents are gone as well as two of those Texas friends. If this house
catches on fire I'm grabbing these treasures on the way out.

But . . . read that verse again, Luci.

Isn't it easy to put our valuables before God's virtues? Although we may
have silver and gold, it is nothing compared to the wealth God wants to
bestow on us. You and I could own all the rings and goblets in the world but
still be poverty stricken. What good then is all that "stuff"? Only God can
make us wealthy in what really matters: wisdom, patience, endurance, joy. His
bounty comes from a storehouse of riches that is unlimited.

Polished sterling, gold bracelets, silver earrings, or family heirlooms can
never give us the joy that comes from an hour of contentment with Christ.
None of life's trappings make our "treasuries full." Only fellowship with the
divine does that.

*Speak to my heart, Lord Jesus. Show me where I am focusing
on the wrong things, and redirect my vision. I want my life
to reflect your values and my heart to overflow with joy. Amen.*

L u c i   S w i n d o l l

Beyond "How to ..."

You have made known to me the path of life; you will fill me with joy in
your presence, with eternal pleasures at your right hand. —PSALM 16:11

I love this verse. I love all that it promises for you and me.

Go into any bookstore in your community and look at how large the self-help section is. Move over to business and you will be inundated with a million ways to make it in this world, how to get ahead, how to make an impact, how to be number one. Even within the religion shelves the "how-to" section is substantial. There are books written on how to know the will of God, how to discover your spiritual gifts, how to find your place in the body of Christ. If you have any kind of musical inclination there are seminars and workbooks to show you how to launch your career for Christ. I realize that I may be overstating things here, but I love the simplicity of the psalmist's heart: "*You* have made known to me the path of life; *you* will fill me with joy."

I wonder if in our technical age we have substituted time alone with God, reveling in his presence, with books and other aids telling us "how to do it." I bought in-line skates for Christian recently. We sat down and I read the instructions to him and gave him a litany of warnings about potential disasters till he finally said, " Mom, can I just do it?"

A Christian's joy is not found in a book or a tape or a video; it is found in God's quiet and mighty presence.

Father of all life, thank you that in your presence there is joy forever.
Amen.

Sheila Walsh

Sappy Happy

Yet I am always with you; you hold me by my right hand.
—PSALM 73:23

There are certain simple delights in life that are guaranteed to produce a state of sappy happy in me: a great book, an innovative soul-talk, homemade lemon pie, chocolate fudge made with cocoa and not chocolate chips, golf cart racing with Patsy and Luci, and the sappy happy of all time—tickets to the "Tennis Masters Series Indian Wells." The Tennis Garden is only a few moments from my house, and I have tickets for tomorrow. I can hardly wait!

Now the happy side of sappy could be instantly lost if the book is dull, the soul-talk isn't soulish, the pie has a commercial filling, the fudge is grainy, Patsy's cart is faster than mine, and my seat at the tennis match is not in the main stadium. The maintaining of "happy" is a pretty perilous thing; it can be lost almost immediately.

Conversely, if I add joy to the consideration of what makes me sappy happy, I am more secure. Joy is not changeable as happy is. I can still have joy even if the fudge is made from chocolate chips. Why? Because joy is a state of being; it's steady and dependable. It is the spiritual foundation upon which I race my golf cart or read a book or have a conversation.

Joy comes from the fact of God's presence in me through the Holy Spirit. Joy comes from knowing he will never leave me under any circumstances. Joy is the assurance of his intimate availability to me: "Yet I am always with you; you hold me by my right hand." Joy is not even remotely related to fudge.

Lord, thank you true joy is in you alone.
Amen.

Marilyn Meberg

Ding-Dong

Come before him with joyful songs.
−PSALM 100:2

My doorbell plays music that matches the holidays. It's programmed with everything from "Happy Birthday" to "God Bless America" to "Joy to the World." I think that's so cool because I'm a musical dweeb. I have a deep appreciation for music but absolutely no talent. (Trust me; this has been validated by the best.) So the thought that my doorbell would strike up a happy tune for my guests pleased me.

But, here was my surprise: After I had met a number of guests at the door, I realized the person pressing the doorbell was oblivious to the melodic sounds, and I was the one receiving the benefit of the tunes as I traipsed through the house to greet guests. Hmm.

That scenario is reminiscent of other misconceptions I've had. For instance, regarding apologies, I'm not fond of saying, "I was wrong. Will you forgive me?" It's way too, uh, revealing. I've been quick to mumble "Sorry" on any number of occasions to my hubby after he's pushed my button—only to realize that my tart apology was more for me than for him. I needed relief from my guilt, but I didn't actually feel regret for the way I had treated him. My "Sorry" was more about my discomfort than the pain I had caused Les.

Guilt is no friend to me. Instead, guilt gains a stranglehold on my self-esteem, convincing me that I *am* sorry—a sorry mess. Whereas, when conviction comes knocking, it reveals my weaknesses so I can take responsibility for my conduct and then open the door to restored relationships and spiritual healing. Now, that will put a song in my heart every time!

Lord, may I ring with authenticity and resound with joy!
Amen.

Patsy Clairmont

Fueled by Joy

The LORD your God will bless you in all your harvest and in all the work
of your hands, and your joy will be complete. –*DEUTERONOMY 16:15*

Sometimes something happens to me, and I get so wound up I'm like a drop
of water on a hot frying pan, jumping excitedly all over the place. That's the
way I felt one night in Tulsa. I'd met some young men who were working as
ushers at our conference there. They were homosexuals and wanted to know
more about my encouragement to parents to love their children unconditionally, as Christ loves us.

I called them that night, and we talked nearly an hour. Then they asked
me to call their mothers, so I did. We talked and cried and laughed, exchang-
ing stories about what it's like being the mothers of homosexual sons. Afterward, I was eager to write down the story so I wouldn't forget anything. But
writing it out in longhand would be so cumbersome.

The next morning when my helper met me in the hotel lobby, she took
one look at me and realized I was wearing exactly the same clothes I'd had
on the night before. In fact, I hadn't been to bed! Finally I had to confess
that I'd been up all night writing. "I even went to the all-night Wal-Mart
around midnight, hoping to borrow a typewriter!" I confessed.

"You went to Wal-Mart?" she asked incredulously.

"It's just a few blocks," I assured her. "I was about halfway there when a
nice policeman stopped and asked if I was okay." (I guess in Tulsa they're not
accustomed to seeing seventy-year-old ladies walking down the four-lane after
midnight.) It was a night packed with encouragement and fueled by joy.

Oh, Lord, keep the joy coming!
Amen.

B a r b a r a   J o h n s o n

"I'm Not Pleased with You"

Throw away the foreign gods that are among you
and yield your hearts to the LORD. *–JOSHUA 24:23*

Preparing my wardrobe for the 2001 Women of Faith conference tour became a challenging experience. I opened one of my four closets crammed with wall-to-wall clothes and heard in my spirit, "I'm not pleased with you."

I closed the closet door hoping the voice would go away. When I opened it again, I got the same holy nudge. The Lord wanted me to clean out my closets!

I started laying mountains of clothes on the bed. When I thought I was finished in one closet I went to another, and then another. Designer suits, dresses, T-shirts, casual clothes—bunches had to go.

Frankly, I didn't like this one bit. I wanted to keep my clothes. But three times he sent me back to each closet.

I finally asked him what I *could* keep. "Anything that has your logo on it," I heard in my spirit, "and some of your speaking suits, and all your junky stuff." I was grumbling when I heard him add, "Cheerfully." Cheerfully? *I wanted my stuff!*

But I started smiling and acting cheerful. Pretty soon I felt cheerful. When I finished my task, I was relieved and dancing joyfully around the house.

All my clothes now fit in one closet. I'm quite satisfied with the ones I have.

When was the last time you cleaned out the closets in your mind and heart? I suspect you have garments hanging around that you need to discard. When God says, "I'm not pleased with you," listen. He has a plan to renew your joy.

God, you see into all the closets in my life.
Help me to clear out the clutter—cheerfully.
Amen.

Thelma Wells

Branching Out

A tree is recognized by its fruit.
—MATTHEW 12:33

One sunny day Les and I strolled through town at our leisure. In our journey we discovered a café tucked inside a nook of shops and decided to stop for lunch. The waitress guided us to a window table in a cove, and we placed our orders. As we contemplated the sweetness of the day and each other's company, I noticed a tree outside the café. My eyes traced the branches as my mind tried to make sense of what I saw. Let me describe it and see what you think....

One branch held a profusion of buds, as if it were springtime and the tree was ready to break forth in blossoms. The branch just below flourished with summer-green leaves and full blossoms. These branches were in direct contrast to the lower ones that were starkly barren. Meantime the very top branches boasted the orange, yellow, and rust-colored leaves of autumn. This tree appeared to have an identity crisis!

Come to think of it, I've been like that tree. Sometimes I've tried to be all things to all people—perky, colorful, fruitful, soothing, creative, and— here's a stretch—reserved. Whew! Now that's exhausting, if not impossible. I'm also tempted to be like that tree with my time, trying to be everywhere with everyone. And guess what? It can't be done without rupturing my joy. Or looking out of place like a seasonally confused tree.

To bloom where we are planted brings joy to us and those who encounter us. It doesn't mean we lose our identity, but instead we respond appropriately out of who we are, whatever our situation.

Jesus, thank you that you have a fruitful plan for my life.
Amen.

Patsy Clairmont

Enough Love to Last a Lifetime

Give, and it will be given to you. A good measure, pressed down,
shaken together and running over, will be poured into your lap. For with
the measure you use, it will be measured to you. –LUKE 6:38

It's been more than sixty years since I got to wish my dad a happy Father's Day. I was only twelve when he died unexpectedly of a heart attack. But he packed those twelve years full of enough love and sweet, fun memories to encourage and inspire me the rest of my life.

Dad was associate pastor of a large church in Grand Rapids, Michigan, and I often accompanied him to tent revivals around the area. He would lift me up on a chair at the front of the tent to sing "specials," and beam proudly as I performed. As we rode together in the car, he'd drill me on Bible verses I had memorized. Sometimes when there were dips in the road, he'd tell me to sit on the floor in the back of the car, then he'd *zoom* over the humps and plunges so I could have my own personal roller coaster ride. We'd laugh to the verge of hysterics. When Daddy died, he was carrying in his pocket several packs of Black Jack Gum—my favorite—that I had asked him to bring me.

On Father's Day, and most days, I think of my dad and still feel embraced by love and laughter, all these years later. It's the kind of legacy I hope to pass on to my sons and grandchildren.

Father of all, your love carries me through
the roller coaster of life. Hold me tightly in the plunges
and push me always upward toward heaven. Amen.

Barbara Johnson

Oh, Baby!

Your love for me was wonderful.
—2 SAMUEL 1:26

I confess I'm a mushy-gushy grandma, the kind who will accost you with volumes of photographs and tales galore. And, yes, my grandson, Justin, is the cutest, most brilliant baby in the world. Actually, the possibility of his growing up normal with the way Grandpa and I hover over his every move is somewhere between "no way" and "fat chance."

When Justin was six months old, his grandpa and I flew to the California desert for a couple of months to escape the wintry blasts in our home state of Michigan. We were relieved to bask in the sunshine, but as the days passed we missed our darling grandson. So after three long weeks my son, his wife, and Justin flew out for a visit.

I was concerned, however, that Justin wouldn't remember us. I kept reminding myself it might take a while for him to get used to us. I repeatedly cautioned myself not to scare him with a sloppy greeting. (He was in the "I don't like strangers" stage.)

As the plane pulled up to the gate, I was there waiting. My daughter-in-law deplaned, holding Justin face forward. I was amazed by how much he had grown in less than a month. As they came closer, Justin spotted me and locked his eyes on my smiling face. His inquisitive look turned slowly to recognition and then to glee as he laughed aloud and stretched out both arms for me to take him. I immediately embraced him and we giggled our way through the airport.

What joy!

Lord, thank you for the joyous gift of loving others
and being loved in return. Amen.

Patsy Clairmont

For the Good Times

Rejoice and be glad, because great is your reward in heaven.
–MATTHEW 5:12

I've been in one of my "nameless elemental yearning" periods for the past few days. It's just a basic longing, but for what I'm not sure. This time it can't be satisfied by chocolate or pepperoni pizza with the grandkids. It just lies there on the floor of my soul.

Years ago, that nameless yearning was satisfied by going trout fishing with my father in the icy lakes amidst the grandeur of Colorado's Rocky Mountains. Other times that yearning was met by my mother during one of our many richly deep and philosophical or theological exchanges that left me pondering and sweetly satisfied.

Every Friday night while I was married, my husband, Ken, and I had "date night" where we'd settle in and catch up with each other. One evening after dinner in Laguna Beach we were strolling along the boardwalk. Suddenly he said, "Follow me, Marilyn, and don't stop until I do." He walked straight into the ocean; his shoes, slacks, and shirt were no hindrance. Neither was my canary-yellow pantsuit. As I followed him, sloshing and giggling all the way back to our car, I said, "Ken Meberg, you are the most delightfully crazy person I know." "And so are you, Marilyn Meberg . . . isn't it fun?"

It was fun. I miss him.

Maybe it's good I can't satisfy this yearning. Maybe it's good I simply remember what was, feel its sweet loss, and know the day is coming when there will be no more losses. There will instead be a reuniting in the presence of the One who has called us all together in eternal joy.

Thank you, God, that with you good things
are never really over. Amen.

Marilyn Meberg

There Will Come a Day

Your love has given me great joy and encouragement, because
you ... have refreshed the hearts of the saints. –PHILEMON 1:7

Last week I ran across three little schoolbooks my niece, Gloria, made when she was eleven. She's now forty, married, and the mother of four children. These books are full of her youthful handwriting and artwork. Priceless treasures! I had the fun of watching her face when I returned them to her to pass them along to her children. She had completely forgotten she'd given them to me.

An old college friend did something similar for me. She sent the large, framed illumination from "The Hound of Heaven" I had made for my senior art project. There was a note attached: "You gave me this forty-two years ago, and now it's time for you to enjoy it." When I look at it hanging in my hallway my heart fills with gratitude. I had no memory of where it was.

Shakespeare expresses my point: "Praising what is lost makes the remembrance dear." Indeed it does. Both Gloria and I rejoiced with thanksgiving over the object and the fact it was returned. What a thrill!

Hang onto those little treasures that will one day bring encouragement to the original owner. Maybe it's a childish drawing, or a personal journal. Perhaps it's an old piece of jewelry or handwork. At some point, putting those treasures back into the hands of those who made it or gave it away will "refresh" them. Watch their faces glow with the joy of remembrance.

Dear Lord, guide me with discernment about things
I might be tempted to throw away. Help me remember who
gave them to me, and to rejoice in their love. Amen.

Luci Swindoll

A Leap of Joy

Your joy will be complete.
—*Deuteronomy 16:15*

My favorite moments are those that spring up when I least expect them and draw from a reservoir of joy deep within. Now, not everyone receives joy from my reservoir because it's unique to me.

Last night I had one of those unexpected joy-drenchings. It was a balmy, citrus-scented evening, and I was driving my friend Pat to her condo just four streets from mine. We were, of course, in my golf cart (christened "Celeste").

"Don't turn yet, Marilyn," Pat said. "It's too nice to go in yet. Just stay on Morocco." Obediently I stayed on track and agreed it was "too nice to go in yet." Then it happened.

A garage door was up on one of the condos, revealing two spectacularly shiny collector cars: a red 1940 Ford coupe and a deep blue 1920 Ford two-door convertible. My heart rate increased, I began to salivate on my blouse, and Pat groaned, "Marilyn . . . don't turn around . . . you don't even know that guy bent over the engine . . . just take me home . . . please." *Not a chance, sweetie!*

After a brief introduction, my new pal Hal began to describe the Corvette engines he had in both cars and regaled me with their racing triumphs. Gratified by my enthusiasm and interest he asked, "Hey, you wanna drive the convertible around the block?"

Leaving Pat in Celeste with a look of grim-faced disapproval, I tore out of Hal's garage and was soon at full throttle (which doesn't last long because my gated community has short streets). Within minutes I was back, but not before the sound of that deep-throated engine and quick accelerator's power had splashed joy all over me. Then . . . I took Pat home.

Lord, every good gift is from you. Thank you.

Marilyn Meberg

Take the Plunge!

There is a river whose streams make glad the city of God,
the holy place where the Most High dwells. —PSALM 46:4

I didn't learn to swim until I was sixteen years old. It was humiliating: I lived by the ocean and couldn't swim. I knew how to do it in theory; I was just too afraid to take the plunge.

One day, I decided that this was the day. I went to the swimming pool by the beach and jumped off the diving board into the deep end. There was nothing gracious about my performance, but I swam. I was terrified and thrilled and alive!

In *Mere Christianity*, C. S. Lewis writes, "If you want joy, power, peace, eternal life, you must get close to or even into the thing that has them." In other words, you must take the plunge! God is not a stagnant pool but a mighty river running faster and faster, suddenly curving in a different direction, resting a while, then racing off again in breathtaking power and beauty. Those who describe their relationship with God as dull and dusty have never plunged into his river of mercy. There is no greater adventure for a man or woman than throwing everything they have in with God, without reservation.

How sad it would be to stand on the edge of the water of life and never get wet. Jump in! The Most High will be there and you will be terrified and thrilled and alive!

Dear Father, thank you for the gladness I feel when
I'm immersed in your presence. Amen.

Sheila Walsh

Lavish Love

How much more will your Father in heaven give good gifts
to those who ask him! –MATTHEW 7:11

Every day I live in my house, I send up a cheer. I *love* it here. Before I bought this place in 1994 I'd never owned a home. The few times I moved, it was always into apartments.

I had heard that renting had advantages—mobility, liquidity, and if you stayed put till you died, morbidity. They'd carry you out in a pine box so you'd never have to pack again. I was all for that. I'd read an article in the *Los Angeles Times* entitled, "Psyching Oneself Up to Be a Renter for Life," and I had psyched.

Then, I saw this house. It was small, in a safe, gated community, full of possibilities, and available. *Can I afford this?* I wondered. *Are my hopes too high? Am I nuts?* At that moment I thought about how God continuously pours out his love. He delights in lavishing us—me!—with gifts we haven't even asked for. What joy to be the recipient of such an overflowing love!

So . . . at the age of sixty-one I took out a thirty-year loan. Why not? If I'm raptured before my mortgage is paid up, some unbeliever can finish the payments. I'm outa here!

Don't stay in mediocrity just because you think you don't deserve something better. God has great things planned for you. Rejoice!

> *Oh Lord, thank you for your lavish gifts, specially*
> *chosen just because you love me. Being your*
> *child makes my heart overflow with joy. Amen.*

L u c i   S w i n d o l l

Night-lights

Arise, shine, for your light has come.
—*ISAIAH 60:1*

Ever try to catch a firefly? Those little rascals are flickery. They flit around like they have a case of the giggles. Now you see them, now you don't. Since they're night-flyers, they cleverly tote their own flashlights. Little polka dots of brilliance, these evening darters ignite the landscape.

Ever danced with a firefly? Then you know their comedic style is reminiscent of a skittish cha-cha. I love their flair. And get this: A firefly won't leave you laden with itching lumps like a mosquito or wincing pain like a yellow jacket. Instead, fireflies just dazzle.

Did you know that if you pull the light off a firefly's bottom (ouch! I hate it when that happens), the light glows for several seconds before it fizzles out? You can actually wear it like a jewel until it fades. That was a childhood game we played in my neighborhood. (Aren't you glad you didn't live there?) The poor firefly got the yucky end of that deal.

Fireflies replicate some Christians with their playful behavior and their flitting antics. In fact, our Women of Faith speaking team probably looks that way, with our back-and-forth jaunts to conferences throughout the land. Here we are; there we go—like we have the giggles (and often we do).

I'm grateful our light is permanently affixed (no fizzling), as is our joy, thanks to Jesus. We, like you, are called to be ablaze amidst life's dark landscapes.

So glow, girlfriends, glow!

Lord, cause me to glow with your joy. And may I not leave others wincing but dazzled by your light even in the bleakest night. Amen.

Patsy Clairmont

God Doesn't Discriminate

I will pour out my Spirit on all people.
Your sons and daughters will prophesy. —JOEL 2:28

A preacher asked a woman I know to teach Bible study at his church in January, 2001. He hoped it would be appropriate, as congregations all over the world were inviting her to speak. He made sure she knew, however, that *he* did not believe women should teach in the church.

She told me that he sat in the front row during Bible study but kept his head cocked toward the audience to see what their reaction would be to a woman minister. Frankly, he seemed to be the only person with an "issue." Once he felt assured that people were listening and participating with enthusiasm, he started doing likewise.

At the end of the evening he approached the speaker and asked her if this was the kind of thing she'd been doing all over the world. "Yes!" she replied. "Well, this is powerful," he admitted. "If you keep this up, you might make even me change my mind about women preachers!" She graciously assured him that it was not up to her to make him change his mind; that was the Lord's business.

Isn't it wonderful that God doesn't discriminate? He uses men, women, boys, and girls to carry his message and minister to people. Perhaps those who have hang-ups about women in ministry don't know much about Miriam, Deborah, Huldah, Isaiah's wife, Anna, and the daughters of Philip.

It is God's good pleasure to use everyone who is willing to carry his gospel with humble joy.

Lord, I praise you for being a perfect Parent who has no "favorite"
children. Please use me today to share the joy of belonging to you. Amen.

Thelma Wells

Who Wants It?

Consider it all joy ... when you encounter various trials.
—JAMES 1:2 NASB

Rare is the person who in the midst of physical pain, emotional hurt, financial deprivation, or threats to personal safety will respond with, "What a joy! I'm so glad not to have missed it ... thank you so much!"

The Greek philosopher Simon Weil says, "Pain is the root of knowledge." There seems to be a universal understanding that pain feeds the mind, expands the spirit, and deepens the soul. But who wants it? And how on earth can Scripture claim that suffering comes with a joy pack?

Oddly enough, when we see a painful experience in our rearview mirror, we can usually say, "I truly am glad I didn't miss it because of what I gained ... and yes, there's even joy that attends the memory."

Last year when my health challenges threatened me on every level of my existence, I learned what everyone else probably already knows; and that is, nothing, absolutely nothing, is more important than my relationship with God. I've been inclined to believe that I was created simply to serve him, but I've learned that my service is secondary to my sweet communion with him. I was created for a relationship with him, to connect with him, and in so doing receive comfort, encouragement, support, tenderness, and the assurance that he's with me always.

That knowledge gave me joy during some dark days. It still gives me joy today. Without the pain I might have continued in the mistaken belief that my simply *being* in relationship with him is secondary to what I think I can do for him.

> God, trials reduce me to one consideration, and that is you.
> Thank you for the joy of our relationship. Amen.

Marilyn Meberg

June 26
Crowns Galore

Be faithful, even to the point of death, and I will give you the crown of life.
—REVELATION 2:10

While salvation is a free gift of God and not a result of works, when we get to the judgment seat of Christ our works we will be judged and rewarded accordingly (1 Corinthians 3:6–15).

Whether we visit the sick, feed the hungry, comfort those in loss, clean up the church, drive a shut-in to the store, or tell someone about Jesus, we have a choice about how we will perform the deed. We can do it begrudgingly just because we're supposed to or because someone expects us to, or we can perform it cheerfully for the glory of God.

If we have a bad attitude while we're serving others, our "good deeds" will be burned in the fire of judgment like wood, hay, and stubble. But if we have a compassionate and loving attitude, our works will come forth from the fire as gold, silver, and precious stones. If what we have "built" on this earth survives the fire of God's judgment, we will receive our reward. What joy!

I want all the rewards! How about you?

The Crown of Life is for those who have been faithful until death.
The Imperishable Crown is for those who deny themselves and run the race of life with patience.
The Crown of Exultation is for those who have won souls for Christ.
The Crown of Righteousness is for those who yearn for Christ's return.
The Crown of Glory is for the faithful and obedient minister of the gospel.

Since you know the qualifications, groom yourself for the crowning moment.

Righteous Judge, please give me a pure and
cheerful heart as I work for you. Amen.

Thelma Wells

Laughter amid the Tears

He has sent me to bind up the brokenhearted.
—*ISAIAH 61:1*

We hear some heartbreaking, hair-raising stories at my book table during Women of Faith conferences. Women who have read my books often come to tell me how they've worked through their own harrowing heartaches. My helpers and I share many tears with freshly hurt mothers who have lost children to accidents, disease, alienation, or some other calamity.

God, in his mercy, balances out these sad moments by also sending broadly smiling women wiggling through the crowds. These are the heartbroken moms "in recovery" who are eager to share a funny tale. For example, one woman patted the book that told my sad and sometimes ridiculous story of how I coped with the estrangement of our homosexual son. "Barb, your book saved my daughter's life," she said solemnly.

"Oh?" I answered. "Did your daughter read the book?"

"No," she said, her face breaking into a grin. "*I* read it, and it kept me from killing her!"

Another woman said, "Barb, you really should put a warning on your books: 'Do not read in a public place. When you burst out laughing, folks will think you're crazy!'"

Two sisters told me they had read one of my books aloud to their elderly mother as she lay dying. The sound of her laughing on her deathbed was something they would always cherish, they said. "Ohhh," I responded sadly, "when did she die?"

"She didn't!" one of the sisters exclaimed. "She recovered. We think it was all that laughing. She'd be here today, but it was her turn to deliver Meals on Wheels."

Thank you, Father, that you can replace my tears with joy,
and that you send other laughter-loving people my way. Amen.

Barbara Johnson

We Could Sing

Be joyful always; pray continually; give thanks in all circumstances,
for this is God's will for you. −1 THESSALONIANS 5:16−18

What can we do, Mommy?" Christian asked.

We were stuck yet again in an airport during a winter storm, and it didn't look good for getting out that night. Tempers were frayed in the departure lounge. The agents behind the counters were being bombarded by a million complaints, but they had little power to change anything.

"We could sing?" I suggested. Christian wouldn't always respond to that idea, but on that evening in a cold airport he grabbed hold of it and lifted his little voice high.

This little light of mine, I'm going to let it shine.
This little light of mine, I'm going to let it shine.
    Let it shine, let it shine, let it shine.
Hide it under a bushel, no! I'm going to let it shine.
Hide it under a bushel, no! I'm going to let it shine.
    Let it shine, let it shine, let it shine.
Won't let Satan blow it out, I'm going to let it shine.
Won't let Satan blow it out, I'm going to let it shine.
    Let it shine, let it shine, let it shine.

I watched people turn to listen to him and smile. A little girl joined in. An old man began to tap his foot as Christian gave the performance of his lifetime.

"I'm going to sing until something good happens, Mom."

I looked around. "I think it already did, darling."

Thank you, Father, for the gift of joyful singing and how it can
transform my sagging spirit. Today I lift my heart and voice to you.
Amen.

S h e i l a   W a l s h

Freeway Chorus

With singing lips my mouth will praise you.
—PSALM 63:5

That Barbara Johnson . . . what a sweetheart! A few years ago when my birthday rolled around she gave me a fabulous gift: two cassette tapes with piano and organ accompaniment to great hymns, plus a hymnal with this note attached:

> This Celebration Hymnal has all the pages turned down that I thought YOU would enjoy . . . they are my selections especially for you. Took lots of time to go through this book because I wanted to sing every song myself. (By the way, old hymnals are hard to find—I had to steal this one.)

I keep those cassettes in my car, and whenever I want to praise God or need a touch of peace in the middle of frustration, I put one in and sing my heart out. Mine is the only voice to all that fabulous accompaniment. It's great fun!

Barb knew I would love that gift because we both enjoy singing and come from the same background where these classic hymns were sung in church:

"I Love to Tell the Story"
"Rock of Ages"
"To God Be the Glory"
"Have Thine Own Way, Lord"

. . . and on and on and on—eighty different hymns, with which I can sing melody or harmony, whichever I choose.

I was singing in the car the other day and passed a woman on the freeway who was doing the same. Driving alone, her mouth was open and she was rocking back and forth. We caught each other's eye and laughed.

Singing to the Lord is a wonderful way to lift our spirits and find harmony when things are out of whack. The situation won't necessarily change, but we'll sure feel better.

Joyful, joyful, we adore thee!
Amen.

Luci Swindoll

Look!

The LORD delights in those who fear him,
who put their hope in his unfailing love. —PSALM 147:11

Man, just look at that boy!"

I looked. That boy, my son, was sitting on the grass with a magnifying glass, gazing at a ladybug.

"What is it, Pop?" I asked William, my father-in-law.

"Just look at him. He's brilliant! How does he know how to use one of those?"

"You just look through it," I said.

"Well, I know that, but look at *how* he's looking through it."

I looked. It looked pretty standard to me. Not to his papa, though. Everything Christian did was special, from the way he ate his cereal to the way he flushed the toilet. William died unexpectedly in November 2000, and every day when Christian is doing even the most simple of tasks, I hear in my head, "Man, look at that boy!"

Do you know that's how God feels about you? Sometimes as we grow older we lose that sense of being special—or perhaps you never had it to begin with. To God, you are a delight and a joy. He watches over you, marveling at you— his beloved child. When you go to sleep he is with you, and when you wake up to begin a new day he is right beside you. When you speak a kind word, reach out and help without being asked, refuse to take offense, cover a sister with love and grace, listen carefully. You might just hear him say, "Just look at that girl!"

Abba Father, thank you for the joy in knowing that you
delight in me and that your love never fails. Amen.

Sheila Walsh

JULY

Freedom

I run in the path of your commands, for you have set my heart free.
—PSALM 119:32

This wonderful little verse is tucked away in the longest chapter of the book of Psalms. The day I found it I was fretting over something not going my way. Out of sorts and heavyhearted, I complained to God about my disappointment. Then, this little jewel showed up! *Luci, look at this verse*, my inner voice beckoned. *You know why your heart is heavy? Because you are in your own way! Step aside, kid, you're blockin' the light.*

So often we don't experience freedom because we're convinced our way is best, and all our effort to make our "best way" work out becomes a dark spot on God's liberating path. We can't get around it, over it, or under it. And we sure can't go through it. But when we step aside and out of the way, there is no shadow. We're free to run forward!

Freedom is the most wonderful feeling in the world. It comes from the realization that even though control is out of our hands, but the One in charge is a lot bigger and smarter than we are. We can relax . . . if we'll just do it. When we do, we gain a sense of tranquillity, immunity, liberty, even lightheartedness.

As you read about freedom this month, remember your hands are not tied. You are not in prison. You do not have to believe you are trapped, without hope. You are free to be absolutely complete in Christ and to run the race set before you with confidence, power, and pleasure. So get out of the way and go for it!

Luci Swindoll

True Delight

I will walk about in freedom, for I have sought out your precepts.
—PSALM 119:45

There is liberty in knowing the Word of God and walking freely in its truths. Psalm 1 describes the pure happiness that comes from this intentional way of living: "But his delight is in the law of the LORD, and on his law he meditates day and night. He is like a tree planted by streams of water, which yields its fruit in season and whose leaf does not wither" (vv. 2–3).

Living with a clear conscience and a light heart has nothing to do with our own rules or judgments or small confined perspectives. Rather, the key to personal liberty is *delighting* in God's Word. In *Mere Christianity* C. S. Lewis writes, "To become holy is rather like joining a secret society. To put it at the very lowest, it must be great fun."

What a wonderful perspective! We make our lives so much more complicated than they need be. We wonder where the narrow road is. We wonder if the person to our right or left is "doing it right." We wonder if anyone is noticing how hard we are trying.

God says, "Focus on *me!* Love me, delight in my ways, and be free!"

Father, thank you for the gift of your precepts
that give life and liberty. You light my path and guide
my way. What a delight it is to follow you! Amen.

Sheila Walsh

It's Never Too Late

Stand firm, then, and do not let yourselves be burdened
again by a yoke of slavery. –*GALATIANS 5:1*

One of the greatest ironies in all of human history is that God granted freedom, and freedom gave rise to enslavement. Adam and Eve lived in a perfect environment. They had perfect bodies, a perfect climate, and were surrounded by health sustaining perfect food. Each day and night was spent in perfect marital harmony. God, their loving and perfect Creator, communed with them each day, and yet . . .

When that chaos-producing, tragedy-inducing decision was made to disobey God's one simple requirement, freedom was lost. Human beings have been enslaved by their own sinful nature ever since.

That would be a heart-rending, tragic story if that was the final chapter, but it is not. God, in his relentless love for his creation, offers freedom anew. He offers us Jesus. "It is for freedom that Christ has set us free," states the apostle Paul with confidence (Galatians 5:1). Through Christ's atoning sacrifice on the cross, we are liberated from the bondage of sin that condemns us to an eternity of separation from God. Christ also offers us freedom from fear, joylessness, and poverty of soul. Because of Jesus, the perfect sacrifice for sin and mediator to God for us, it is never too late to reclaim our lost liberty.

Lord Jesus, how I thank you that your perfect plan includes
a way to remove the heavy yoke of history. Thank you
for setting me free from all forms of bondage. Amen.

Marilyn Meberg

Disobedience Doesn't Pay

Live as free men, but do not use your freedom as a cover-up
for evil; live as servants of God. —1 PETER 2:16

Zipporah and her husband were on their way to Egypt when God was mad
enough to kill him. You see, for some unknown reason, Moses had not fulfilled
the Hebrew law to circumcise his son on the eighth day after birth. Whatever the reason, the whole family discovered that disobedience doesn't pay.

Maybe Moses and Zipporah had discussed the Hebrew laws, so when God
got mad she knew what was wrong and immediately took action to set things
right. Taking a sharp instrument, she cut the foreskin off her boy. But she
was as mad as a wet hen. She took the foreskin and threw it at Moses' feet,
calling him an unflattering name: "You bridegroom of blood!"

Aren't you glad that God doesn't repay us according to what we deserve?
Even if there is something in your life that makes God angry, he's not going
to kill you over it, or even call you rude names! Because Jesus spilled his blood
on Calvary, you have the freedom to be the imperfect human being God knows
you are. He gives you chance after chance after chance to follow him instead
of evil. Then, he forgives you for all the times you've been wrong and wipes
your slate clean.

Doesn't that make you want to just fall down on your face and worship?
Use your freedom to serve him!

*Lord of liberty, help me to discern what I need to do to get
in step with your will. I want to obey you all my days.*
Amen.

Thelma Wells

For You and Me

Be not afraid, O land; be glad and rejoice.
Surely the LORD has done great things. –JOEL 2:21

Ever heard of a woman named Janina Atkins? As a Polish immigrant she came to America with $2.60 in her purse, a few clothes, old letters, and books. She loved it here because she could buy a needle at the nearest store and didn't have to stand in line for food; her mail wasn't censored and her phone wasn't tapped. She was free.

Ever heard of Emma Lazarus? At the age of thirty-four this Jewish poet wrote a sonnet called "The New Colossus." It is inscribed at the base of the Statue of Liberty:

Give me your tired, your poor,
Your huddled masses yearning to breathe free,
The wretched refuse of your teeming shore.
Send these, the homeless, tempest-tost to me,
I lift my lamp beside the golden door!

Ever heard of Geraldine Ferraro? She was the first woman to run for Vice President. She said, "If you take advantage of everything America has to offer, there's nothing you can't accomplish." It's a free country.

Ever heard of Christa McAuliffe? As a social studies teacher she was selected by NASA to be the first private citizen in space ... an ordinary woman on an extraordinary mission. When *Challenger* exploded, her freedom took her into eternity.

"This land is your land, this land is my land," Woody Guthrie's song tells us. *This land was made for you and me.* We can be anything we want to be. By the power of God the sky's the limit. Don't wait to enjoy your liberty. It is yours today. Remember Galatians 5:1— "It is for freedom that Christ has set us free."

Dear Lord, this is the day you have made. Help me enjoy
it freely and pass my personal sense of liberty on to someone else.
Amen.

Luci Swindoll

July 5
Soaring

No discipline seems pleasant at the time, but painful.
Later on, however, it produces a harvest of righteousness and peace
for those who have been trained by it. –*HEBREWS 12:11*

It was supposed to be a picture-perfect moment, a touch of romance and grace. At the end of the music video of the old Welsh hymn, "The Love of God," I would release a white dove into the sky, symbolizing the liberty of God's love.

"What will happen if they don't capture it in the first shot?" I asked the bird handler on the set of the video shoot. "Will the dove be gone?"

"Oh, no! I pull a couple of his tail feathers out and he can't fly far. It don't hurt."

Easy for you to say, I thought.

I was horrified and apologized to the bird in a private moment. When it came time for me to release the dove, it became clear to all involved that Mr. Bird Man had been a bit overenthusiastic in his plucking. I released the bird with the admonition, "Fly!" The dove flapped his wings once and plummeted to the ground.

God's trimming of our feathers is not like that. He trims us perfectly so we can fly to heights we know we are not capable of. The prophet Isaiah assures us: "Even youths grow tired and weary, and young men stumble and fall; but those who hope in the LORD will renew their strength. They will soar on wings like eagles; they will run and not grow weary, they will walk and not be faint" (Isaiah 40:30–31).

As we put our hope in the Lord, he will make us soar.

Lord, teach me to wait patiently for your strength
that lifts me to new heights of freedom. Amen.

Sheila Walsh

The Freedom of Letting Go

I have set before you life and death, blessings and curses. Now choose life.
—Deuteronomy 30:19

Hook-and-line crab fishing is a lesson in the art of decluttering our lives. The crab fisher baits a hook with a big blob of chicken liver. Then he drops the bait into the water and waits. When the crab grabs the bait with its claws, the crab fisher reels in the bait. The crab doesn't want to let go. But unless it does . . . it is somebody's lunch!

That analogy reminds me of a recent article that urged readers to "Free yourself from clutter!" The writer noted that most folks use only about 20 percent of their belongings. The remaining 80 percent is "just in case" stuff—just in case we lose fifty pounds, move back to that other climate, have another child, decide to start a garden, or get the urge to go back to college. All that unused stuff causes clutteritis, slowing us down and becoming oppressive.

My husband, Bill, is an expert declutterer. Occasionally he will go on a binge of closet cleaning, and inevitably he talks me into letting go of things I really don't want to give up. But when it's over, the things I use frequently are so much easier to find that I feel as if I've been freed from an onerous burden!

The same is true in my life. It is not easy to turn loose of old habits or resentment, but when I do, I am rewarded with a great sense of freedom, as though my spiritual "closet" has been decluttered. And I can more easily find the good things of God that I'm seeking!

Dear Jesus, help me choose to declutter my life
and focus on you alone. Amen.

Barbara Johnson

Shackled by Love

Love must be sincere.
—ROMANS 12:9

My three-year-old grandson, Alec, is showing an inclination toward bigamy. You may remember he was very much in love and talking marriage a couple of months ago. So I wasn't prepared for what I saw when I picked him up at preschool yesterday.

He and a little girl (not his betrothed) were sitting very close to each other on the grassy section of the playground. He looked very debonair in his bright yellow Donald Duck sunglasses, and I must admit her Mickey Mouse tennis shoes provided a pleasant matched-couple look. Nonetheless I wondered if Debbie knew her wedding plans were in jeopardy.

Alec greeted me enthusiastically and then introduced me to Heather. Ignoring me she leaped to her feet and shouted, "Alec . . . hug me!" He obeyed but then asked if he was coming home with me. "If you want to. . . ," I said, glancing at the other woman. She shouted, "Alec . . . don't leave me!" I told him to think about it while I went to check him out of the preschool office.

When I returned to the playground, there wasn't a sign of either Alec or Heather—or Debbie, for that matter. Another little girl with bright red shorts and a chartreuse tank top sang out, "They're hiding!" Alec then sheepishly emerged from behind a tree and announced, "I'm ready, Maungya." As we made our way to the car, Heather could be heard shouting, "I don't love you anymore, Alec!"

Buckling Alec into his seat I realized that at some point we'd need to talk about some big concepts like loyalty and possessiveness, real love and freedom. But certainly not before our McDonald's Happy Meal.

Thank you, Lord, that your love is generous and spacious.
Amen.

Marilyn Meberg

Games People Play

You have been set free from sin.
—ROMANS 6:18

I love word games—crosswords, Scrabble, Upwords, and computer Boggle. Right now I'm into Boggle, a word game based on visual speed. My opponent is Maven, the unseen, all-knowing computer challenger. One of my favorite features of the computer version is that, at any point during the timed challenge, I can restart the game. In fact, I can wait right up to the last seconds, assess my progress, and decide to restart the game to improve my score. I push that button frequently.

Now, if only we had that option in real life. I think of different conversations I've had in which I needed a button to push to take back my existing score with people and start anew to improve my standing. Even if that button only existed in my home, it would be invaluable. I've said so many things in heated moments, in careless exchanges, in hormonal escapades, that didn't need to be said or could have been expressed in wiser, more genteel ways.

Alas, life is no game. No button allows us to rewind, erasing our conversations so we can begin again. Here, though, is the good news: Jesus offers us a fresh beginning every (any) hour of the day or night. He won't wipe away what we have said to another person, but he will guide us toward reconciliation. He will give us the humility to ask for forgiveness and the internal grace to walk through the painful renewal process.

Our all-knowing resource is Jesus, who offers us as many chances as we need to succeed. Now that, folks, spells f-r-e-e-d-o-m!

Jesus, grant us the ability to gamely try to mend relationships,
including our relationship with you, that we've broken. Amen.

Patsy Clairmont

No Strings Attached

How great is the love the Father has lavished on us, that we should be called children of God! And that is what we are! —1 JOHN 3:1

My daughter Lesa made a comment the other day that spoke right to the deepest longing we have as Christians—as human beings, for that matter. She said that as she has danced this year at the Women of Faith conferences and spent time with the speaker team, she has experienced for the first time in her adult life what it's like to feel free to be herself without the judgment of individuals or cliques. She explained that she had not found this kind of freedom in church and among some friends and acquaintances. But the Women of Faith team—each of us so different, yet so authentic—is able to love, support, correct, tease, and pray for each other with no strings attached. You can exhale on that!

Jesus came that we might have this kind of no-strings-attached relationship with each other and with him. It is liberating to know that you don't have to walk on eggshells when you are with other people. It is a relief to know that even though you dress differently, are a different size, talk funnier than someone else, or whatever, you are free to live unencumbered by the bondage of phoniness. Besides that, phoniness is ultimately revealed.

Take a reality check to see if you give people the freedom to be themselves when they are with you. Jesus accepts us completely and unconditionally. He gives us the freedom to be ourselves all the time! We ought to do the same for each other.

*Father, thank you for the precious freedom to be myself
with my friends and with you. Help me to graciously allow
others the same freedom. Amen.*

Thelma Wells

The Great Escape

Oh, that I had the wings of a dove! I would fly away and be at rest.
—PSALM 55:6

Sometimes there is nothing left to do but run away. We are tired, sick of the stress, and want a change. Actually, we're looking for a place to hide. I know the feeling very well. I've had it many times.

When that happens here's what works for me. Take a trip. I don't mean on a plane. I mean in your mind. Go to your favorite chair with a pint of ice cream, a big spoon, a good book, and fly away.

I did that today. The book I chose was about a woman's trip to Africa, and it was fascinating—all about the pictures she took, the villages she stayed in, the people she met, her escapades with wild animals. I was with her every minute and the ice cream was gone in no time. What a delicious way to spend an afternoon.

Groucho Marx says, "Outside of a dog, a book is man's best friend. Inside of a dog, it's too dark to read anyway." There's nothing like a good book. My favorites are those that teach me something new and take me far away. Through books I've been into the minds and cultures of people all over the world. I've left home and flown through the air without ever getting out of my chair.

Generally speaking, when we are ready to quit, the best thing is a change of venue. We need to get out of ourselves. We can do that with a good book. There's no tellin' where the Lord might take you when you ask him to map out your trip. He's full of surprises as well as the best traveling companion ever.

Lift my spirit, Lord, on the wings of your Holy Spirit.
Amen.

Luci Swindoll

July 11
No Ball and Chain for Me

But we have the mind of Christ.
−1 CORINTHIANS 2:16

Have you ever wondered how we can have the mind of Christ when so much of what goes on in our minds is not Christlike? I'm slowly beginning to grasp the wonderfully liberating truth about this concept.

Because I've accepted Jesus' invitation to receive him as my personal Savior, he's cleansed me of all sin. As a result, I am a holy person. A holy person cannot have unholy thoughts. Jesus lives in my cleansed and holy mind; however, thoughts from the Enemy, who wishes nothing more than my stumbling and failing, can still come to me from the outside. The thoughts he brings with him are not sin; they do not prove that Christ does not inhabit my mind. Those thoughts simply mean that the Enemy is alive and well and ever seeking to destroy God's children. I am his child.

So what do I do about those thoughts? First, I live in the assurance that the person of Christ continues to indwell me; and second, I follow Paul's prescription in 2 Corinthians 10:5: "We demolish arguments and every pretension that sets itself up against the knowledge of God, and we take captive every thought to make it obedient to Christ."

I love the image of those rascally thoughts being dragged to Christ, complete with ball and chain. They literally become captives, but they are *his* captives, not mine. I have no power over them; he has all power over them. Because of his indwelling, victorious-over-all-sin presence, they are defeated.

What is my job? Turn them in to the Authority. Then I am free to think Christ's thoughts.

Lord Jesus, I revel in the knowledge that you live in my mind.
Amen.

Marilyn Meberg

July 12
Perfect Harmony

Now the Lord is the Spirit, and where the Spirit of the Lord is, there is
freedom. And we, who with unveiled faces all reflect the Lord's glory, are
being transformed into his likeness with ever-increasing glory, which comes
from the Lord, who is the Spirit. —2 CORINTHIANS 3:17–18

My husband and I love to watch dog shows on television. Our favorite is
the Westminster Dog Show, which has been in existence for over a hundred
years. In 2001 the "Best in Show" was a Bichon Frise. I have never seen a
dog more delighted about winning than this perfect little bundle of fluff. He
looked like he was bursting to make a speech. As his trainer was receiving
the prize cup the little dog was waving his front paws as if to say, "Yo! Hello!
Over here with the microphone."

It's an old joke, but I do believe there is some validity to the theory that
people look like their dogs. The tall slim woman loping beside the elegant
Afghan and the short stocky man puffing his way around the ring beside the
bulldog look like they were made for each other. That's how I want to be
with God: transformed into his likeness as I run with him.

The more we commune with God, the more like him we become. The
more time we spend meditating on his Word, the more like him we sound. It
is a beautiful sight to watch a dog and trainer who love and trust each other
work together. There is no push and pull—just the graceful freedom that
comes from running in tandem.

Father God, teach me to run in perfect harmony with you
so that all who watch know I belong to you. Amen.

S h e i l a   W a l s h

Who's the Boss?

He is the Rock, his works are perfect, and all his ways are just. A faithful
God who does no wrong, upright and just is he. –DEUTERONOMY 32:4

Get up right now! Don't just lie there. It's time for you to be up. Get up right
this minute, wash your face, brush your teeth, and put on your clothes!
Mamma's gone to work. I'm the lady in this house today, and you're taking me
to the park. If you don't get up right now, I'm going to spank you."

He didn't get up until he got spanked.

On a vacation day from school, my five-year-old granddaughter imitated
exactly what her daddy says to her when she won't get up. She actually
spanked her dad though. (He doesn't spank her.) He was laughing so hard
he couldn't get upset. Guess where they spent the day? At the park and the
Golden Arches.

Vanessa's authority was short-lived, however. Things went back to normal
pretty quickly.

We often think we're in control of things. We yell and demand and
threaten. And God just sits back sometimes and lets us think we are in charge.
Before we get completely out of hand, however, he steps in and shows us who's
the boss. I love that, 'cause I know that when the rubber meets the road, I'd
rather have him driving!

Vanessa couldn't drive the car to the park or pay for the hamburgers. The
real authority figure had to. She just had the illusion of control. Her freedom
to be a child came in the form of a daddy who loves her.

*Father, when I want to act like the boss in my life, remind me that
I am your beloved child and you're a perfect Parent. Amen.*

Thelma Wells

July 14
Respecting God's Boundaries

Above all else, guard your heart, for it is the wellspring of life. Put away
perversity from your mouth; keep corrupt talk far from your lips. Let your
eyes look straight ahead, fix your gaze directly before you.... Do not swerve
to the right or the left; keep your foot from evil. –PROVERBS 4:23–25, 27

Christ's love frees us, but with that freedom comes responsibility. In striving
to live Christlike lives, we must guard our thoughts, words, and actions so that
we stay within the boundaries God set for us.

It's like the story of the dog whose owner gave his beloved pet free range
on his property. The owner diligently trained the dog to stay within the boundaries, and in that space the pet enjoyed complete freedom to run, chase bun-
nies, lie in the sun or the shade, swim in the pond, and do whatever else a
dog likes to do. But occasionally the dog just couldn't resist slipping onto the
neighbor's property and causing problems. Eventually, the dog's master built
a large pen, and although the dog still had plenty of room, he repeatedly dug
under the fence and escaped. Finally, the owner sadly chained the dog to a
stake he'd driven into the ground. And there sat the shackled dog. By his
actions, he had exchanged freedom for imprisonment.

Like the dog in this story, we enjoy great freedom. But to have the greatest serenity and influence as Christians, we must live within God's boundaries,
because it is there, embraced by his love and protected by his grace, that we
enjoy the sweetest liberty.

*Lord, guard my heart, keep me focused on your Word,
guide my steps . . . and set me free! Amen.*

Barbara Johnson

Splendor

Tremble before him, all the earth! The world is firmly established;
it cannot be moved. —1 CHRONICLES 16:30

The headline that caught my attention was "Distant, Oversize World Causes Cosmic Confusion." The newspaper write-up was about a solar system 123 light-years away that harbors one ordinary planet and another one so huge (seventeen times as massive as Jupiter) that scientists can't quite figure out what it can be.

Also recently discovered is a pair of planets, each about the mass of Jupiter, that whirl around their home star fifteen light-years from earth in perfect lock-step. One takes thirty days to complete an orbit, the other exactly twice as long. This is the first time such a configuration has ever been seen.

According to scientists these discoveries make it clear how little they know about planets and add to the dawning realization that our solar system may be a cosmic oddball. One astronomer conceded that not a single prediction for what scientists expected to find in other systems has turned out to be correct!

I love the majesty of Isaiah 45:12: "It is I who made the earth and created mankind upon it. My own hands stretched out the heavens; I marshaled their starry hosts." There is such security, such freedom from fear, at the realization that not only did the planets burst into being at his command, but God is also completely in control of his entire creation.

Lord, I praise you for the inner freedom I experience every time
I meditate on your splendor and might. Thank you for holding
everything and everyone so securely in your sovereign hand. Amen.

Marilyn Meberg

Delightfully Different

The LORD your God loves you.
—*DEUTERONOMY 23:5*

Being a grandmother is interesting and delightful. As I observe the differences in my grandchildren, I am amazed and charmed.

Vanessa, my six-year-old, is a thinker who prepares before she speaks. And she expects to get back well-thought-out answers. One day she said, "Grammy, you give such good advice; I need your help. There is a girl at school who looks at me with evil eyes. What should I do when she looks at me like that?"

After pondering and praying for a few minutes I said, "If she doesn't do anything but look at you, continue to smile at her. Pray in your mind for her to be nice and kind."

"I knew you'd tell me something good, Grammy," Vanessa replied. "Thanks!"

Alaya, my four-year-old, is quick, impulsive, and dramatic. The little drama queen is always at work for an Academy Award. The world is a stage and she's the only actress.

Alyssa, my three-year-old, is the fashion model. She's discovering that whining and crying make you look ugly, and her goal is to be cute. She rejects clothes that don't make her look cute.

Bryna is only sixteen months old and seems to be the one who really doesn't want to be bothered. She wants peace and quiet and can be perfectly content playing all by herself. When the other girls get in her face, she takes her little hand and swats them away.

Each of my granddaughters is so different, and I love it that way.

Praise you, Father, that you didn't make anyone alike and you
give me freedom to be exactly who I am. Everyone's personalities
are as different as toe prints, and you love it that way! Amen.

Thelma Wells

Someone's in the Kitchen

I would like you to be free from concern.
—1 CORINTHIANS 7:32

I love kitchens. Their warmth makes them natural gathering places while the wafting aromas and circular tables entice people to sit a spell. The most nurturing conversations seem to take place over romaine salads, swirls of pasta, and hunks of French bread dipped in olive oil.

Oh, but wait, in case you misunderstand, let me clarify: I don't cook. Well, it's not that I don't or won't, but those who know me best have suggested that I shouldn't. My feelings would be hurt except that I agree.

Last Christmas I invited my daughter-in-law, Danya, and our friend Amy to bake holiday goodies with me. The plan was for each of us to make our own items and then to share the wealth. The girls agreed, and I searched my cookbooks for some dainties. I decided to try a candy recipe. All started out well. I stirred the ingredients in a pot for thirty minutes and then, with lightning agility, I poured the mixture onto waxed paper. Halfway through the pouring, my candy set into the shape of a mud puddle.

My second recipe was for cookies. The resulting product looked suspiciously crude. In fact, as the three of us stood over both of my efforts, we agreed that the cookie batch looked like Kibbles 'n Bits and the candy batch appeared to be Puppy Chow. The girls said I didn't have to share.

I love kitchens. And where I excel is in inviting guests, setting the table, and calling the Colonel. It's all in knowing your gifts and feeling free to express them.

Lord, thank you for setting me free from concern about my limitations,
and for giving me the pleasure of using the gifts I have. Amen.

Patsy Clairmont

Be You

> The LORD does not look at the things man looks at. Man looks at the outward appearance, but the LORD looks at the heart. —1 SAMUEL 16:7

I gave my friend Debbie Petersen a new hat. It was darling: one of those Helen Kaminski skimmers made of natural fibers in Australia. Colorful. I bought it in California and took it to Deb in West Virginia where she packed it for Florida. She had a fit over that thing.

But you know what I liked more than the hat? The box it came in. I'm not kidding—what a piece of clever engineering. It had a little round cardboard extension inside to keep the hat upright, stylish lettering outside with a spiffy leaf logo, and a rope handle. I wanted that box.

I'm a sucker for packaging. I'll buy almost anything if it's packaged cute. Not long ago I came home with a box of cigars because I liked the lettering on the front. I don't smoke but I had to have the box. Then there are bottles of ink. It's their shape I enjoy even if I'll never write anything in "purple mosque." I could go on, but I'll spare you.

Ironically, one of my favorite things about the Lord is that he *doesn't* care about packaging. He's not hung up on our grooming or clothes or the kind of car we drive. He's not concerned about the box. He's concerned about the contents. Our hearts!

I've heard my brother Chuck say, "Give yourself permission to be you . . . then soar!" We are not bound to this earth or its trappings. Christ has given us the liberty to be who we are, like what we like, wear what we want, and feel what we feel. I love that!

Cigar, anyone?

Father, help me give myself permission to be me.
Amen.

Luci Swindoll

The Grass Grows Greener on Liberty Street

So if the Son sets you free, you will be free indeed.
–JOHN 8:36

Imagine mowing your way across America. One man took the challenge of riding a lawn mower from Atlanta, Georgia, to the Pacific Ocean. He drove ten hours per day for a daily average of eighteen miles. Through eighteen states he cut a path, driving five thousand miles over a twenty-month period. He did all that to raise $200,000 to help clean up America.

A guy would have to have a lot of internal freedom to take on such a task. I mean, this wasn't the newest Harley, fastest Lamborghini, or some macho Hummer. He was riding a sure-enough grass-green lawn mower. Can't you see him now—inching along while children on tricycles passed him? That takes a lot of moxie!

I admire folks who step outside the lines to color. Consider John the Baptist, who lived in the desert and dined on big grasshoppers. Note I said I admire such people, not aspire to behave like them. While I might ride a lawn mower through, say, my hometown, for charity, I'm not available to eat locusts. Of course, who's to say if times were hard and food scarce? Grasshoppers might start to look good on a cracker.

In our look-alike world in which we can identify each other's labels from a distance by the cut of the cloth, lawn mowers and locusts look liberating. While I understand some lines are necessary to maintain order and human dignity, I think other lines are born of our rigidity and fear. Those are the ones I'd like to mow down and step across, even if it means I'd have to ... gulp ... eat a grasshopper.

Lord of liberty, help me to walk in greater freedom.
Amen.

Patsy Clairmont

Keys to Freedom

Do not forget my teaching, but keep my commands in your heart.
—*PROVERBS 3:1*

Consider these keys for living an effective life, liberated inside and out:

1. Free your heart from hatred.
2. Free your mind from worry.
3. Free your home from clutter.
4. Free your life from hurry.
5. Expect less.
6. Give more.
7. Exercise daily.
8. Laugh out loud.
9. Rest.
10. Pray without ceasing.

And finally, remember *whose* you are. "And whatever you do, whether in word or deed, do it all in the name of the Lord Jesus, giving thanks to God the Father through him" (Colossians 3:17).

Dear Father, I long to be free from hatred, worry,
clutter, and hurry, and I strive to live an effective life for you.
Thank you for my freedom in Christ. Amen.

Barbara Johnson

Can't Miss

He guides me in paths of righteousness for his name's sake.
—PSALM 23:3

Bondage is defined as a state of subjection to a force or power. Freedom is defined as a condition of being liberated from restraints. We would all love to live free of restraints, and yet many of us live in a state of subjection.

One restraint that keeps us in bondage is the fear many of us harbor that we'll "miss" the will of God. But that worry need not exist for us when we belong to Jesus, simply because when the Spirit of Christ expresses his life through us we *are* living in his will. Does it make sense that when we abide in him and trust him to guide us, he would have a lapse and let us veer off course? No! That's not his nature.

But when we experience an unpleasant surprise or disappointment, we tend to wonder if we have missed out on his perfect plan. In those moments we must remember that his plan is not the same as ours. In his plan we may experience what seems to be all wrong, but because it is truly his plan we can be assured it's all right! On a human level of thinking, who would ever believe that the crucifixion of Jesus was God's will? It was too brutal, too unthinkably unjust, to be God's plan. But what followed that horror was the wonder of the Resurrection and the new covenant between God and his lost people.

Jesus didn't miss God's will, and neither will we.

Lord, what security I have when I place myself in the center
of your will. As I choose to trust in your plan instead of my own,
I welcome freedom from anxiety and doubt. Amen.

M a r i l y n   M e b e r g

Messes Welcome

In him and through faith in him we may approach God
with freedom and confidence. –EPHESIANS 3:12

Mom, can I have an ice-cream cone?" my son asked one night.

It was close to bedtime and past the usual sugar cutoff zone—that well-defended line that is supposed to contribute to a long, restful night of sleep for Christian and the whole family.

"Please, Mom. It's a special day," he said with eyes like a Golden Retriever puppy.

"What's special about it?" I asked.

"You are my mother!" he pronounced, his hand on his heart.

"Oh, brother!" I said as I headed toward the freezer.

He disappeared into his room with the ice-cream cone. Five minutes later he was back with a sorry look on his face.

"Oops! Mom?" Christian called.

"What's wrong, darling?"

"I dropped it!"

I followed him back to his room just in time to see the cat walking through a puddle of melted French vanilla. Christian and I cleaned up the ice cream and the cat took care of herself.

"Can I have another one?" he asked with those puppy-dog eyes.

Once more he trotted off, happy as a clam.

"You're never going to believe this," he said as he reappeared with an empty cone. I believed it.

I love that you and I are invited to come to the throne of grace with all of our messes. We don't cower as we approach. We're coming to a Father who loves us, so we approach with confidence, knowing that he will receive us. He will welcome us, clean us up, and fill our empty cups once more.

*Thank you, Father, that because of your love for me I can
approach you today with total freedom from fear. Amen.*

S h e i l a W a l s h

Going Nowhere

Do not conform any longer to the pattern of this world,
but be transformed by the renewing of your mind. —ROMANS 12:2

Merry-go-rounds, carousels, and Ferris wheels decorated the parks and amusement areas of Paris, France, whose theme for the new millennium was "Wheels of Time." When I thought about the circles of pleasure used to depict the theme, I thought about life. Sometimes we are suspended on a Ferris wheel, looking down at the bustling world below. When we finally come down from the ride, we really haven't gone anywhere.

Life seems like that when your bills roll around month after month and the balances on your credit cards remain the same. Or when you think you have some extra money at the end of the month, only to discover that your month is longer than your money. Or when you go to work and it's the same routine day after day. Or when a relationship continues to be strained for months.

To change your destination, I suggest you get off the Ferris wheel that's taking you nowhere and get on the bus that transports you from one place to another. Drive your bills down by paying more than the minimum monthly installment. Spend a little less so you'll have a little more. Change the way you do things at work so it won't feel like such a relentless grind. Substitute positive responses for negative ones with people you're having trouble with.

Seek God's wisdom in making all these decisions. Let God drive; he never takes you on a dead-end ride.

*Father, please give me a renewed mind and determination
to make changes that will get me off the rides that are taking
me nowhere. I want to be free! Amen.*

Thelma Wells

Do Something for Yourself

No eye has seen, no ear has heard, no mind has conceived what
God has prepared for those who love him. —1 CORINTHIANS 2:9

One of the sweetest pleasures of singleness is coming and going as I please. I had lived in my new home for six weeks when I noticed a small article in the newspaper. *Lucia Di Lammermoor* was being performed that very night at the McCallum Theater. *Lucia* is an opera that I had sung with Maria Callas, and the McCallum was five minutes away. I was ecstatic.

Not knowing if I could get a ticket, I left home with time to spare, dressed to the nines! Unbelievably, I was able to sit on the eighth row, right in the middle. As I read the program I learned this was the Dallas production "on loan" to Palm Desert. That meant all sets and costumes came from Dallas. I smiled because this was where I had sung opera. "Callas in Dallas," I used to say! This was *my* production.

The houselights dimmed, the orchestra began to play, and in a matter of moments I was transported back twenty years. One of the choristers even had on *my* costume. Three hours later I drove home, triumphant.

If you are single like I am, don't spend one minute of your precious time today regretting your single status. You are independent, my friend . . . free to do what you want. Free to come and go, as you like. Decide on something fun to do tonight all on your own. Plan it. Look forward to it, and then enjoy it triumphantly. You have no idea what God has up his sleeve . . . just for you.

Lord, thrill my soul today with a special surprise.
Amen.

Luci Swindoll

Share the Gift

Do not use your freedom to indulge the sinful nature;
rather, serve one another in love. –GALATIANS 5:13

My mom loves to sit beside people on airplanes who want to chat. I, on the other hand, dread people like my mother! I am usually reading or writing a book or playing tic-tac-toe or Go Fish with Christian.

I almost never fly alone, but recently I had to travel to Las Vegas to speak at a church. The first leg of my flight was from Nashville to Dallas. I sat beside a man who looked busier than I, so I assumed God was giving me the day off for good intentions.

"What do you do?" he asked.

I thought you were busy, I thought to myself, but instead I answered, "I'm a writer."

"What do you write?"

"I write books for women about joy and hope and freedom."

"Freedom from what?" he asked.

"Freedom from ourselves to be able to love God and love other people."

"That's what I need."

We talked for a while. It turned out he is a Hollywood agent. "I live in such a self- obsessed world," he confided. "There has to be something more."

I took down his address and sent him a couple of books, along with an invitation to his wife to attend our next Women of Faith conference.

That leg of one of many annual trips was a reminder from God not to hug my faith to myself and live selfishly but to liberally share the gift of freedom that only a relationship with Christ can bring.

Father God, give me your heart to love
all the people around me. Amen.

Sheila Walsh

Fill My Cup

If anyone is thirsty, let him come to me and drink.
–JOHN 7:37

The TV sitcom *Cheers* tapped into a primal need of every human being. The camaraderie, authenticity, and place of safety where "everybody knows your name" beckons one to pull up a stool and settle in.

For many of us a few hours in a neighborhood bar is not an option, but a few hours in a church coffeehouse is a great alternative. I was heartened to read about the Family Christian Center in Munster, Indiana, where a Starbucks has been opened in their church lobby. Their desire is to offer a wholesome and relaxing environment—a place where people can learn each other's names.

Family Christian is just one of many churches around the country starting businesses on their property in an effort to make church a warm and inviting place. If church is to be a haven for the hurting, what better place to express one's heart than over a non-threatening mocha latte with lots of whipped cream.

A cup of shared coffee might prove to be a person's introduction to the concept of spiritual liberty—a gift of grace from God that says we are acceptable, safe, and welcome to live in authenticity and freedom. When that person then enters through the sanctuary doors and takes a seat, he or she will learn who it really is that offers such freedom. We learn his name and find out he has always known ours.

Lord Jesus, may the love that fills my cup splash over
into the cups of those around me. May I ever be sensitive
and available to be a conduit of your grace to those
who are searching and longing to be free. Amen.

Marilyn Meberg

Home-Field Advantage

If the LORD delights in a man's way, he makes his steps firm; though
he stumble, he will not fall, for the LORD upholds him with his hand.
–PSALM 37:23–24

Athletes competing on their own turf are said to have a "home-field advantage," but it is not really the familiar playing *field* that gives them the advantage. In most cases it is the crowd of familiar fans in the stands, cheering for the players, that motivates the team to work harder and compete with more enthusiasm.

Most of us respond the same way. When our efforts are applauded and cheered, we are motivated to work harder and do better. Think how parents teach a child to walk. The baby manages to stand while tightly clutching the coffee table, and the parents hold out their hands and beckon encouragingly: "Come on. You can do it. Take a step. We're right here. We'll catch you. That's the way. Good girl!" Knowing her parents are there with love and kisses no matter what happens, the baby feels free to turn loose of the table and take that first wobbly step.

God wrote the book on positive parenting techniques! He sets us down somewhere and then gently beckons us to go forth and serve. "You can do it. I'll be with you. Take a step . . . ." Because we know he'll love us no matter what, we turn loose of our fears and take that first wobbly step in faith. What freedom we enjoy, knowing that any failures we face need not be final. With God in our grandstands, we always have a home-field advantage.

Oh, God! Your love and grace free me to do your work
in ways I could never do on my own. Amen.

Barbara Johnson

First Things First

"Bring the whole tithe into the storehouse, that there may be food in my house. Test me in this," says the LORD Almighty, "and see if I will not throw open the floodgates of heaven and pour out so much blessing that you will not have room enough for it." –MALACHI 3:10

Normalcy is when you run out of money; insolvency is when you run out of excuses; bankruptcy is when you run out of town."

I didn't make that up, but I wish I had. It's true. Every normal person has been broke and tried to explain it with excuses. When we can't rise above it, we want to move. Nobody likes money problems. They're embarrassing. They affect every aspect of our health: material, emotional, physical, intellectual, and spiritual. If we can't leave town, we'd like to retire ... but we could live only until 2:00 P.M. tomorrow. We're stuck!

Let me suggest a dozen ways to help you get unstuck:

1. Tithe off your gross income.
2. Live within your means.
3. Take care of what you have.
4. Wear it out.
5. Do it yourself.
6. Anticipate your needs.
7. Research value, quality, and multiple uses.
8. Make gifts by hand.
9. Shop less.
10. Buy used.
11. Pay cash.
12. Do without.

There is nothing selfish about the Lord. He blesses freely. When we realize everything is his and we give because we've been given to, it's easy to tithe off the gross. This is God's #1 priority in the stewardship of handling money. Putting first things first enables us to see his goodness at every turn. There's blessing all over the place!

Lord, keep reminding me I cannot outgive you. Amen.

Luci Swindoll

It's Too Hot!

Father Abraham, have mercy on me, and send Lazarus,
that he may dip the tip of his finger in water and cool off my tongue:
for I am in agony in this flame. —*LUKE 16:24* NASB

My husband brought home a pound of fat, juicy Texas Hotlinks. The first bite of sausage didn't seem hot, so I chowed down. Suddenly my eyes and nose started watering. My tongue told the rest of my body that it was on fire. Ice and water didn't cool it. Time was all I had to soothe my scorched tongue.

My husband, on the other hand, was popping Hotlinks like nothing was happening. I think George's taste buds have burned off because he eats spicy food so often. He judges the quality of a restaurant by whether or not they offer hot sauce with every entrée. Only once do I remember hot sauce being too hot for George. Some friends brought him a bottle from Jamaica. His whole body felt like it was on fire. *Heh-heh.*

Now y'all, if hell is any hotter than that, I don't want to go. I don't want to be anywhere I can't get ice water or have time to cool off. I understand from the Bible that hell is a mighty hot place. When the rich man begged for Lazarus to bring him a drop of water to cool his tongue, he got no satisfaction. Poor soul. He was in torment for eternity.

That's not going to happen to me. I've done what it takes to keep from burnin' up. I've accepted Jesus as my Lord and Savior.

What about you? Will you avoid the heat?

Savior, you made a way for us to spend eternity with you,
free from the fire. Hallelujah! And amen.

Thelma Wells

Passing Through

You are no longer foreigners and aliens, but fellow citizens with
God's people and members of God's household. —EPHESIANS 2:19

I just had visa photos taken for a trip to India with World Vision. (Don't
ever do that on a day you're already depressed . . . cameras don't lie.) Last
year we went to Ghana and the year before, Guatemala. As I was leafing
through my passport I was amazed at the places I've traveled all over the world.
No one ever stopped me at a border or questioned why I wanted to go. Six
expired passports are proof of my adventures. I've had the freedom to leave
my own country, going anywhere I chose.

Every time we get in a car or hop a bus, train, or plane, do you know that
it's a gift? We do it because we *can*. Rarely are we stopped because of lack of
freedom.

I've traveled so much that I've "adopted" families in Greece, Europe, and
Africa. It is amazing how traveling has changed me from being a foreigner to
a fellow citizen with all these folks. That little passport gave me the right to
get there.

My sojourn on earth is kind of like that. I'm on my way someplace else.
That rite of passage takes more than a passport or a visa photograph. It takes
being a member of God's household, believing he went before and paid the
price for me to come later. One day the Lord will call me and I'll fly away—
free of this earth, finished with my work, and finally with him. I won't even
have to pack.

Want to come with me? Your ticket has already been paid for.

Lord, thank you for what you have done to set me free from
all the things that would hold me down, or back. Amen.

L u c i   S w i n d o l l

Home at Last

To live is Christ and to die is gain.
—*PHILIPPIANS 1:21*

In the human heart is a vacancy that we, in our neediness, lease out to a reckless world. And that's who moves in: an unkempt, raucous community. With doors splayed open, our interiors abound with folks who breeze through, folks who hang out for a season, and folks who linger on and on. We soon learn to secure the entrance and to be more discriminating. We learn something else as well: Loneliness is a terminal condition.

Jesus came to be our Divine Companion, but he chooses not to free us from the nagging ache of our solitariness. Yes, he is ever present, and he will never abandon us. Yet we still feel the pangs of our hollow humanity. Actually, the ache might be our longing for a larger freedom. In a place called Eternal, we will finally feel safe, finally whole, finally free.

Until then I've learned not to see loneliness as a chiding enemy but as tinder to flame my spiritual passion. Loneliness is often birthed in brokenness and therefore senses the unspoken signs in others who may be too paralyzed to speak. Let us use our ache as a bridge to reach their stained-glass hearts. We will not release them from their human condition; yet for a wisp of time we will both feel connected.

Loneliness doesn't alter God's changelessness or his nearness; it merely defines a fleeting aspect of our condition. Don't give loneliness greater credence than it deserves, for just around the next bend, my friend, is freedom, is home.

Lord, help me to come to terms with my temporary soul aches, because they will soon be salved in your eternal presence. Amen.

Patsy Clairmont

Humor

A cheerful heart is good medicine. —*PROVERBS 17:22*

There is nothing better than a good laugh to lighten a dark situation. They say laughing is like jogging on the inside, and I try my best to get all the internal exercise I can!

Laughter has been proven to speed recovery from illness and injury, and it has magnetic powers as well. Find something that makes you laugh, and others will flock to you. (Of course, they may be wearing white coats and carrying a straitjacket, but that's something to laugh at right there, isn't it?)

I have shed my share of tears during my life, and I know it is never easy to plaster a smile on your face and pretend to be happy when you're not. As someone said, "Always keep your chin up—and you'll bang your head on the door frame!" But sometimes a little pleasant pretending can help jump-start your recovery. When you're stuck in the pit and mired in the cesspool, hold on to hope—and humor. Be open to opportunities to laugh, and anticipate a happy future. The worst grave of all is a closed heart.

When times are hard, find something to laugh about, and feel God's blessing envelop you. Don't hold back. Laughter is the pole that helps us balance the bad and the good as we walk the tightrope of life. When anxiety engulfs us, it is a tranquilizer with no side effects. Laughter is a powerful weapon against hopelessness and a reassuring comfort blanket of God's love. Cherish the gift—and use it often!

Barbara Johnson

Yuk, Don't Snicker

They raise their voices, they shout for joy.
—ISAIAH 24:14

That humor heals is not a disputed fact for most people. Norman Cousins chronicled his personal experience of recovering from a debilitating illness in his book *Anatomy of an Illness*. He says that watching Marx Brothers movies and favorite cartoons and *I Love Lucy* sitcoms were powerful contributors to the healing that took place in his body.

There has been an enormous amount of energy spent in the study of laughter and its healing properties since Cousins' work. One recent study of 300 people, half of them heart patients at the University Medical Center in Baltimore, concluded that big guffaws are more effective than dainty tee-hees in fighting heart disease. Michael Miller, M.D., who led the research team, reported that anger and mental stress impair the endothelium, which is the protective lining of the blood vessels. This can cause fat and cholesterol buildup in the coronary arteries. But laughter, the study suggests, may have the opposite effect; it appears to stimulate elements that protect the endothelium.

For the sake of the "big yuk" and the health of my endothelium, I asked my three-year-old grandson last night if I could teach him to "play" the kazoo. Alec was hesitant because he had never seen nor even heard of a kazoo. I explained that basically you just hum into it and then it makes the "kazoo sound." I did an impressive rendering of "Old MacDonald Had a Farm" as an introductory warm-up.

As we traded the kazoo back and forth, Alec and I were soon rolling on the floor in helpless giggles. In no time, my endothelium felt better.

Lord, thank you for big yuks, guffaws, and belly laughs.
Amen.

Marilyn Meberg

Two Pigs and a Giraffe

For I was hungry.
–MATTHEW 25:35

I'm on a food program spelled d-i-e-t. I'm trying to lose the weight I gained during my last pregnancy, which was twenty-nine years ago. Actually, I've lost it before, but being conscientious, I found it again. This yo-yo tendency has left me with inflated issues: fluffy thighs, chubby knees, and puffy upper arms. My dietary consultant has assured me, though, that the overlapping folds between my chin and necklace will remain regardless of my efforts. Oh, great.

The menu I'm on allows for snacks. In fact, it demands them. I like that in a program because I'm a snacky girl. "Snack," for me, is a hot caramel-marshmallow sundae, while this program allots eight olives. Not chocolate chips or M&M's, but sour *green* olives. Amazingly, however, when one is on a limited menu one's enjoyment-range can expand. Why, those little Spanish marbles actually seem like rare delicacies.

My husband is offended that I've become protective of my food. While I used to share freely, now I threaten anyone who touches a morsel of my provisions. Trying to be a nice guy, Les brought home a small box of animal crackers, knowing they were low in calories. I carefully counted out a bounty . . . one giraffe, two pigs, and a sheep. I savored each one.

The following day I decided I'd consume two water buffalo and a lioness, but when I strode to the kitchen, my cookie stash was gone. I bellowed at my hubby. Wide-eyed, he informed me my friend who stopped by with her child had innocently taken them. I wondered if I should sue.

Discipline is never easy.

Lord, help me keep my sense of humor in the midst
of appalling deprivation. Amen.

Patsy Clairmont

Pie in the Sky

So I commend the enjoyment of life, because nothing is better for a man
under the sun than to eat and drink and be glad. *–ECCLESIASTES 8:15*

Summer in Palm Desert, California, is more than a challenge ... it's a commitment to staying alive. The hottest day I've experienced was 128 degrees. Nothing moves or stirs. The plants don't wither, they're electrocuted—they just turn brown and crumble.

One such day a friend and I decided to go out for dinner after it had cooled off ... to 100 degrees. We looked forward to it all day—our big outing. I picked her up and we ate and visited leisurely, then took dessert to go. A lemon meringue pie. Great choice!

When we got to her house, I asked, "Where's the pie?"

"Oh gosh. I thought you had it. You were the last one holding it."

We looked in the car, the garage, even the kitchen ... and then I remembered: I'd put the pie on top of the car while I threw my purse in the backseat. Forgetting it was there, we took off.

Piecing all this together we gasped at first, then started laughing. We could picture that pie sailing through the air, and the look of amazement on people's faces as it flew by. Retracing our steps just to satisfy our own curiosity, we found it on the side of the road. Lemon meringue was splattered in gutters and on curbs and sidewalks all along the route. The empty pie pan was leaning against a fire hydrant. We howled!

When life throws you a little curve today, throw it right back with a hearty laugh. This too shall pass.

When the going gets rough, Lord ... give me a laugh.
Amen.

Luci Swindoll

Weird Laughter

There is a time for everything, and a season for every activity under heaven:
. . . a time to weep and a time to laugh. —ECCLESIASTES 3:1, 4

I have known Christian author and humorist Lee Ezell for years. She is the queen of props with the largest collection of weird hats and glasses west of Vegas.

We met up recently at a women's conference in Bossier City, Louisiana. When the conference was over on Saturday night, Barry and Christian and I were in our room eating chicken strips and watching Tarzan. There was a knock at the door. Christian wanted to answer it. He came back with a puzzled look on his face.

"Mommy, there is a weird woman at the door with a green lizard hat on."

"Tell Lee to come in," I said.

He was fascinated by her. After we finished our chicken she asked him if he wanted to go to her room and see the rest of her hats. He was out of the door quicker than a used car salesman after you've given him your check. He came back with an umbrella hat on his head. Lee was dressed like a porcupine.

"We went down to the lobby, Mom," he said. "People looked at us like we were cool."

I wasn't sure he had read that absolutely right, but I love that Lee loves to laugh, loves to laugh at herself, and loves to bring others into the party. Regardless of her many personal heartaches and losses, Lee chooses to look at life through a "weird" lens. Her perspective cheers everyone around her.

Father, thank you for those who bring laughter and humor
into my life. May I pass on the gifts. Amen.

Sheila Walsh

Make 'Em Laugh

But the fruit of the Spirit is . . . joy.
–GALATIANS 5:22

Long before Marilyn Meberg was entertaining the world with her witty, wonderful prose, she was writing funny notes to me. She'd drop by my house or ride in my car or seek out my purse. . . and later I'd find a scrap of paper with her words:

> Looking forward to our next event—whatever that might be—half a grapefruit or filet mignon! Loving you warmly, Marilyn.
>
> Hi Baby. Jeff and I had a hamburger at Coco's and rather than go home we came to your house where I brushed my teeth, combed my hair, and drank a beer. Do you mind that I made myself at home? You are loved, Pearl Mitsubishi.
>
> Enjoy your trip to the Caribbean (that spelling is the latest for that part of the world. It looks unfamiliar because it has yet to experience common usage).
>
> Beth and I came over here for a short spell because the bug man came for a repeat spray. (Meberg pests are hard to kill.) We have to stay out of the house for two hours so we're now going to lunch.—Sara Teasdale

And my favorite, found stuck on my refrigerator:

> Loving you till the day you die. Yours truly, Margaret Thatcher.

What fun! Each note gives me a quiet little giggle of remembrance. When Marilyn stands on the Women of Faith stage now and I see thousands of faces responding to her unique, utterly delightful humor, I think, *Do it, Marilyn: Make 'em laugh.* And she does.

By the way, Marilyn hates beer.

Give me the eyes to see those who need a laugh today, Lord.
Help me make it happen. Amen.

Luci Swindoll

The Gift of Goofiness

Blessed are you who weep now, for you will laugh.
–LUKE 6:21

You don't have to be a clown to stick a geranium in your hat and be happy (although it does help if you are a little bit off-balanced to begin with!). But you do need a sense of humor. I have an advantage in the humor department because God has blessed me with the gift of goofiness.

That's how I end up in ridiculous situations like the time my pal Andy and I slipped into an invitation-only gathering at the Crystal Cathedral by claiming we were doing a "bomb check." We took my little phone-dialer, the gizmo I use to retrieve messages from my answering machine while I'm away from home, and solemnly marched down the aisle to aim the little gadget at all the potted plants along the edge of the platform. As it beeped and clicked we nodded and smiled, then headed for a side door. I happened to spy one of my friends in the audience as we were leaving, and her eyes nearly popped out of her head. "Barb, what were you doing?" she asked me later. I confessed that Andy and I were just having fun.

Security has increased at the Crystal Cathedral since then (I wonder why?), but my love for goofiness hasn't changed. With each new day, my craving for humor begins anew. How blessed I am to have similarly afflicted goofy friends who are always ready to help me search out the humorous side of nearly every situation.

There are at least two sides to every issue, and one of them is bound to provoke a giggle. That's the side I'm on. Won't you join me?

Lord, thank you for creating me (and allowing me) to be goofy.
Amen.

Barbara Johnson

This Is Only a Test

You will laugh at destruction and famine.
–JOB 5:22

How can you tell if you have a sense of humor? Is it when you tell a funny story or joke, you're the life of the party, you laugh easily at someone else's mistakes as well as your own? Or, is it when life tests you with pain and sorrow?

A person who has truly passed this test is my friend and speaking comrade Barbara Johnson. When the doctor told her he regretted delivering the most disturbing news of her life, she remarked, "You evidently don't know anything about my life."

Barbara has a brain tumor. "I'll get some treatments," she told me, "and then I'll be back speaking and spreading my joy somewhere."

When I visited her in the hospital after surgery, her head was shaved and silver staples ringed her head from ear to ear. "I'm going to get that guy who gave me this hairstyle," she quipped.

Many people would have crumbled after nearly losing a husband to an accident, identifying the bodies of two sons killed tragically five years apart, and being disowned by another son for more than a decade. But Barbara pulled out of the recesses of her redeemed heart the ability to use her sense of humor as a balm of healing that destroyed the bitterness of despair. She's a great example to the world that you can find joy and spread humor even when everything around you is falling apart.

Master, how brilliant you are to give me a sense of humor
that can buoy me in even the most traumatic experiences of my life.
Please help me pass the humor test. Amen.

T h e l m a   W e l l s

Get Your Ducks in a Row

You who dwell in the dust, wake up and shout for joy.
—ISAIAH 26:19

My heart was heavy as my dear friend and colleague Barbara Johnson faced brain surgery. There was a "deeply embedded tumor" the size of a golf ball in her frontal lobe. I hate the phrase "deeply embedded"; she hates the golf ball metaphor. She prefers a Ping-Pong ball comparison because it sounds softer, friendlier, and "easier to get out." Whatever the metaphor, we pray fervently that in the midst of her latest trial she will be filled with an extra measure of the hope and humor she has so generously given to millions.

Last year when I was suffering from the effects of toxic silicone slithering throughout my body, I was one of those millions; she pulled alongside me and never left. She phoned me every day, made countless calls to doctors all over the country (she knows everyone), and kept telling me I "needed to get my ducks in a row" to survive. We laughed repeatedly over that wacky theology and wondered if there was a verse to support such a principle.

Every now and then a package would be delivered to my front door. In it would be yet another ceramic grouping of ducks lined up in formation with the familiar admonition, "Remember, Marilyn, keep your ducks in a row." Each duck gave me a much needed giggle. Each duck lifted my spirits.

As I sit here today, I can see one of those many duck arrangements on my kitchen counter. So in all reverence and love I say back to you, Barb, "Get those ducks in a row."

Lord, even when I am afraid, you can lift my spirit with something silly.
Thank you for knowing just what I need. Amen.

M a r i l y n   M e b e r g

Color Me Fortunate

I have set my rainbow in the clouds.
—GENESIS 9:13

My husband, Les, is a colorful character. He sings almost constantly—when he isn't lovingly annoying his family with his old jokes. We never know what kind of outlandish gift he will haul home next. (The latest was a motorized motorcycle with kickstands for his nine-month-old grandson, who only has to wait four years to try it out.) Les is drawn to the ridiculous and is fond of the absurd (which explains the ten hip-swinging, yodeling Santas he gave away one Christmas). It makes me giggle to think his mom named him Les, when he is most certainly more, more, more!

If I were to color Les, I'd have to use all the crayons in the biggest Crayola box to capture his personality. And here's the kicker: He's color-blind. Most of his world is green—whatever "color" his green is. I find it perplexing when I stand next to one of autumn's blazing red maple trees, and he can't tell any color difference between it and the evergreen next to it. That does, however, explain the times Les has walked out of the bedroom dressed in green pants, blue shirt, one brown sock, and one gray, asking, "Does this work?"

Yet who cares how many flavors his wardrobe is when his heart is bursting with rainbow generosity, individuality, and humor? Who minds if he can't tell a bluebird from a redbird when he fills our home with song? Who cares how antique his jokes are when he never fails to make his family laugh?

Color him outrageous, color us blessed.

Lord, may I reflect your vibrant hues.
Amen.

Patsy Clairmont

Laughing All the Way

She is clothed with strength and dignity; she can laugh
at the days to come. —*PROVERBS 31:25*

Growing older is one of the easiest things to laugh about. (Just be sure you're wearing your Depends before you get too carried away!) For example, there's that list that suggests ways childhood games are renamed as we age. My favorites are:

Sag, you're it!
Kick the bucket
Musical recliners

You do know how to tell when you're *old*, don't you? Old is when you think about sex and your pacemaker opens the garage door! It's when you'd fall apart completely if it weren't for elastic and static cling. President Dwight Eisenhower once defined life as happening in three stages: youth, maturity, and "My, you're looking good!"

And then there's menopausal mirth—the laughs you get when you consider selling your home heating system at your next yard sale or when you have to write your kids' names on Post-It notes so you don't forget them.

It doesn't really matter what age you are; learn to laugh at your stage of life, and you'll make that stage the best.

Oh, God, I know you understand. After all, you are elderly too! Amen.

Barbara Johnson

Lock Her Up!

You created all things, and by your will they were created
and have their being. —REVELATION 4:11

Plato thought humor was sufficiently dangerous to warrant carefully regulating it in his republic. Socrates believed humor fell into the category of salt; it should be used sparingly. Pythagoras swore it off entirely and forbade his followers to indulge.

Laughter was serious stuff for the ancient Greeks. Some, like Plato, thought it could stir up violence and upset the social order. Can you imagine a more deadly time for me to live? I would have continually upset the social order; ultimately, the word "doomed" would have been branded on my forehead.

The question of whether Jesus had ever laughed so consumed medieval Christian scholars that the University of Paris devoted an entire conference to the topic in the thirteenth century. Since good evidence was lacking, Louis IX (later canonized) decided, just to be on the safe side, never to laugh on Fridays.

I cannot imagine why it should be difficult to imagine if Jesus laughed. Of course he laughed! How can I say that so dogmatically? Very simply: because we laugh. We are created in his image. For example, our capacity to appreciate the beauty of nature came from him; he appreciates beauty and he imprinted that same appreciation on our souls. Our capacity to appreciate humor is also from him.

I think the issue for sober-minded scholars to work on is this: If the inherent human ability to appreciate humor didn't come from God ... then from whom did it come?

Thank you, Lord, for my capacity to find humor in life.
I can't help it! And neither can you. Amen.

Marilyn Meberg

August 12
My Little Joker

For you have been my hope, O Sovereign LORD, my confidence
since my youth. —PSALM 71:5

It was time for my son's annual checkup. Visiting the doctor is always a challenge for both of us. I was hugely relieved to discover that no shots were due until he turned five. Christian was so ecstatic that he couldn't contain his exuberance.

"Do you want to know a joke?" he asked Dr. Ladd.

"Sure!"

"Ask me how poor I was," Christian said.

"How poor were you?" Dr. Ladd asked.

"I was so poor that I had to get married for the rice!"

"I've got more," he said. "My computer crashes so often that I had to get a helmet!"

Christian doesn't have a clue why either of these jokes is funny; he just knows they are and laughs his head off at how clever he is.

As we were leaving the office and Christian had run on ahead to get his free sticker, Dr. Ladd told me it was unusual for a four-year-old to tell a joke. "We use that as a test at age six to measure confidence," he said.

When I was pregnant, my prayer for my son was that as a young boy he would have a heart tender toward God and that his strength and confidence would be in God alone. How gracious our Father has been to capture my boy's heart, and to give him a sense of humor besides!

We don't even have to understand our own jokes to laugh and spread delight. All we need to know is that we are secure in Christ.

Dear Father, you make me laugh!
Amen.

Sheila Walsh

August 13
Hidden Treasures

Your barns will be filled to overflowing, and your vats
will brim over with new wine. –PROVERBS 3:10

Much of my mail comes from heartbroken moms who pour out the misery they're feeling because of something about their children—a child has died or is homosexual or is in jail or ... well, you get the picture. I'm blessed to think God uses me in small ways to offer encouragement to these hurting parents. And I'm also blessed to find, in nearly every batch of mail, a day-brightener to offset the many notes of sorrow.

For example, recently someone sent me a silly story about a preacher who visited an elderly woman from his congregation. As they talked, he nibbled from a bowl of peanuts on the coffee table. They visited for nearly an hour, and by the time the preacher was ready to leave, he had eaten the whole bowl of peanuts. A little embarrassed, he told the woman, "I have to apologize. I really just meant to nibble a few peanuts. . . ."

"Oh, that's okay," the old lady reassured him. "Ever since I lost my teeth all I can do is suck the chocolate off them anyway."

Whenever you get mired down in the miseries of this life, search for the funny story, the day-brightener, buried in the muck. Think of it as a treasure hunt, and find something joyful hidden in every batch of mail, every errand you run, every person you meet. Ask God to help you find these hidden treasures. He will!

Dear God, guide me in seeking out the treasure trove
of humor you have hidden in my life. Help me find joy
and laughter in some part of each day. Amen.

Barbara Johnson

A Twinkle in His Eye

*For those God foreknew he also predestined to be conformed
to the likeness of his Son.* –ROMANS 8:29

He's called Teacher, Rabbi, Master, Lord . . . but few call him a humorist. Yet a look at Scripture demonstrates just how quick, witty, and playful he was. Why else do you suppose little children flocked to him?

"It is easier for a camel to go through the eye of a needle than for a rich man to enter the kingdom of God," he told his disciples (Mark 10:25). I think they couldn't help but laugh at the absurdity of the image. But today we take Jesus so seriously that we miss his robust sense of humor and the twinkle in his eye.

His humor could bite too. "You strain out a gnat but swallow a camel," he challenged the Pharisees (Matthew 23:24). Jesus enjoyed hanging out with ordinary and disreputable people. He facetiously described his critics: "They're like spoiled children complaining to their parents, 'We wanted to skip rope and you were always too tired; we wanted to talk but you were always too busy'" (Luke 7:32 MSG).

The Creation account tells us, "When God created man, he made him in the likeness of God" (Genesis 5:1). And the apostle Paul encourages us: "And we, who with unveiled faces all reflect the Lord's glory, are being transformed into his likeness with ever-increasing glory" (2 Corinthians 3:18). If we don't have a twinkle in our eye and a humorous perspective on life, then we are not being as much like Christ as we might think.

Don't miss out on one of the best parts of being his child. Laugh with him!

*Lord Jesus, please put a twinkle in my eye
and humor in my heart. Amen.*

Thelma Wells

August 15
Huh?

At Parbar westward, four at the causeway, and two at Parbar.
—1 CHRONICLES 26:18 KJV

Isn't that the weirdest verse? A Dallas Seminary professor told me it was his favorite.

"What does it mean?" I asked.

"I haven't a clue."

It is refreshing to find a theologian who doesn't take himself too seriously. So many people are afraid to laugh. (God'll get 'em.) That drives me crazy!

William James says, "We don't laugh because we're happy, we're happy because we laugh." If we can't laugh at things that don't make sense, how will we enjoy old age?

San Jose State University holds an annual contest to find lousy writers. Thousands of people send in their hilarious pieces of putrid prose . . . opening paragraphs for a would-be novel. This was my recent favorite by a librarian named Janice Estey:

> "Ace, watch your head!" hissed Wanda urgently, yet somehow provocatively, through red, full, sensuous lips, but he couldn't, you know, since nobody can actually watch more than one part of his nose or a little cheek or lips if he really tries, but he appreciated her warning.

Look around your neighborhood for signs that make you laugh. Write down stories your kids tell with made-up words. Have fun with poorly edited prose. Best of all—listen to *yourself*. You are funny whether you know it or not. So let go and loosen up!

If you go through life taking everything literally, you will "feel like a buzzard on a desert where nothin' dies" and quickly everybody will "enjoy about as much of you as they can stand." I learned this from Country Western music . . . and it's true.

Heavenly Father, one of your greatest gifts is a sense of humor.
Please don't let me take life, especially myself, too seriously. Amen.

Luci Swindoll

humor

Humor in Unlikely Places

*I know that there is nothing better for men than to be happy
and do good while they live.* –ECCLESIASTES 3:12

I love Luci Swindoll's sense of humor. She and I have great fun with television and radio interviews. As we drive over to the station we give each other impossible words to fit into a sentence during the pending interview. The bet might be for a few dollars or a free meal. I have discovered that there is no such thing as a word that Luci can't fit into a sentence. It has cost me dearly. She could feed the poor in Africa with the bets I've lost. And she does!

Luci has taught me to have fun in every day, to make the best of circumstances I haven't chosen. It is wonderful to be around people who make the best of things, who find humor in unlikely places.

When we were in Phoenix, the television station was kind enough to send a stretch limousine to pick us up. If you have ever tried to get into one of those things, you know it's no easy task. They are low to the ground, perfect for wiener dogs.

"How do you get into one of these?" Luci asked as she grabbed hold of the door handle—which came off in her hand with wires and pieces of fabric trailing like pathetic streamers in a cheap parade.

I answered helpfully, "Well, not like that!" Of course, Luci thought it was hilarious.

I have taken up Luci's challenge to have fun while doing even the most mundane of tasks. A sense of humor lightens every load.

*Father, today help me to look for humor in unexpected places . . .
and to celebrate every precious moment. Amen.*

Sheila Walsh

Seasick

A violent storm arose.
—*JONAH 1:4*

Jonah was a little fishy, if you ask me. In fact, I'll bet he reeked once he got thrown up on the beach. Imagine all that seaweed matted in his hair, and who knows what that fish ate last (besides Jonah). Then mix in the acid from the fish's stomach... *Oh, yuck, somebody stop me!* Obviously, Jonah needed hosing down, not to mention a powerful mouthwash, a hairdresser, and a haberdasher.

I've been in a few putrid situations myself. Ones in which I felt engulfed by my circumstances or swallowed by my emotions. Untangling emotions can be as tedious as trying to extract seaweed from one's tresses. And I've always had more emotions than there are fish in the sea.

I appreciate feelings of love, joy, and peace, but I'm not as fond of jealousy, depression, or hatred. I'll bet Jonah understood, for he wasn't fond of the folks in Nineveh. They were the neighborhood bullies. So when the Lord said, "Arise and go to Nineveh," Jonah fled.

Have you ever run away from people you're not terribly fond of? Do you think God was unaware of Jonah's feelings when he asked him to go to Nineveh? Or is it possible Nineveh wasn't the only problem God was untangling?

Nothing like a little getaway to refresh one's emotions; Jonah's proof of that. "But I, with a song of thanksgiving, will sacrifice to you" (Jonah 2:9). What a change. Of course, that was A.D. (After Digestion).

Feel swallowed up by your emotions? Engulfed by your circumstances? Annoyed at the bullies in your neighborhood? Fleeing from the Lord?

My advice: Avoid boat rides.

*Thank you, Lord, that even when I stink with sin
and bad humor, you don't give up on me. Amen.*

Patsy Clairmont

August 18
Slam Dunk

With joy you will draw water from the wells of salvation.
—Isaiah 12:3

This past holiday season I was attending a social gathering that had all the potentiality of escorting me into a coma. Desperate to keep myself from such a lapse, I leaned over to the woman seated next to me and said, "Did you know that a slam dunk is not a rough baptism?" Settling back into my chair I waited for her response. Since I had only met her that evening I didn't know what to expect.

She reared around in her chair and stared at me with that bifocal tilt known and used by all of us over fifty. "What are you talking about?" she asked mirthlessly.

"Nothing really . . . I just read that somewhere and found it amusing."

After an uncomfortable silence she finally said, "Well, I guess I just don't see anything funny about baptism, that's all!"

I could have made matters worse and told her that as a Presbyterian I ran no risk of a slam dunk because we sprinkle; but even I had sense enough to choose the coma instead of the comment.

I firmly believe God has created within each of us a capacity to appreciate humor, and we get to choose mirth or misery. That being the case, there really is no reason to miss out on laughter in life . . . unless of course you see nothing amusing about slam dunks.

Lord, thank you for all the potential you have given me
to see the funny and quirky side of life. Help me lighten up!
Amen.

Marilyn Meberg

humor

247

Facelift for Free

The LORD make his face shine upon you and be gracious to you.
—NUMBERS 6:25

A stranger called me one day and asked if I would like to have a facelift.

"Who is this again?" I asked, dumbfounded that such a call came from out of the blue. As I spoke, I leaned around the corner so I could peek at my face in the hallway mirror. I puckered my mouth just a little, trying to find my cheekbones.

The woman laughed and said she worked for a plastic surgeon who had just performed a facelift on a friend of mine. She explained that when the doctor did a facelift, he offered a big discount to any patient who gave him the names of four friends who were also interested.

"Sh—she thought I needed a facelift?" I stuttered, lifting my chin indignantly to smooth out the creases in my neck. "She said I would be interested?"

"Well . . . I guess she did," the woman said, a little embarrassed when she realized my friend (*former friend,* I was thinking) hadn't prepared me for her call. "But it sounds like you're *not* interested, huh?"

"You got *that* right!" I answered. I hung up the phone, trying to decide whether to feel hurt, angry—or old. When I glanced into the hall mirror again, my face had contorted into a disgusted frown. For one brief moment I saw the droopy eyelids, the neck creases, the wrinkles everywhere. Then, just as quickly, I decided to laugh about the whole thing. And what do you know! My face lifted all by itself!

Dear Lord, you put the twinkle in my eye and the humor
in my heart. I can overlook the wrinkles. Amen.

B a r b a r a   J o h n s o n

Wrong Word!

But from everlasting to everlasting the LORD's love is
with those who fear him. —PSALM 103:17

Christian and I often revisit a familiar discussion on manners. He does well for a four-year-old boy, but he seems to have the Walsh trait of brain leakage and occasionally all my reminders slip out.

We were flying to Dallas and the flight attendant asked Christian if he would like to have wings to pin on his ball cap.

"Yes, I would!" he replied enthusiastically.

"Yes, ma'am," I reminded him.

"Yes, ma'am," he mimicked, looking at me as if I was ruining his chances of having a meaningful relationship with this darling blond flight attendant.

Later that night he sat on my lap while we sang our favorite nighttime songs. When we were finished I asked him if he remembered our discussion on the plane.

"Yes, ma'am," he replied with a grin.

"I know you think I make a fuss about things like that, Christian, but it's important to show respect for your elders."

He looked at me and laughed. He waited for me to join in. I didn't.

"Mommy, that was funny," he said, a little confused.

"Why was that funny?" I asked sternly.

"How can I show respect for my elbows?"

How often do we do that with the Lord? He says, "Trust." We hear, "Try." He says, "Rest." We hear, "Strive." He says, "I love you just the way you are." We hear, "I love you, but I'd love you a bit more if you'd change a few of your bad habits."

Dig deep into the Word of God. All the right words are in there!

Thank you, Father, that you're willing to keep talking
to me even when I don't get it! Amen.

Sheila Walsh

Live!

Sing to him a new song; play skillfully, and shout for joy.
—PSALM 33:3

I found a clever poem. I don't know who wrote it but there's a lot of truth in it:

There was a very cautious man
Who never laughed or played;
He never risked, he never tried,
He never sang or prayed.
And when he one day passed away
His insurance was denied;
For since he never really lived
They claim he never died.

For those of us who "really live" it is hard to imagine why some people don't. I'm amazed at those who tell me they can't remember when they last laughed. They confess, "We were never allowed to laugh in our home while I was growing up, so I don't know how."

Playfulness is one of my favorite attributes in people. One morning a simple phone call cheered me up in the middle of paying bills. It was from some little kid who had the wrong number.

"Hello," I said.

"Hi."

"Well, hi . . . who is this?"

"Me."

"Oh . . . okay. Who would you like to speak with?"

"You."

"All right! How ya doin'?"

"Good. How *you* doin'?"

"I'm doing great. How old are you?"

"Four. How old are you?"

"I'm sixty. Would you like to marry me?"

"No. I gotta go now. You're too old. Bye."

"Bye."

You may feel too old to get married, but you should never feel too old to have fun. Laugh. Play. Risk. Try. Get out there and really live!

Lord, help me to be playful today . . . not only with the people around me
but with the circumstances I face. Remind me that humor is simply a way
of seeing and of being. Amen.

Luci Swindoll

humor

Hup, Two, Three ...

Get up ... and walk.
–MARK 2:9

I thought after five decades of hoofing my way through life that I knew how to walk, but, nay, 'tis not the case. After listening to taped messages by a walking instructor, I'm surprised I've managed to trek this far.

Well, see what you think. First, when you walk, you should step forward with your toes pointing toward the sky so that you land on your heel and then roll up onto the ball of your foot, pushing off for your next step.

Huh? I just sling one foot in the direction I want to go, followed by the other, and *voilà*, I'm there.

Second, pull your shoulders back and down. Suck in your abdomen, and then, as the instructor coos on the tape, "Relax."

You've got to be kidding. Who can relax with shoulders pasted back, rib cage inflated, and breath held? (Which is the only way I can keep my ribs from slipping into my tummy.) Hello! Somebody work with me here.

Third, breathe from your abdomen. Excuse me, but isn't that the stomach? Mine is preoccupied with the knot of peanut butter and bananas I just scarfed down. No room for something as filling as air, thank you.

Scripture also gives us insights on walking. Listen in: "This is the way; walk in it" (Isaiah 30:21). Now, that's simple. See the path? Yep. Then walk. Okay!

And what about this? "They will walk and not be faint" (Isaiah 40:31). Feel faint? You've walked too far. Find a bench. Chill.

Also, "walk in the light" (Psalm 89:15). Makes sense to me: walk in the day; sleep in the night.

I think I'll change instructors!

Lord, teach me to walk in your ways.
Amen.

Patsy Clairmont

Laugh Away the Calories

He sees God's face and shouts for joy.
—JOB 33:26

There is nothing like a good belly laugh to lift our spirits, restore our hope, and ease our sorrow. And now scientists realize it's a great weight-loss tool too. I read somewhere that one hundred belly laughs are equal to working out on a rowing machine for ten minutes! (This idea came from the same person who said jumping to conclusions was a great way to boost your heart rate.)

Even though I do my best to laugh my way through every day, I haven't lost any weight doing it. So I'm thinking about starting a new diet I heard about. You can eat all you want . . . of everything you don't like! Of course, exercise is important too. But motivation is my problem there. Finally I came up with an incentive for doing sit-ups. I squeeze an ice-cream cone between my knees and take a lick every time I reach for my toes!

Caution: There *is* a drawback to laughing off too much weight. The problem was illustrated by an old lady in a rest home who told her friend, "It's my birthday. I'm eighty-five years old, and by golly, I want to do something fun today, something shocking. I'm gonna streak through the cafeteria in my birthday suit."

Sure enough, she ran naked through the dining hall. Two old men, leaning over their soup bowls, watched stone-faced as the old gal trotted by. Then one of them commented to the other, "Say, Alma's jogging suit is kinda wrinkled today, isn't it?"

Oh, Lord, thank you for the opportunities you give me
each day to enjoy a healthy belly laugh! Amen.

Barbara Johnson

A Respite of Joy

A cheerful heart is good medicine.
—*PROVERBS 17:22*

Have you ever been down in the dumps and someone told a joke or said something funny that made you laugh? That was a respite for your spirit, wasn't it? Instantly, your body and brain rushed with hormones and enzymes that foster healing.

Both medical science and common sense have proven that people who smile a lot and have a good sense of humor are not as prone to depression as people who don't. People who laugh a lot respond more favorably to every kind of medical and psychological treatment and get over sickness faster than people who don't.

In my customer service seminars I ask people to smile and say, "I'm having a great time." Then I ask them to stop smiling abruptly. They find it difficult to stop even if they didn't want to smile in the first place! Then I ask them to frown and say the same thing. They find that even more difficult to do because the medicine that heals the soul is already flowing in their body from the smile they so recently enjoyed.

God is a masterful creator. He gave our bodies and souls the ability to get back in balance through the power of humor. So why don't you resolve to smile instead of frown, laugh instead of cry. If you have a difficult time smiling, just put a mirror on your desk or anyplace where it's convenient for you to watch yourself. Then, every time you feel down, look into the mirror and smile. (Nobody wants to see herself looking ugly.) I guarantee that you will feel better instantly!

God, I choose to rejoice in you.
Amen.

Thelma Wells

Dog Days of Summer

*You have filled my heart with greater joy than
when their grain and new wine abound.* —PSALM 4:7

Geneen Roth wrote a sassy little book called *When You Eat at the Refrigerator, Pull Up a Chair*. It's a list of fifty ways to feel thin, gorgeous, and happy.

I love lists . . . getting things done. Write it down, do it, check it off! So on this hot August day let me suggest a few ways to get through the heat of whatever challenge you have in front of you. They're simple attitude adjustments that can lower your internal temperature.

First—

Refresh your day by reading Scripture. Find a passage that will be strengthening or comforting and read it aloud. Let it sink into your mind and soothe your heart.

Second—

Swim in the encouragement of God's love. No matter how down you are or how much you'd like to give up, hang on. God has a plan for you. Today's test is part of the plan.

Third—

Breeze through your chores in the power of the Spirit. There's no way you will be able to deal successfully with things apart from God's Spirit. The Lord doesn't give us a task without enabling us to get it done.

Fourth—

Drink in the blessings that are already yours. When you accepted Christ, a bunch of promises came with your salvation: peace, joy, endurance, victory, courage, hope. Pick one and believe it.

Fifth—

Chill out! God's in charge.

After trying all these things, if life is still just too hot to handle, go to the refrigerator. Open the door. Pull up a chair.

*Believing you are in charge is the hard part for me, Lord.
Give me more faith. Amen.*

Luci Swindoll

humor

Humor by the Hour

He will yet fill your mouth with laughter.
–JOB 8:21

Is there anything more dull than a day without humor? But if we look for humor on the hour, as I like to do, it generally falls into the category of what I call the "quick-pick."

For example, yesterday I was talking to the administrative assistant to Steve Murray, senior pastor at La Jolla Presbyterian Church. Since I was slated to preach their three services the next weekend, the assistant and I were going over some necessary details. Though I have frequently filled in for Steve, the assistant was a recent hire and we'd never met.

As we concluded our arrangements, she said she understood I was quite tall and she'd be looking for a robe for me. I told her I usually wore Steve's robe, but that didn't seem to satisfy her. She asked if she could get back to me.

A short time later she called and triumphantly told me she'd arranged for me to wear the robe of one of the other pastoral staff persons who happened to be 6 feet 5 inches tall. I couldn't control my outburst of laughter. The picture of me staggering down the aisle dragging wads of velveteen fabric, attempting not to knock over candles or lurch into the pipe organ as I struggled to mount the steps to the pulpit was more than I could stifle. She waited for me to finally "get over it." I apologized for my lack of self-control and informed her that I am 5 feet 6 inches, not 6 feet 5 inches.

That one quick-pick lasted all day. In fact, it's working today as well. I'm putting it into the "count-on-it" file.

Lord, I thank you for hourly doses of humor.
Amen.

Marilyn Meberg

The Old Lady with the Baby

Sarah said, "God has brought me laughter, and everyone who hears
about this will laugh with me." And she added, "Who would have
said to Abraham that Sarah would nurse children? Yet I have borne
him a son in his old age." –GENESIS 21:6

You have to admire Sarah. I would not be laughing if I discovered at ninety that I was pregnant. I would be hiding from the *National Enquirer* paparazzi! The old couple had wanted children forever, but now that Abraham was one hundred he wouldn't be much help during the midnight feedings.

When reading biblical accounts, we tend to forget that they are stories of real people like you and me—people who walked every day through the unknown. They didn't have the benefit of the whole story the way we do as we observe them in retrospect.

In spite of some pretty outrageous circumstances, Sarah said that everyone who heard about the old lady with the baby would laugh with her. I love that. She said *with* her, not at her. That's because she started the laughter herself.

God's ways are so unpredictable. I never thought I would have a baby, so when I became pregnant at forty I was amazed. Now I realize I don't hold a candle to Sarah, being fifty years younger, but it was still a surprise. So Barry threw a surprise party for me. I walked in to forty friends waiting to laugh and celebrate with me.

When Sarah got pregnant in her old age, she might have cried; but she chose instead to laugh at God's outrageous surprise.

Father, thank you for divinely planned—and perfectly timed—
surprises. You do have a pretty wild sense of humor! Amen.

Sheila Walsh

That's the Way the Cookie Crumbles

A happy heart makes the face cheerful, but heartache crushes the spirit.
–PROVERBS 15:13

All I wanted was some milk for my cereal, but when I opened the refrigerator door, a panful of cookies slid off the top shelf and headed south. The pan hit the floor with an aluminum explosion that caused every cookie in the pan to fly north and then tumble back to earth. Cookies landed willy-nilly across the kitchen's unforgiving stone floor.

Oh, wait a minute. Let me back up and explain the significance of these cookies. My daughter-in-law, Danya, was visiting along with our son, Jason, and their baby, Justin. Danya and I decided that since Valentine's Day was approaching, we would bake sugar cookies for some friends. As we mixed the batter, rolled the dough, and cut out the different-sized hearts, we chatted about how we would wrap the cookie packages, make some valentines, and hand deliver our surprises.

Then Danya and I decorated the cookies, using colored sugars, food dyes, and icing. I have to admit youth displayed a tad more flair than my conservative approach. Even though mine were pleasing, many of Danya's cookie creations were sensational.

By the time we cleaned up, we were impressed with our results. Carefully selecting the loveliest sweets, we placed them in a pan and slid them onto the refrigerator's top shelf.

Later, as I stood ankle-deep in broken hearts, Danya came around the corner, spotted the debris, and giggled. Her lighthearted response helped me not to take the cookie crumbs too seriously.

Having a crummy day? Try a good giggle.

Lord, thank you for the relief in laughter.
Amen.

Patsy Clairmont

Treasures of the Heart

*The house of the righteous contains great treasure, but the income
of the wicked brings them trouble. —PROVERBS 15:6*

One of my fondest memories of my childhood is of laughter. We didn't have
a lot of money, but we all had a sense of humor.

My brother, Stephen, and I take great delight in teasing my mom about
the trips she made us take to the airport. If you take children to the Dallas airport, they might find it interesting. Planes take off and land every few seconds.
Not so in Ayr, Scotland! There might be one plane a day, on a good week.
Stephen and I would stand on the balcony of the observation tower and
exclaim, "Hey, I think I see one! No, it's a bird. Oh look! There's one! No,
it's just a cloud."

Treasure comes in all sorts of packages. My greatest childhood treasures
were laughter and time. We laughed together and we spent time with one
another. We played board games and rode our bikes together, even in the
rain (which was my favorite time). We were all frequent visitors to the library.
We couldn't afford expensive trips, but we could check out books on travel
and go wherever we wanted to in our minds. We told each other jokes and
performed at the drop of a hat. We had an old beat-up piano and Mum could
only play the black keys, but we sang the great hymns of the faith with gusto.

Our culture tells us that treasure can be measured in dollars, but all the
money in the world can't buy the gift of laughter or the gift of time.

*Father, thank you for laughter, for time,
for memories that warm my heart. Amen.*

Sheila Walsh

The Bonding Laugh

Make my joy complete by being like-minded, having the same love,
being one in spirit and purpose. —PHILIPPIANS 2:2

Have you given much thought to psychoneuroimmunology lately? That's the study of how emotions and thoughts affect our health. Many researchers consider this study the richest area of science right now.

We have learned that when we change our attitudes, we change our body's basic chemistry, and we change it in a way that promotes healing. There have been many studies that considered the degree to which a positive attitude can bolster the immune system. Studies also show that laughter unleashes chemical neurotransmitters and hormones that contribute to an overall sensation of well-being.

There is no doubt that humor can augment individual health, but I've noticed that it is especially powerful in its effect on a group. Through laughter, we not only connect with ourselves but also with others. The contagious element of united laughter is a breaking through of the feelings of isolation and alienation we may have brought to the group.

Much has been written about why Women of Faith conferences are so enthusiastically received. I think one of the reasons is that because there is so much laughter, and laughing together reconnects hearts that long for a sense of belonging.

As a society that is becoming increasingly isolated by technology, our opportunities for interaction diminish. All the more reason to laugh together whenever we can. It isn't even necessary that we can spell or say *psychoneuroimmunology*. The healing is in the laughter.

Lord, grant me a light spirit today so I can recognize opportunities
for connecting with others through humor and laughter.
Don't let me be a stick-in-the-mud, but allow me to be one
that stirs the pot of mutual joy. Amen.

Marilyn Meberg

Spontaneous Laughter

In this world you will have trouble. But take heart!
I have overcome the world. —JOHN 16:33

My editor told me of her surprise at how difficult it seemed for us "funny" Women of Faith to write about humor. We could crack her up with some of the stuff we wrote, she said, but when assigned to write *about* humor, some of us floundered a bit at first.

I found that as disconcerting as she did. But then I realized that maybe it's because humor is a natural, spontaneous element of effective communication. We can't manufacture laughs in others; we can only elicit a tickled response by being spontaneous and authentic.

For example, I was well into my speech about God's extravagant grace at a conference when I looked down on the stage and saw my shoulder pad. I stopped my speech in midsentence and muttered, "I lost my pad! It's lying on the stage!" After I stooped down to pick it up, I held it up for all to see and said, "I mean my shoulder pad."

The surprised look on my face and my muffled but audible declaration of distress evoked a knee slapping moment for the crowd. The episode wasn't planned; it was just spontaneously funny!

Real humor is not pretentious or contrived. Rather, it is a gift from God that helps us express our reason for joy in a world that yearns for something to laugh about.

Jesus, what a gift to be able to find humor within, without having
to manufacture it. Thank you for the indwelling of your Holy Spirit,
who fills me up with everlasting joy. Amen.

Thelma Wells

Vitality

I have come that they may have life, and have it to the full. *–JOHN 10:10*

Someone asked me how I have so much energy, more vitality than anyone he knows. I told him that it isn't me who has all that zest, it's the Lord. I simply love life! Each day is another day to live life to the fullest.

People have asked my daughter, "Is your mother full of life all the time?"

"Yes," she says. "It makes me sick. I can't even have a bad day."

But who really wants to have a bad day? Someone who doesn't have a life, I guess.

Vitality is the infusion you receive:

When you are fully aware of who you are—and whose you are.

When you know how to make lemonade out of the lemons of life.

When you learn how to share yourself and your possessions with others, expecting nothing in return.

When you understand *real* wealth.

When you *really* care about others.

When you can laugh at yourself and this crazy life.

When you have a vision, a personal mission, and a passion for life.

When you have hope.

When you are honest and trustworthy.

When you know how to pursue good and resist evil.

When you learn not to worry.

When you keep a song in your heart.

When you quickly get over your mistakes.

When you treat other people better than you treat yourself.

When you live in the present, not agonizing over the past or anxiously anticipating the future.

When you trust in the Lord with all your heart.

When you let his strength be perfected in your weakness.

May you receive an abundant infusion of vitality as autumn leaves start to fall!

Thelma Wells

When Your Get-Up-and-Go Has Gone

It is God who arms me with strength and makes my way perfect.
He makes my feet like the feet of a deer; he enables me to stand on
the heights. —PSALM 18:32–33

To me the word *vitality* sounds like something you would find in an aisle of a drugstore, so I was curious as to how a dictionary would expand my understanding. The words *energy, strength, life, vigor,* and *get-up-and-go* were just part of the list.

The latter definition took me back several years. I was living for a time in London with my pastor and his wife and their three sons. The youngest boy, Joe, was about to turn five. His mother and I decided to throw a cowboys and Indians party for him and all his darling friends, who turned into marauding hoards within minutes of arriving. I was tied to a tree and left to be pecked to death by the local sparrows.

When everyone finally went home and I was untied, I sank into the sofa with a glazed look on my face. Joe came and sat beside me.

"Cool party, huh?"

"Very cool," I lied.

"Well, I don't know about you," he said, "but since I turned five, I just don't have the same get-up-and-go!"

Do you ever feel like that? You crawl into bed at night, and before you have even closed your eyes the alarm is going off. I identify more with the face of a deer than the feet of a deer; you know, that startled look?

But God has promised to be our strength and to enable us to accomplish what could not be done without him.

Father of life, today I come to you for strength.
Set me on the heights! Amen.

Sheila Walsh

Give Your All

Six days you shall labor and do all your work.
—*EXODUS 20:9*

I work hard for my money, honey. And that's what Labor Day is all about. It is a one-hundred-year-old American holiday celebrated annually on the first Monday in September. It originated from labor unions as a testament to their cause, and President Grover Cleveland signed it into being.

With the decline of the labor unions in America, Labor Day has taken on a different emphasis. It is viewed by many Americans as simply the day summer ends and the school year begins. But as a young girl, I remember Labor Day as one of the most important days of the year in our black community.

St. John Missionary Baptist Church was the place where my community gathered on the Sunday before Labor Day to present speeches, give awards, and sing patriotic songs and Negro spirituals signifying the role that black people played in shaping this country. Businessmen, doctors, nurses, lawyers, morticians, pharmacists, educators, cobblers, barbers, beauticians, and preachers all showed up to commemorate this proud day of recognition.

My friends and I were taught that work is honorable; we were ingrained with a dedicated work ethic. We were taught to always give an honest day's work for our wages. Old folks would say, "Do your work well. If you're a garbage man, be the best garbage man you can be. You'll be able to sleep at night, knowing you gave your all."

That was great advice, and its tangible rewards continue to flow in my life as I give my all to my work and to my God.

Lord, for the strength to work and serve you with vigor,
I give you thanks. Amen.

Thelma Wells

The God of Fresh Feet and Strong Fiber

*For forty years you sustained them in the desert; they lacked nothing,
their clothes did not wear out nor did their feet become swollen.*
–NEHEMIAH 9:21

Never mind the miracle of crossing the Red Sea on dry land. Forget the manna that appeared every morning to nourish them with divine sustenance. The really amazing thing God did for the Israelites for forty years—at least in my opinion—was to keep their clothes from falling apart and their feet from failing! (Keep in mind, this astonished observation comes from someone whose buttons are held on with safety pins and whose ankles have been known to resemble fire hydrants after standing a few hours at the book table.)

Athletes talk about needing "fresh legs" when they face competition. That means their legs need to feel rested and strong when the contest begins. As the Israelites awoke each morning in the desert, that's the miraculous gift God gave them: fresh feet to carry them through that day's journey, as well as "jogging suits" that never wore out.

It is the same gift he gives to us today. Our God is the Father of miracles, great and small—as enormous as the creation of the universe and as intricate as the threads of our clothes. He enables our steps and strengthens the fabric of our lives. Remember that fact today, no matter what desert you're facing. Let God, the creator of fresh legs and strong fiber, sustain you!

*Dear Father, thank you for this day. Please guide my steps
in your appointed direction, and strengthen my fiber so that
as long as I live I can serve you with joy and vitality. Amen.*

Barbara Johnson

Wonder Bread

Give us this day our daily bread.
—MATTHEW 6:11

The taste of fresh bread triumphs over any food experience I can have. Bread is without a doubt the most virtuous of foods, proof being that above all else it is the best antidote to a growling stomach. Any decent restaurant puts bread on the table first. Only a foolish restaurateur would put out bad bread. One who puts out crackers deserves twenty lashes from the closest and longest purse strap. I have risked public disdain by burying my face in freshly baked bread that I might inhale deeply the incomparable smell of the yeast that causes the bread to rise to palpable plumpness.

Bread is also the prime metaphor for serenity and vitality. Historically many have prayed for it, rioted for it, and, at times, stood in line for it. Appropriately, Scripture makes repeated reference to bread. Elijah was nourished by God-delivered bread in the morning and evening (1 Kings 17:2–6). The children of Israel were satisfied with the bread of heaven, yet God warned that "man does not live on bread alone but on every word that comes from the mouth of the LORD" (Deuteronomy 8:3). Jesus used a bread metaphor to underscore his own role as the ultimate provider for the needs of humankind: "I am the bread of life. He who comes to me will never go hungry" (John 6:35).

I have been privileged to savor some of the best breads in the world (my favorite being in Paris). But not once have those breads satisfied my hunger for more than a few hours. It is Jesus and Jesus alone who is the true Bread of Life.

Lord Jesus, thank you for the rich sustenance
of my daily bread—you. Amen.

Marilyn Meberg

The Bread of Life

*Taste and see that the LORD is good; blessed is the man
who takes refuge in him.* —PSALM 34:8

Pinto beans smell so good when they're slowly cooking on the stove and the savory aroma wafts through the house. Today is one of those cold, rainy, dark days outside. But inside it is warm, comfortable, and smelling like good eat'n.

When my husband stopped by home on his way to the bank, he smelled the beans cooking and had to have some for lunch. I served them with some tasty sweet cornbread and a crisp green salad. While we were eating and talking, I began to think, *Taste and see that the Lord is good. He's bread when we're hungry and water when we're thirsty. How sweet he is!*

Even though George and I ate lunch, we were going to be hungry again that evening. Oh, but when you fill yourself with the Bread of Life, you never hunger again! Jesus is that bread. He has promised to give us spiritual sustenance every single day. This promise never fails even in the horror of terrorism and the uncertainty of war.

Taste the bread of forgiveness when you ask for it. Taste the bread of mercy when you really deserve judgment. Taste the bread of contentment when things are not working out the way you want. Eat at Jesus' table daily and be filled. This is the way to peace in your soul.

*Bread of Life, please continue to break bread with me even
when I come to your table empty-handed and fearful. I need
the vital nourishment that only you can give. Amen.*

Thelma Wells

Get Up and Get Going

Diligent hands will rule.
—PROVERBS 12:24

The great interpretive dancer Martha Graham was quoted as saying, "There is vitality, a life force, an energy . . . that is translated through you into action. And because there is only one of you . . . this expression is unique."

Think about it. You are you and nobody else. You are alive physically, and if you are a follower of Christ, you are fully alive spiritually as well. There is nothing you can't do through him . . . out of your own vitality and originality.

I love the word "energy." It is that capacity for action that lifts us out of the chair and moves us forward. It's the intensity that makes us produce. Let's say we want to do something but have no energy for it. Like putting up bookshelves, writing a story, losing weight, or . . . even making dinner. Unless our motivation gets sparked, we'll sit there all day and nothing will happen.

Maybe you need to clean out your garage, but you haven't started before now because it's just too far gone. A total mess! Here are a few tips:

First of all, picture how it will look when you're finished.
Second, tackle small areas in manageable increments.
Third, clean up as you go so you have a sense of accomplishment.
Fourth, sing and dance while you work.
Fifth, quit thinking, *This is too time consuming and too boring.*
Sixth, remember the Lord is with you and he will see you through.
Seventh, celebrate being done!

The hardest part of any project is the first step. So, get up and get going. The garage may look so good when you're finished, you'll paint the house.

Father, help me live fully out of my own energetic
originality . . . which comes from you. Amen.

Luci Swindoll

You've Gotta Show Up

When you walk, your steps will not be hampered;
and when you run, you will not stumble. —*PROVERBS 4:12*

Some women were talking about their attempts to get into shape. One of them shook her head in exasperation. "I paid four hundred dollars to join a gym two months ago," she said, "and I haven't lost a single pound. Apparently, you actually have to *show up* to see any results!"

Sometimes we look at a problem and think we know all the answers. Then we find out we actually have to *show up* to make a difference. We can't just belong to a gym; we actually have to participate to get fit. And just as it takes determination and conscious effort to keep our physical bodies fit, it also takes dedication and focus to keep our spiritual lives in shape. We can't just carry a Bible around and become spiritual "jocks"; we actually have to open God's Word and study it to understand how he blesses us.

One woman I know reminds herself of the double motivation to keep physically and spiritually fit by keeping a little sign taped to the mirror in the room where she exercises. It is a drawing of a thin, cross-shaped opening in a high wall. Below the picture, my friend has underlined a couple of words in Jesus' warning in Matthew 7:14: "*Small* is the gate and *narrow* the road that leads to life, and only a few find it."

Dear Jesus, your promises empower me, and your love upholds me.
Thank you for showing up for me. Amen.

Barbara Johnson

Bingo and Hula Hoops

Praise the LORD, O my soul ... who satisfies your desires with good things
so that your youth is renewed like the eagle's. −PSALM 103:2, 5

How many ninety-year-old women do you know who hula hoop every day as well as ride ten miles on a stationary bike each morning? Alberta Bailey, mother of my dear friend Ney, is so "on the go" that Ney has trouble finding her at home. Alberta is either reading to a group at a rest home, doing hospital visitation for her church, or tutoring disadvantaged children in her community. When her schedule allows, she loves to play Bingo. She generally balances sixteen cards at a time.

About six months ago, Alberta's car was broadsided by a driver who ran a red light. She escaped injury, but her car was totaled. The policeman on the accident scene recognized Alberta as an elderly driver and assumed she was at fault. With a degree of condescension, he asked her if she knew where she was. Not only did she give him the cross street names of where she was, she corrected him as he wrote his report, which cited incorrectly the streets preceding the intersection.

This petite little dynamo reads several newspapers every day. Several months ago we were discussing the pros and cons of a particular bill before Congress. Thinking I had a fairly good handle on it all, I expressed my opinion. After a few gently spoken words from Alberta, I realized how ill-informed I was on the issue. At the conclusion of our evening I told her she should run for president. With a twinkle she said she didn't have time.

*Lord God, fuel my spirit with a zest to fully live the life
you've given me. Amen.*

Marilyn Meberg

September 9
Wash-and-Wear

They have washed their robes and made them white
in the blood of the Lamb. —REVELATION 7:14

Recently I purchased a pair of black, cotton-knit slacks for everyday knock-around wear. The first time I laundered them and pulled them from the dryer, I found they had become an abbreviated version of the original. They had shrunk to knickers fit for a Keebler elf.

Discouraged that I had wrecked my new purchase, I whined about my goof to Marilyn Meberg. She replied, "No problem. Just rewash them and don't put them in the dryer. Instead, stretch them while they're damp, and then let them air-dry."

Impressed with her sage advice and hopeful I could redeem my brief britches, I rewashed them. Then, while they were damp, I stretched and pulled on them with vigor. When I hung my slacks to dry, I realized I had been a tad zealous in the stretching. Now the legs cascaded down and appeared a bit too long for the Jolly Green Giant. I mean, I could have knotted the waist on my head and still had pant legs to spare.

Does life ever leave you feeling out of shape? Do people pull on you until you have stretch marks? Do you feel reduced in size because of the heated environment you're in?

Here are three thoughts on shaping up:

1. Tumble your cares upon the Lord.
2. Shrink your ego by owning your mistakes.
3. Stretch your faith by learning to handle difficulties with maturity.

You might be more "wash-and-wear" than you realized.

*Dear Lord, use my circumstances today
to make me more like you. Amen.*

Patsy Clairmont

September 10
Getting Healthy

Do you not know that your body is a temple of the Holy Spirit,
who is in you, whom you have received from God? You are not your own.
–1 CORINTHIANS 6:19

Barbara Johnson told me about a fiber drink that could help lower cholesterol. My husband and I tried it and found that Barbara was right. (She's always right!) George and I began to feel better. That started an uphill climb toward more energy and better health.

After doing more research and consulting with holistic health care providers, I also started eating more "live" foods and very few "dead" foods. I began feasting on raw vegetables and fruits, minimizing my meat intake, drinking more water, and exercising. Now I can march up and down the stairs without feeling like I'm going to pass out! I can handle more projects during the day with greater vigor. I sleep more soundly and I'm getting more hours of sufficient rest.

Our bodies are not just vessels that carry us around; they are temples in which the Holy Spirit of God Almighty chooses to dwell! God has given us stewardship over our bodies, to keep them in good working condition. Eating the right foods and getting the proper exercise are the cleansing agents for our temples. When they are kept tidy, we are able to do more for him with strength and gusto, not tiring easily or needing to sleep on the job.

God, show me clearly today how you want me to go about getting
healthy and strong so I can do the work of your kingdom with vigor.
Amen.

Thelma Wells

vitality

271

September 11
Bringing Fragrance to the World

*But thanks be to God, who always leads us in triumphal procession
in Christ and through us spreads everywhere the fragrance
of the knowledge of him.* – 2 CORINTHIANS 2:14

September 11 has become a day that will forever stand alone in our calendar. It is a day when the unthinkable came into our homes through the media and the unbearable visited New York and Washington, DC and altered the once familiar beloved landscape through the brutal force of terrorism. For many it was a wake up call to the reality that evil exists in our world. For those of us who love and trust God, it was a reminder that our enemy is not simply in human form, but he is a constant spiritual reality, one who roams around seeking whom he may destroy.

When the fires were out in New York, the memorial services over, books written, and songs sung, what was the lasting legacy that God birthed out of the ashes of destruction? People turned to God to not only bless America but to heal our great nation. At Women of Faith we saw unprecedented numbers of women make first time commitments to Christ. Perhaps we began to treasure each day a little more, to tell those in our lives we love them, and to let go the little petty frustrations of life. There has never been a greater time to live as the people of God, to show what it looks like to know peace, grace, and love in the midst of fear. For too long in our nation the Church has been defined by what we stand against. It is time to show in whose lovely name we come with arms stretched out to love. As we will never forget this day, let us never forget that other day of utter barbarism when the Lamb of God took on himself the worst that hell had to throw at him. He did it for you and for me. He did it so that we could be free. Evil will never have the last say in our lives or in our nation because of his sacrifice. There will be a day when every knee will bow and every tongue confess that Jesus Christ is Lord. Until that day we bring his fragrance to a world that has lost hope, that has lost heart. In his name we come.

Father God, let me be used by you for your glory.

Sheila Walsh

vitality

Don't Be a Slug

Wake up! Strengthen what remains and is about to die, for I have not
found your deeds complete in the sight of my God. –REVELATION 3:2

There is a club for procrastinators whose motto is, "Time is too valuable to
fritter away on the essentials." I'm not kidding—the club was established in
the mid-fifties.

Are you a member? To some degree, we all are. We are overwhelmed. We
dislike what has to be done. We don't believe it is possible. We are lazy. We
wait to be prodded, hoping if we wait long enough, it'll go away.

But here is an unpopular truth: When there is a hill to climb, waiting
doesn't make it smaller. Don't you hate that? Fortunately, God has given us
the ability to do what he's placed before us. He even promises we'll finish if
we persevere.

If you're feeling stuck in slo-mo, try this:

Divide your job into little parts. Start small ... think big. Little efforts add
up. It burdens the spirit to have too much staring us in the face. Remember,
every accomplishment is a process.

Draw a picture of it if you can. Envisioning what we have to do keeps it
from looking like such a monster chore. It is easier to tackle something we
can see.

Decide what is yours to do. Sometimes we are trying to accomplish things
that are actually God's job, not ours. Ask God to help you figure out your part,
and then trust him to do the rest.

Wake up! Don't be a slug. Step out today by faith, and watch what God
will do through you when you get in step with him.

*Help me, Lord, to utilize the power you have already
given me to overcome procrastination. Amen.*

Luci Swindoll

Red-hot

Those whom I love I rebuke and discipline. So be earnest, and repent.
—REVELATION 3:19

Girl, the sickest I've ever been is when I had an upset stomach a few weeks ago. One minute I was feeling fine, and the next I thought I was going to faint. I lay down and everything kept spinning. I took my temperature and I was burning up. Finally, I threw up. *Yuk!*

Can you imagine God being so sick to his stomach that he feels like vomiting? That's a gross thought, but he said he's felt that way—about his own children! Listen to this: "I know your deeds, that you are neither cold nor hot. I wish you were either one or the other! So, because you are lukewarm—neither hot nor cold—I am about to spit you out of my mouth" (Revelation 3:15–16). It is pretty clear that God wants us red-hot for him, or not at all.

Before I really gave God all of me, I wonder how many times I made him sick to his stomach. Sick enough to spit me up! I can't retrieve those former days. But I can make sure today and in the future that I remain on fire for God.

If you want to increase your passion for God, you have got to get where the heat is. Snuggle up to Jesus in quiet, quality meditation. Put on some good ol' praise music and sing along. Assemble yourself with people who are red-hot for Christ. Stoke your mind with books and tapes that keep your spiritual fire blazing.

Heavenly Father, I'm sorry for the times I've made you sick.
I will do my part to keep the fire burning in my heart for you forever.
Amen.

Thelma Wells

"Whatever, Lord!"

To this end I labor, struggling with all his energy,
which so powerfully works in me. —COLOSSIANS 1:29

Everyone is blessed in different ways, and one of the most precious gifts God has granted me is the gift of energy. It simply cannot be explained any other way; it is as amazing to me as it is to all my friends who continually comment on it. I just have days when I feel like that silly bunny that advertises long-lasting batteries, especially when I'm on a mission to "spread my joy," as I like to say.

My life hasn't always been this way. After the deaths of two of our four sons, and the long estrangement of another, I spent nearly a year in my bedroom, just counting the roses on the wallpaper. During that time I felt so lifeless that blinking my eyes nearly wore me out! It wasn't until I prayed a surrendering prayer of relinquishment—"Whatever, Lord!"—that I regained any hope for facing the next hour, let alone the next day or month or year. I turned over all my heartaches and worries to God, and he replaced the massive burden I was carrying with a bubble of joy and vitality that has uplifted my life for years now.

Give your grief and despondency to God and see what wonderful gifts he gives you in return!

Thank you, Jesus, for bearing my burdens and filling my life
with the gifts of love, laughter, and exuberant energy!
Amen.

Barbara Johnson

Strength for the Heart

My flesh and my heart may fail, but God is the strength
of my heart and my portion forever. —PSALM 73:26

Charlie Wedemeyer is one of the most vital men I have ever met. He lives
in a wheelchair. He can't breathe on his own. Charlie has Lou Gehrig's disease.

I first met him when he was a guest on *The 700 Club*. Knowing that I
would be interviewing him, I read his book beforehand. It was a very honest,
challenging book, but it still didn't prepare me for Charlie himself. At first
sight Charlie's whole getup is a little intimidating. His wheelchair is very high-
tech, with a breathing machine attached that noisily provides Charlie with
every breath. His story is amazing, his courage humbling; but it was his wicked
sense of humor that caught me off guard. His wife tried to prepare me, but I
fell into that old trap and forgot that just because someone's body has failed
him doesn't mean that his mind or personality is any less razor-sharp.

We laughed and joked, but what I enjoyed most was meeting a husband
and wife devoted to each other and to God. I can't imagine what it must be
like to feel so helpless. I'm sure it is very difficult for a man to feel as if there's
nothing he can do for his wife and that she must do everything for him.

*Charlie's body no longer listens to him; his physical strength is gone. But what
I saw in him was a spiritual vitality far beyond the limitations of his body. The glorious power of God shone through him.*

> *Father, help me to remember today that even if my body
> is strong physically, you alone are the strength of my heart.
> Amen.*

Sheila Walsh

Pedal to the Metal

Is not wisdom found among the aged?
—JOB 12:12

Last year I turned the same age as the speed limit for trucks, which was ever so helpful. When folks would ask me how old I was, I'd simply hang my head out the window, check the road sign, and rattle off the number.

For some reason over the past ten years my two-digit status has eluded me. I can remember my social security number (well, okay, most of the time) but not my age. This year will be a real challenge since I don't have a natural hook unless someone ups the truckers' speed.

Speaking of speed, while my numbers are going up, my pace is slowing down. What's that about? Seems like it should be the other way around so that the older we get, the faster we boogie. That way we could back up our ever increasing wisdom with physical endurance. But alas, I wasn't in on the meeting when they made the decision that mounting years would come with decreased stamina.

Do you think increased energy reserves would cause us aged ones to become too high-minded? Then we would be in the young folks' faces with way too much information, getting on their last nerve. Nothing worse than a know-it-all with energy—at any age.

In the 1800s Henry Cuyler Bunner wrote,

It was an old, old, old, old lady,
And a boy that was half-past three;
And the way they played together was beautiful to me.

Perhaps that's what it's really all about. Not speed or spouting knowledge but how loving is our interplay ... at any age.

> *Lord, forgive me when I speed and spout. Help me to give*
> *up my need to accelerate so I can live more lovingly.*
> *Amen.*

Patsy Clairmont

Now, Where Was I Headed?

The LORD is my strength and my song; he has become my salvation.
—*EXODUS 15:2*

When my doctors emphasized how important exercise was to maintaining my health, I enthusiastically set up a daily regimen. For several weeks Bill and I walked twice a day, every morning and every evening; but eventually we had to discontinue that routine because, quite mysteriously, we were both *gaining* weight. (It could have had something to do with *where* we walked. Each morning, we walked to the donut shop, and in the evening we hiked to the ice-cream parlor. It turns out two twenty-minute walks do *not* cancel out a maple-frosted pastry and a double dip of pralines and cream!)

Isn't life just like that? Sometimes we smugly announce we're stepping out in righteousness—and then find ourselves feeding at the trough of temptation. Unless we keep our ultimate goal constantly in mind, it is easy to lose our focus and forget where we *really* want to end up.

At those times when our feet threaten to propel us in a direction our heart knows is wrong, it helps to meditate on the reassuring words of the psalmist: "Yet I am always with you; you hold me by my right hand. You guide me with your counsel, and afterward you will take me into glory" (Psalm 73:23–24).

I, for one, am counting on the Lord to get me where I really want to go. Because sometimes I forget!

> *Oh, Father, hold me by the hand and guide my steps*
> *so that I always walk with you. Amen.*

Barbara Johnson

Returning

"Return to me," declares the LORD Almighty, "and I will return to you."
—ZECHARIAH 1:3

The twentieth-century playwright Eugene O'Neill defined life as a bad dream between two awakenings. With equal cheerfulness Shakespeare proclaimed, "Life is a tale told by an idiot, full of sound and fury, signifying nothing." Obviously these two highly esteemed writers lost their esteem for living.

I cannot begin to say what happened to those men, but I'd like to suggest that one thing that saps our vitality is the hesitation to "return" to the God who loves us and longs to reconnect with us. We may not be living in overt sin, but our personal determination to make life "work" the way we think it should moves us away from the loving partnership God offers us. Whether conscious or unintentional, our various forms of self-reliance keep us from divine intimacy.

This "disconnect" can start first thing in the morning when we read the paper instead of the Bible; talk on the phone instead of to God; make business decisions based on a gut instinct instead of a Spirit prod. Before long we hear the faithful voice of God calling, "Return to me."

The advantages of returning are innumerable, but specific to our personal challenges in life is God's promise about those challenges: "'Not by might nor by power, but by my Spirit,' says the LORD Almighty" (Zechariah 4:6). What a relief! My power and might accomplish nothing; but the almighty God, by his Spirit living in me, accomplishes everything.

Life is not a bad dream, nor is it a tale told by an idiot. But with all due respect, we are idiots when we wander from our source of power and vitality.

Lord, thank you for always calling me back.
Amen.

Marilyn Meberg

You Choose

Finally, brothers, whatever is true, whatever is noble, whatever is right, whatever is pure, whatever is lovely, whatever is admirable—if anything is excellent or praiseworthy—think about such things. –PHILIPPIANS 4:8

Great power lies in what we choose to think about. In fact, we are the product of our choices. And sometimes when we are unaware, we chose negative over positive. This happens because we don't think. It's that simple. Given a conscious choice, everybody I know would opt for a happy life. But when we don't actively choose the thoughts and experiences that create a happy life, the opposite is often our lot. Our lifestyle ends up reflecting the very things we hate.

When we are negative or critical, we have said yes to unhappiness. When we refuse to forgive someone who hurt us, we have said yes to lugging a heavy burden into our future. Every time we are legalistic in our theology, we forfeit grace. And when we are always rigid, we miss out on playfulness. We may not even be aware we've said yes to these negative ways, but our behavior mirrors our unconscious choices.

God has given us the power to change. He's given us the will to choose. The late Eudora Welty once said, "All serious daring starts from within." And it is within ourselves that this power is located.

I challenge you to be different today from the way you were yesterday. Make up your mind. Others will notice the changes in you and ask how you made them. Then you can tell them, with God's help, it was your choice.

Enable me, Lord, by your Spirit's revitalizing power within, to make the changes that produce a positive life. Amen.

Luci Swindoll

A Fine Oak Tree

The LORD is my rock, my fortress and my deliverer;
my God is my rock, in whom I take refuge. *–PSALM 18:2*

Thelma Wells is a vital woman. In my eyes she is like a fine oak tree—strong and upright, giving shade to all who will gather close.

As I have traveled with Thelma, I have grown to love her dearly and lean on her more and more. In the fall of 2000, William, my father-in-law, had a heart attack and died. We were all in shock. He seemed so healthy. He was never sick. He traveled with us everywhere we went, including to every Women of Faith conference.

Our friends gathered around us and carried us through the unreality of the funeral and the next few days. But Thelma wanted to do more. A couple of weeks after we buried William, she e-mailed me and asked if she could come from Dallas to Nashville and cook for us and hug us for a while!

Now, Thelma is a busy woman. She has a husband and children and grandchildren and books to write and an office to run, yet I never get the impression from her that it is ever getting too much. Part of that is just who Thelma is, but I'm convinced it is also a direct result of the way she lives her life. She listens to praise music all the time. She constantly feeds on the Word of God. No wonder she is strong like a fine oak tree; the spiritual nutrients she takes in build her up inside like a rock.

Lord, thank you for human examples of your rocklike strength.
In the fortress of your love I will take refuge. Amen.

Sheila Walsh

September 21
Diving Fearlessly

I can do everything through him who gives me strength.
—*PHILIPPIANS 4:13*

Platform diver Laura Wilkinson was definitely the underdog in the 2000 Olympics in Sydney, Australia. After all, she was competing with a serious injury. She had broken three bones in her right foot three months earlier during a training accident while practicing the inward 2-1/2 somersault. Having surgery to set the bones would have knocked her out of the Olympics, so she postponed the surgery and let the bones heal in their jumbled position. Then she continued her training, wearing a temporary boot to climb the ladder to the diving platform.

In Sydney, in the glare of the world's spotlights, she miraculously worked her way to the top of the standings. Then there was just one more dive to go. And wouldn't you know? It was the inward 2-1/2 somersault.

There Laura stood, balancing precariously thirty-three feet above the water . . . balancing painfully on the ball of her foot—her *broken* foot. Her face froze in a mask of concentration. Her lips moved slightly. And then she spiraled through the air, twisting, folding, straightening, knifing her lean form into the water. And she won the gold!

When a reporter shoved a microphone into her face, Laura ignored whatever question he posed and simply blurted out the verse she had recited before every dive for years and years: Philippians 4:13. She said later that she'd prayed before going to Sydney that God would use her. And in front of millions of viewers, God did exactly that.

Dear Father, I'm so thankful you've given me
a platform to use me on. Amen.

Barbara Johnson

Puddle Hopping

*Whatever you do, work at it with all your heart, as working for the Lord,
not for men. —COLOSSIANS 3:23*

In the summer of 1996, Mary Graham and I were in England. We read in the *London Times* that John Stott, the British theologian, was speaking at All Soul's Church on Sunday night. I had met Dr. Stott before and respected him and his work. We decided to go hear him preach.

Just as we left the hotel to catch one of those London buses, it began to rain . . . and the nearer we got to the church, the harder it poured. Unfortunately, we had to get off a couple of blocks from the meeting hall and puddle jump . . . without an umbrella.

We finally found two empty seats in a packed congregation of young and old, men and women—every nationality and color. Some folks were dressed beautifully and others of us looked like drowned rats. We sang heartily, and Dr. Stott preached from 1 Timothy, where Paul encourages young leaders in ministry. You could have heard a pin drop. It was a wonderful sermon!

When everything was over, Mary and I stood in the rain once again, waiting for the bus to come, talking about how glad we were we went. We still talk about it.

You may want to do something meaningful that's utterly inconvenient. Are you willing to put the effort into accomplishing it? Remember this as a rule of thumb: Anything of value cannot be had for nothing.

*Dear Lord, help me to discern what is really worth going for in life,
and then help me to be willing to put in the effort. Amen.*

Luci Swindoll

The Sixth Sense

Whoever heeds correction shows prudence.
–PROVERBS 15:5

A somewhat playful definition of *guilt* is that it is a sixth human sense instilled in children by parents and in congregations by the clergy. If the sense is well instilled, it may not prevent people from sinning, but it will prevent them from enjoying it.

Yesterday my grandson Ian arrived at my door at 7:30 A.M., too sick to go to kindergarten but well enough to avoid hospitalization. I set him up next to my desk with his own little table and chair. He practiced making his letters, and we chatted intermittently about his classmates—both those he liked and those who "got in big trouble."

Around 10:00 we both needed a juice break because we'd been working extremely hard. During our break he decided to confess that he didn't think he was really sick. (His energy level and bright eyes had made me wonder about the seriousness of his infirmity, but I had not questioned it audibly.) We talked then about the wisdom of him going to school (there was still time since it started at 11:30), and we also talked about guilt and how it could nudge us into better actions. Ian decided he should probably go to school even though it meant not going to McDonald's for lunch with me.

When we got to his classroom he said, "This is a good idea, Maungya; I think my 'wilt' is gone." I'm assuming he meant guilt but I didn't correct him. After all, he'd experienced a lot of teaching for one morning.

Lord, the feeling of guilt gets a bad rap, but sometimes it's a divine nudge, directly from you, that can help me take positive action. Please enable me to respond with energetic obedience. Amen.

Marilyn Meberg

True Wealth

Seek first his kingdom and his righteousness, and all these things
will be given to you as well. –MATTHEW 6:33

The Queen of Sheba heard about the wisest man who ever lived and wanted
to know if he was "real" or not. So she loaded up her caravan and headed to
Israel. The queen was beautiful and rich, yet she knew deep within that there
was more to life. At Solomon's feet, she learned the truths of God and acquired
divine wisdom that opened her heart to a life of serving the true and living God.

Some people have said that their problems would be over if they could just
win the lottery, or make that big sale, or inherit some of Uncle Henry's fortune. But the Queen of Sheba reminds us that the most valued possession in
life is understanding and accepting God and the things of God. She went to
Solomon with a hungry heart and mind. She gave the wise king a large portion of her possessions and wealth because he had given her eternal wealth
through knowing God. The beautiful, wealthy queen went home and revo-
lutionized her nation.

When we depend on our appearance or our possessions to give us a sense
of security, we miss the point. Those things are only temporary and can be
given to us or taken away. True wealth is in knowing who the wealth-giver
is, and living accordingly.

*Wise Heavenly King, thank you for providing me with people who
give astute counsel from your Word. Cause me to hunger for your
righteousness and to live every day with zeal for you. Amen.*

Thelma Wells

One Day at a Time

This is the day the LORD has made; let us rejoice and be glad in it.
—PSALM 118:24

On the first of March, 2001, John Painter died. He was 112 years old. Mr. Painter was a hero in our Tennessee community, the oldest survivor of World War I. He was never bedridden but remained active until the day of his death.

There are all sorts of stories about John. Some people will tell you that if you had a wart on your hand and you shook hands with old John Painter, the wart would disappear. Some say he walked for three days right after he broke his hip. The thing about this dear gentleman that I admired most, however, was his presence in *today*. Patsy, his grandson's wife, said of John, "He didn't look back, and he didn't look forward. He lived one day at a time."

When I read that quote about Mr. Painter in our morning newspaper, I took it as a precious jewel left behind by a wise man. So often I miss what's happening at the moment because I'm anticipating something around the corner. Sometimes the joy of today is shadowed by worry about tomorrow. Too often it takes a tragedy to make us cherish life and savor each day.

Perhaps we can take this gift from an old man who had seen a lot of life yet didn't miss the present moment. We can worship God *today*. We can love our family *today*. We can live fully, *today*.

> *Father of today and every day, thank you for this day.*
> *I give it to you and ask you to live through me and love*
> *through me all day long. Amen.*

Sheila Walsh

Quality Time

The LORD gives strength to his people; the LORD blesses
his people with peace. —PSALM 29:11

My four-year-old granddaughter and I went searching for fast food at midnight, without success. Suddenly, she spotted a donut shop that was open all night. We got the doughnuts and drove to my house where she was going to spend the night. It was about 12:30 A.M. when we decided to boil wieners and eat hot dogs. Grandmothers can do that!

Very full and sleepy, we were on our way to take a bath when Alaya changed her mind about spending the night. She said she wanted to go home. *No way!* I thought. My granddaughter was already here, and there was nothing she could do about it. But this is what Alaya said: "Grammy, I really need to go home to be with my family. My family needs me, and I need to spend more quality time with them. The next time somebody asks me to spend the night with them, I'm going to tell them that if they want to see me, they will just have to come to my house." She almost fell asleep while giving her inspired speech.

Alaya's focus on the people closest to her is what God wants from each of us. He wants us to spend quality time with him. He craves our allegiance and devoted love.

When the stores of life are closed (we can't get what we need from them anyway), we can always get a soulful of strength and peace from God. We can spend quality time with him at Grammy's house or anywhere we are.

Praise you, Lord, that you long to spend your holy time with me.
Thank you for the refreshment you provide me when I focus on you.
Amen.

Thelma Wells

A Whiny Warrior

The LORD, the LORD, is my strength and my song;
he has become my salvation. —ISAIAH 12:2

When the angel of the LORD appeared to Gideon, he said, 'The LORD is with you, mighty warrior'" (Judges 6:12). I see a warrior as a guy with rippling muscles in his arms and legs, a hairy chest, and a flat, taut stomach. I see him as a tall imposing presence who might turn to the angel of the Lord and modestly say, "Well, thank you ... I'll do what I can."

But Gideon, the "mighty" warrior, turned instead to the angel of the Lord and started whining. God was telling Gideon that he'd been chosen to deliver the Israelites from the tyranny of the Midians. Gideon's whiny response: "If the LORD is with us, why has all this happened to us?" (6:13). His response to God's call to deliver his people was countered with a string of excuses: "I'm too weak for the job" (6:15); "How do I know you're really talking to me?" (6:17); "I need a sign" (6:36–40).

Except for the rippling muscles and hairy chest, I identify with Gideon. The fear of not being strong enough or even spiritual enough for whatever God calls me to do is a struggle. And yet, the key to my strength is the same as it was for Gideon: "Then the Spirit of the LORD came upon Gideon" (6:34).

The reality for Gideon and for us is that unless the Spirit of the Lord equips us for a task, we are indeed too weak. We are not born mighty warriors; the Spirit of God makes us so.

Lord God Almighty, my spiritual vitality is found solely in you.
Amen.

Marilyn Meberg

No Trouble

As surely as the LORD lives, who has delivered me out of every trouble, I will surely carry out today what I swore to you by the LORD. *–1 KINGS 1:29–30*

My older brother, Orville, is not only a genius but a sweetheart as well. When I told him I wanted a computer, he said, "Sis, I'll build you one and bring it to you. I know what you need so I'll order everything." He lives in Florida and I live in California, but he made it sound easy so I was up for it.

I gave him my credit card number and before long I had computer parts coming out the wazoo. When I couldn't buy panty hose because I was over my credit limit, I realized this had to stop. So I called Orv.

"No problem, Sis. You already have enough for a great computer."

The date came for Orville to set it all up. I was ecstatic. After a fun greeting at the airport, we went to baggage claim to get his luggage. There were also nine boxes of computer equipment.

"Are you kidding me?" I groaned. "What in the world did you buy? This thing is going to be a moon ship, Orv. Look at the trouble you've gone to . . . *nine* boxes? I'm a beginner, remember?"

He laughed. "Oh, Sis, this was no trouble. I *loved* choosing all this for you. Nothing's trouble unless you let it be."

How often are things "trouble" in your life? They don't have to be! With the right attitude and a little elbow grease, they could even become a moon ship!

Lord, give me an adventuresome spirit and an enthusiastic mind.
I never want to stop being open to challenges. Amen.

Luci Swindoll

Boy, Oh, Boy!

It is God who arms me with strength.
−2 SAMUEL 22:33

I have the joy of spending a portion of almost every day with my grandson, Justin. I eagerly await his arrival, but by the time he leaves, I'm in need of resuscitation. That boy is one bundle of energy.

Changing his diaper is like big-time wrestling. Stopping short of a body slam, it is all his grandpa and I can do to keep Justin pinned down long enough to wrestle off his diaper and Velcro on a new one. He is convinced he has places to go and people to meet—I'd just like him to arrive with clean pants.

Recently Justin has been considering walking. He lets go of the couch, eyes the distance to the chair, then plops down and crawls like a house-a-fire. I'm excited about his achievements, but I'll need roller blades when he starts to ambulate. As it is, he crawls lickety-split up the staircase with the ease of a mountain goat while I huff and puff behind him like a lame hippo.

Justin likes the sound of his own voice (a trait that seems to run in our family). He enjoys yelling at the top of his lungs. Since he doesn't know any words, it's just a piercing sound (attracting dogs from three counties), followed by a volley of giggles.

If life is scampering and screeching along at a pace that exceeds your personal speed limit, just remember that God has provided respite. Eventually night will slip in, and we'll all slumber. *Ah, sweet repose. . . .* In the meantime, ask God for vitality to keep up with all fast-moving vehicles, whether they be babies, business meetings, or big-time deadlines.

I need your strength, Lord. Fill me up.
Amen.

Patsy Clairmont

Choose Life

They are not just idle words for you—they are your life.
—Deuteronomy 32:47

The word *vitality* is defined as the characteristic that distinguishes the living from the nonliving. So it goes without saying those who lie in a morgue lack vitality. However, there are a number of people I've met who, though breathing and occasionally moving, appear to belong in a morgue. They lack verve and vigor!

Moses has a word for those people. He told the Israelites that God's commandments to them weren't idle words scripted in stone to be taken lightly. Instead they were to be viewed as keep-you-out-of-the-morgue instructions for living a long and vibrant life.

So what does that mean for us today? It means when you're laid off from work and financial need threatens to overwhelm you, you don't give up. It means when your spouse bolts out the door and leaves you with children to support, you don't give up. It means when you're diagnosed with a malignant brain tumor, you don't give up. It means when depression washes over your soul, you don't give up.

So often when life's circumstances become overwhelming we revert to behaviors that numb us—that keep us breathing, perhaps, but not vibrant. Moses told God's children that they had a choice: "This day I call heaven and earth as witnesses against you that I have set before you life and death, blessings and curses. Now choose life, so that you and your children may live and that you may love the LORD your God, listen to his voice, and hold fast to him. For the LORD is your life" (Deuteronomy 30:19–20).

What will you choose? Surely you don't want to live in the morgue!

Lord, today I choose life.
Amen.

Marilyn Meberg

OCTOBER

Trust

Now I know that the LORD saves his anointed;
he answers him from his holy heaven with the saving power
of his right hand. —PSALM 20:6

Since life is a journey, I pray the pages ahead will help us to pack up trust so we can take it wherever our roads may lead.

We may need a trunk, for trust is a fragile elephant, and elephants aren't easily transported. Trust is gargantuan; yet one mouse can send it on a shattering rampage. When trust has gone awry, we find ourselves reluctant, if not downright suspicious, of others' motives. While we need to be discerning in our relationships, we don't want to feed a distrustful heart.

We are all needy people, and our tendency is to try to meet our needs through relationships with others. I have a friend whose mother died when she was a little girl. She finds herself drawn to women who remind her of her mom. She latches on and wants these women to be something they can't be. Soon, when she notes their inadequacies, the relationships wane. She feels disappointed and alone once again.

The Bible warns us not to put our confidence in humans but to trust the Lord to meet our needs. That isn't easy when we are looking for someone to hold us and to help us through our muddle of emotions.

Trust is a five-letter word like r-i-s-k-y. It requires us to thrust ourselves into God's care even with our knees knocking. What we learn along the way is that he alone is trustworthy. Others can't fill his place, which allows us to let them off the hook and us to travel lighter.

Patsy Clairmont

Whatever You Please

The king's heart is in the hand of the LORD; he directs it like a watercourse
wherever he pleases. —PROVERBS 21:1

The power of God is an awesome reality. That he makes that power available to us through prayer is an equally awesome reality. That he turns the tide of our hearts and the events in our lives "wherever he pleases" is perhaps most amazing of all.

In her book *L'Abri*, Edith Schaeffer writes about when her son Frankie was stricken with polio. A doctor pressured her to immediately allow him to administer to Frankie an untested serum, which the doctor had invented and in which he had great confidence. Edith didn't know what to do but knew she was desperate to help her son. In a state of panic she pleaded with God to show her what he would have her do. She planned to do what the doctor asked unless God intervened.

Still unsure and frightened, Edith fell upon Proverbs 21:1 and was immediately assured of God's sovereignty and power. Agreeing to allow the doctor to administer the serum, she was stunned to see him pause a few minutes and then suddenly say he had changed his mind. He would not give Frankie the serum after all. Frankie did not experience the predicted paralysis and ultimately was able to walk again.

We can trust God to accomplish his purposes in our lives. Job 9:10, 12 states: "He performs wonders that cannot be fathomed, miracles that cannot be counted. . . . Who can say to him, 'What are you doing?'" No one. We don't have to know what God is doing. We just have to trust him.

Thank you, Sovereign Lord, for being utterly trustworthy.
Do whatever you please with me. Amen.

M a r i l y n   M e b e r g

Nesting

Those who live in accordance with the Spirit have their minds
set on what the Spirit desires. —*ROMANS 8:5*

Once a woman makes up her mind, watch out, honey!

A mama bluebird decided to build her nest in our newspaper slot under the mailbox. My husband removed the nesting material but left it on the ground so Mama could use it to rebuild somewhere else. She was not deterred. She hunted up new nesting material and rebuilt in the same slot. Les removed that woven wonder with care and once again left her supplies nearby. Willful Mama then gathered new twine and twigs and, yep, rebuilt in the paper slot. Seeing he couldn't win, Les hung a bluebird box on the back of our mailbox. It must have been to her liking, for within five minutes Mama moved in.

I love the power of our minds. Once they are set in a direction, lives can be changed. Notice I didn't designate for the good or the bad, which of course depends on which tree we choose to nest in.

I'm sure Mama Bluebird thought her choice was perfect for her family. It was the right height and the right size. Maybe she was the type who wanted to stay abreast of the latest news. But I assure you the first time the delivery person crammed the newspaper into Mama's space, more than her feathers would have been ruffled.

We don't always know best. No matter how certain or persistent we are, sometimes we choose the wrong tree. This is where trust comes in. Will we trust the One who sees the forest for the trees?

Lord, may I set my mind in your Spirit-led direction.
Amen.

Patsy Clairmont

Security under Glass

He will give you rest from all your enemies around you
so that you will live in safety. *–DEUTERONOMY 12:10*

Many years ago, I worked as a field rep for the college from which I graduated. It was my duty to encourage young women to enroll in that school. I
called on many little Texas towns in my '57 Chevy, having a great time.

One late afternoon, driving alone, I realized a stranger was following me.
Every time I turned, he turned. Since it was getting dark, I started looking
for a motel.

Spotting one ahead, I quickly pulled in, signed the register, raced to my
room, and bolted the door. By this time I was scared to death, crying out to
God for protection. I had to force myself through the routine of getting ready
for bed, praying all the while.

Just as I somewhat shakily reached to turn out the light I noticed a hand-
written note under the glass on the dresser. It read, "Come to me all who are
weary and heavy laden, and I will give you rest." —*Jesus*

Unbelievable! Those words were there for ME. I chose with my will to
take Jesus at his word. After a while my heart stopped pounding, and I drifted
off to sleep. The next morning as I drove away, there was no sign of that
stranger. I have no idea where he went.

Trusting the Lord is *extremely* hard sometimes when situations look impossible. But I encourage you today to come to Jesus with your burden. He promises to give you peace and courage to go on.

Lord, may I rely this day on your words of truth. Help me to believe.
Amen.

L u c i S w i n d o l l

O for Grace to Trust Him More!

Do not let your hearts be troubled. Trust in God; trust also in me.
—JOHN 14:1

Some of our most beloved hymns came from songwriters' personal experiences of deliverance. After Louisa Stead's husband died trying to rescue a drowning swimmer, she was left penniless with no way to support herself and her young daughter. On a heartbreaking morning when she had no food and not one cent in her house, she happened to open the front door . . . and found a gift of food and money left by a kindhearted friend. That very day she wrote the hymn, "'Tis So Sweet to Trust in Jesus."

Songwriter Fanny Crosby had a similar experience. One day when she needed five dollars and didn't know where she would get it, a stranger came to her door and handed her that exact amount. The only explanation she had was the prayer she had whispered shortly before the stranger appeared on her doorstep. That day she wrote the hymn, "All the Way My Savior Leads Me." The second verse never fails to inspire and encourage me:

> All the way my Savior leads me; cheers each winding path I tread,
> Gives me grace for ev'ry trial, feeds me with the living bread:
> Though my weary steps may falter, and my soul athirst may be,
> Gushing from the Rock before me, Lo! a spring of joy I see.

> Dear Jesus, though my steps may falter and trials may beset me,
> I trust in you, knowing you "doeth all things well." Amen.

Barbara Johnson

God's Weakness

If God be for us, who can be against us?
—ROMANS 8:31

I have a weakness: my children.

Upon returning to my hotel after speaking one Friday night, I discovered that my grown daughters had not arrived on schedule for the rest of the weekend's Women of Faith conference. I called the airline and discovered their flight had been delayed. Then I called the front desk and confirmed that the hotel would hold their room reservation.

About half an hour later the phone rang. "Hi Momma," my daughter Lesa said. "We're down at the front desk, and they said we don't have a room. They're sending us to another hotel."

"Let me speak to them!" I said furiously. A young man got on the line. I went into BIG MOMMA mode and told him, "Oh, yes, you do have a room! I just called and confirmed their room. YOU *WILL* FIND THEM A ROOM. The correct spelling of my daughter's last name is C-O-H-E-N. Find it!"

"Oh, here it is," the man agreed. "Yes, they do have a room. I am so sorry, ma'am."

I was ready to march down to the front desk with my robe on, barefoot, with no makeup and one curler in my hair, because those were MY children and I did not intend for them to have any problems!

If I care that much about my earthly children, how much more does our heavenly Father care about us? He has gone before us, is with us, and will always protect us. In fact, I believe that if God were to have a weakness, it would be his love for his kids.

Daddy, I know you are always looking out for my best.
Thank you that I can depend on you. Amen.

Thelma Wells

Rust—Er—Trust Away

My eyes are fixed on you, O Sovereign LORD.
—PSALM 141:8

I love autumn's rich palette of golds, reds, browns, and rusts. Speaking of rust . . . at one point in my life, I either pitched in the trash or refinished anything that had rusted. One way or another the rust had to go. But recently I made a significant investment in a rusted floor candleholder because rust, girlfriend, is "in." I'm not talking rust as in the color of maple leaves, but the red-brown corrosion that appears as a sign of age and condition.

Since I'm, ahem, maturing, I hope this designer fling with rust stays popular through several autumns. Then, when I rust up hunched over the computer, my family can just set me in the corner and stick a candle in my hand.

Aging has some benefits, but not many physical improvements occur during the season of corrosion. My bones pop and creak like the floor in a haunted house. I now pay extra to have the thickness of my glasses shaved down so I don't appear to be wearing binoculars. And I've come down off high heels into comfy loafers. Boring!

I'm grateful that our life's quality isn't based on our bones' brittleness but on our faith's soundness. Our value doesn't lessen with our decreased vision, for we are given eyes of the heart that never require bifocals. And no platform shoe could lift us to the heights like knowing that the God of the universe loves us.

So, regardless of our condition or the extent of our corrosion, as long as we trust in the God of eternity, our light is going to shine, shine, shine!

Lord, keep my heart from corroding as it weathers the storms of life.
Amen.

Patsy Clairmont

There's a Whole Lot of Shakin' Goin' On

But the righteous has an everlasting foundation.
—PROVERBS 10:25 NASB

I live in earthquake country. The residents of southern California have been warned repeatedly that the "big one" is not a matter of "if" but "when."

Yesterday two different earthquakes rattled my dishes and jangled my nerves. One gave a quick sharp kick in the morning and the other did a rolling on through in the afternoon. Each had different epicenters and different styles. If I had to choose a style, I'd choose the rolling one. Somehow it seems to have a better disposition.

The reality is I can't choose my style of earthquake any more than I can choose to not have any at all. The other reality is that we all live in earthquake country. Nothing in life is stationary, stable, or immovable. And most jolts are totally unexpected and unwanted.

The violent, sudden shaking of our life is frightening. Those experiences can leave us questioning the goodness of God and the safety of his world. When those jolts knock me off my earthly pinnings, I have a crucial choice to make. God says that in spite of the quaking and the terror, his loving-kindness will not be removed from me. Do I believe his promises and cling to them, or do I refuse to reach out and as a result get buried in the rubble of my circumstances?

I've experienced enough shaking in my life to know I don't want to go it alone; I want the God of all creation to hang onto when all that shakin's goin' on.

God, I can't ride out the quakes on my own.
Thank you for being my sure foundation. Amen.

Marilyn Meberg

No Need to Fear

But I will leave within you the meek and humble,
who trust in the name of the LORD. —ZEPHANIAH 3:12

I looked out at the wasted landscape as our plane landed at the airport in Guatemala. I was there with Operation Rescue, taking food and blankets to those who live on the garbage dump in that city.

As we got closer to the dump in our jeep, the stench of human waste was overwhelming. It was hot and dusty and vultures scurried around the ground like dogs. For a large community of people this refuse pile is home. They sort through the garbage by day and sleep there by night.

We formed a human chain and began to pass out the fresh supplies to people who had been in line for hours. There was great kindness amongst the poverty-stricken community. I saw them help one another, bring a crippled old man to the front, lift children over their heads so they could get to the food first.

I became aware of a girl by my right shoulder who stepped up and began to help me hand out blankets and bottled water. When she spoke I realized she was American. When the day was over and we sat, filthy and exhausted, on the edge of an empty flatbed truck, she told me that she is a missionary there. She is single, in her thirties, and totally committed to serving the Guatemalan people.

"Are you afraid being here?"

"I would be afraid *not* to be here, for this is where God has placed me."

When you know you're where God wants you, there is no need to fear.

Lord Jesus, I thank you that I can trust you right here, right now.
Amen.

Sheila Walsh

Walking with Jesus

When the disciples saw him walking on the lake, they were terrified.
"It's a ghost," they said, and cried out in fear. But Jesus immediately said to
them: "Take courage! It is I. Don't be afraid." —MATTHEW 14:26–27

It was stormy that night. The disciples' boat was "buffeted by the waves because the wind was against it" (Matthew 14:24). The disciples were already rattled by the threatening waves. Then they saw, coming toward them across the whitecaps, a man, walking on the water. And "they were terrified."

Earlier that same day they had seen Jesus feed the multitude with nothing but five loaves of bread and two fish. So in reading this story in hindsight, we wonder why they were terrified when they saw a man walking toward them across the turbulent waters. How could they not have known who it was? Who else could it have been, for heaven's sake?

Maybe they didn't trust their instincts. They needed proof. "Lord, if it's you, tell me to come to you on the water," Peter called out. Then Jesus answered, "Come."

Today we cry out the same stricken plea. *Lord, is it you? Are you there? Show me!* Somehow, we can't quite bring ourselves to trust him to be there when we need him, to help us endure the storms of life and do the impossible, until somehow, when we finally tune out the howling wind and the furious waves that engulf us, we focus completely on his Word. Then we hear him say, "Take courage! . . . Don't be afraid." And the next thing we know we are out of the boat, doing the impossible.

Lord, I trust you! Take my hand and lead me
over troubled waters and into your presence. Amen.

B a r b a r a   J o h n s o n

Something That Sticks

I will redeem you.
—EXODUS 6:6

Who out there remembers S&H green stamps? Yes, I see those hands.

My mom used to collect these green-and-yellow stamps, which she would lick and stick into paper booklets. The stamps were a bonus with grocery and gasoline purchases and could be redeemed for anything from a hair dryer to a clothes dryer.

Mom had redeemed her stamp books for a number of items, but the first time I made a selection at the redemption center was just days before my wedding. Mom loaded up her purse with green stamps, and off we went to find some luggage for my honeymoon. We traded in the booklets for a three-piece set of summer-blue suitcases. They were lovely, and I felt so grown-up. I carried that luggage from place to place for more than thirty years before the last piece cried to be relieved of duty.

My mom understood the value of redemption. She gave her life to Christ in her thirties, and the Lord redeemed her heart. And get this, she didn't even have to save up stamps to get the deal. In fact, the new heart already had been paid for and was simply waiting for her to request it.

After years of lugging around my deep human neediness, I decided to trade it in. And I knew just where to go. Following the lead of my mom, I too gave my life to Christ. I cried as he relieved my years of guilt and failure. Imagine: He unpacked my tattered suitcase full of pain and presented me with a new heart.

Now there's something that sticks!

Bless you, Lord, for paying the price of my redemption.
Amen.

Patsy Clairmont

Taking God at His Word

If you believe, you will receive whatever you ask for in prayer.
—MATTHEW 21:22

I marvel at Marilyn Meberg. She is a shining example of one who totally believes Jesus' words.

When Marilyn was afflicted with the toxic effects of ruptured silicone breast implants, I was heartbroken. Having known her to enjoy good health for years, this malady seemed incomprehensible to me.

Nevertheless, Marilyn trusted God to deliver her. When the prognosis was the worst, she believed she would get better. I watched her courage grow every day . . . and I marveled. All over her house—on the kitchen counter, bathroom mirror, desk, bookshelves—were cards with Bible verses on them, reminding her of God's faithfulness . . . and she relied on it. Rarely was she down.

Little by little Marilyn improved. I noticed she didn't need me as frequently to grocery shop or make her bed. Her energy was returning. One evening she got out of her chair quickly and said to me, "Luci, did you note the alacrity with which I rose?"

Whoa, I thought. *Marilyn's back. My funny, clever, wordsmith friend has returned.*

Now that we are a year away from those difficult, heartbreaking days, I know without doubt that Marilyn is better because she believed getting better was possible. She prayed fervently. She took God at his word. He heard her prayers and honored them.

Does it always happen this way? No. Why not? I don't know. But I do know that watching faith lived out in my friend has increased my own.

Maybe one of the reasons you are going through difficulty right now is to enlarge your faith. And not only yours but the faith of those around you.

Teach me to rely on your faithfulness, Lord. Your mercy never fails.
Amen.

Luci Swindoll

An Outstanding Record

As the Father has loved me, so have I loved you.
–JOHN 15:9

How do I know I can trust you?" asked the teenage girl in front of me in the movie line. Her date responded, "You can trust me because I took you to that chick flick *Chocolat* and didn't even gripe about it." That seemed to settle something, and they disappeared in the direction of where *Gladiator* was playing.

The young man's logic was to remind his girlfriend of how well he'd "come through" in the past, the assumption being he'd do it again and was therefore worthy of her trust. Most of us trust others based on such logic—on their "record" of coming through for us. But when I use that logic with God I can be disappointed.

If it appears my prayers are not being answered and God seemingly isn't "coming through," my trust can be shaken. It is then I most need to remember to place my trust in the immutable *character* of God, not in how his "record" in my history appears to me.

We know the character of God when we know his Son. Jesus claimed, "Anyone who has seen me has seen the Father" (John 14:9). He also said, "I and the Father are one" (John 10:30). It is God's sacrificial, boundless love that I trust, then, and not my own limited perception of his "record" in doing what I want.

God never said we wouldn't have hard experiences, but he did promise he'd never leave us alone in them. I choose to trust in the One whose love for me was demonstrated on the cross. There has never been a more outstanding performance record than that.

God, I trust in who you are.
Amen.

Marilyn Meberg

A Higher View

He founded the world by his wisdom.
–JEREMIAH 10:12

From an airplane window I caught sight of a lake shaped like a great bird with outstretched wings. I thought if I had been sitting on the shore dangling my toes in the water, I wouldn't realize I could be caught in this bird's talons and carried away. If I strolled on the lake's edges, I wouldn't know I had brushed up against feathers, stepped on a wing, and precariously perched on a sharp beak.

Seeing things from on high gives us a new and valuable perspective. Perhaps that's why we are reminded that God's ways are so much higher than our ways (Isaiah 55:9).

I wonder at the vast scope one must have when looking through time and eternity. We are so restricted that even our aerial views are but minuscule snapshots of reality. Trying to comprehend that God looks through time past—and past time—leaves stretch marks on my cranium. Those are thoughts I can't birth, imagine as I might.

Would I try to measure God's fathomless love? My little ruler, my yardstick, or even my longest tape measure is a pathetic device to determine its breadth, height, depth, or length—like a hummingbird trying to sip the ocean dry. That's true too of my bird's-eye view. Binoculars, a telescope, or even a fang-dangled camera atop a space station are not going to provide me with God's expansive, eternal perspective.

What's so important about a higher view? God knows not only my personal alpha and omega but also the entire universe's birthday and the moment of its demise. My all-knowing, all-seeing God offers me his highest counsel. The question is, will I take it?

Lord, speak to me from on high.
Amen.

Patsy Clairmont

Sing On!

In God I trust; I will not be afraid. What can man do to me?
—PSALM 56:11

Last year when Mary Graham, president of Women of Faith, became ill late at night during a conference weekend, I called a doctor friend of mine who lived nearby. After talking with Mary on the phone, he said she needed to eat some bananas. He also called in a prescription to an all-night pharmacy and asked if I could go pick it up. Now, I have to admit I hesitated a moment—especially when he told me this pharmacy wasn't in the best part of town. But my friend Liz volunteered to drive me there in her rental car, so off we went.

Of course we got lost on the way, and as we nervously stopped to consult our directions, a man suddenly appeared beside my window and peered inside! We shrieked and sped away, our hearts leaping into our throats.

Eventually we found the pharmacy and then, incredibly, we spotted a little market that had a big table full of bananas right by the front door. We delivered our items to our friend, and by morning, Mary was feeling fine.

What a lesson in trust that little escapade was! At times Liz and I were shaking in our boots, but we knew if we used our heads and did our best, God would be with us. The experience reminded me of Victor Hugo's remark about a little bird, singing its heart out on a tiny branch. "Though he feels it bend, yet he sings his song," Hugo wrote, "knowing that he has wings."

Dear Father, no matter what today brings, I will trust in you, knowing
you have a perfect plan for my life. Amen.

Barbara Johnson

Fighting with God

You want something but don't get it. . . . You quarrel and fight.
You do not have, because you do not ask God. –JAMES 4:2

As my one-year-old granddaughter, Bryna, and I browsed in Target one day, she was sitting in the cart trying to put the latch of the seat belt in her mouth. I calmly took it away from her and said, "No. No. Don't put that in your mouth." She looked up at me with determination in her eye and started to put it in her mouth. This time I got a little more forceful. I took it out of her hand, and repeated myself. She paused for a few seconds, looked down at the latch, grabbed it abruptly, and proceeded to put it back in her mouth. I got in her face, raised my voice, tapped her little hand, and made her put it down. She stared me down fiercely, then charged at my face to scratch it like a wildcat!

Much to her surprise, I spanked her hand. I was bigger, badder, stronger, older, and wiser than she was. I had to stop her from that kind of behavior before it became a habit.

We try to fight with God. When will we realize that he is greater, more powerful, sovereign, all-wise, and infinitely loving? Our arms are really too short to fight with God. When he tells us, "No, No," why not simply obey? It is a lot easier than getting our hands spanked.

Father, help me to realize that you have already won
all my quarrels with you. Give me the wisdom to ask for your guidance
and adhere to your Word. Thank you
for your perfect discipline and everlasting love. Amen.

Thelma Wells

Not Fair, Lord!

Why are you silent while the wicked swallow up those
more righteous than themselves? –HABAKKUK 1:13

The prophet Habakkuk was having a problem figuring God out when he wrote those words. He wanted God to send revival to his people and shape them up. After all, they were a mess! Instead, people who were an even greater mess (the Babylonians) conquered the Jewish nation, and things sunk to an even lower level of depravity. Why did God allow that?

We have all wondered why it seems as if the good guys lose and the bad guys win. For example, how could God allow that person at work to lie about you and then, based on how you were misrepresented, get the promotion you'd been praying for? How could your spouse get away with his extramarital affair, ultimately divorcing you and leaving you to raise three children with little financial help and no emotional support? Or why didn't God intervene when that medical misdiagnosis was given and you became gravely ill as a result? Doesn't God care about these injustices?

Habakkuk found comfort in reminding himself that God is holy. "O LORD, are you not from everlasting? My God, my Holy One, we will not die" (1:12). Holiness is the highest and most important attribute of God. To be holy is to be perfectly righteous. To be righteous is to meet the standard of what is right and just.

God, who is holy, righteous, and just, is in charge of my life. I asked him to be long ago. Therefore, the one in charge of everything that touches me cares about the injustices I experience. He is holy . . . I will not die.

Lord God Almighty, I put my trust in you
because you alone are holy. Amen.

Marilyn Meberg

Get Up

Then God said, "Take your son, your only son, Isaac, whom you love, and go to the region of Moriah. Sacrifice him there as a burnt offering on one of the mountains I will tell you about." Early the next morning Abraham got up and saddled his donkey. –GENESIS 22:2–3

This is one of the most profound passages in all of Scripture—the ultimate picture of trust. This is the first time in Scripture that the phrase "whom you love" is used. God made it clear to Abraham that he understood what he was asking of him. Abraham had waited a long time for his precious son. He was a hundred years old when Isaac was born. God had promised him the nations of the earth through this boy he now was being asked to sacrifice.

Simple things in this story stagger me. *Abraham got up.* You can almost miss those words, but they are a profound act of faith and obedience. Abraham cut the wood that would consume the body of his son with his own hands. He told his servants to wait at the bottom of the mountain. Then Abraham made a huge statement of faith: "We will worship and then *we* will come back to you" (Genesis 22:5, emphasis added). We?

It is clear as you read on in the text that Abraham intended to follow God's will to the letter; but he trusted Jehovah. He believed that even if he struck his own son down, God could raise him up and still fulfill his divine promise.

That kind of absolute trust in God makes me want to get down on my knees and worship.

Father God, thank you for those who have trusted you
before me and whose example lights my way. Amen.

Sheila Walsh

An Unusual Teenager?

When they reached the place God had told him about, Abraham
built an altar there and arranged the wood on it. He bound his son Isaac
and laid him on the altar, on top of the wood. –GENESIS 22:9

This passage tells us a lot about Isaac. Historians estimate that Isaac was sixteen or seventeen years old when he and his father set off up that mountain. On the way he asked his father where the offering was. "We have the wood and the knife, but we have no animal." Abraham reassured him that God would provide.

When they get to the chosen place, Abraham bound his son and laid him on the altar. Abraham was a century old, Isaac a strapping teenage boy. He must have willingly laid down on the altar. His trust in his father must have been so absolute that he did whatever Abraham asked.

I wonder what the conversation was like as they trekked back down the mountain. Surely they were both changed men. God provided a lamb for the sacrifice and reassured Abraham that through his beloved boy whom he did not withhold from God, his offspring would be as numerous as the stars in the sky.

It is difficult in our culture to even find a frame of reference for this kind of trust. We are so into our individual rights that to see a teenager put his head on the block because he trusts his father is mind-boggling. There are all sorts of ways to model our trust in God to our children. May we do so in such a way that their own faith becomes second nature.

Father God, may my trust in you shine like the stars in the sky. Amen.

Sheila Walsh

A Mother's Love

Give the living baby to the first woman. Do not kill him; she is his mother.
–1 KINGS 3:27

Two women gave birth to sons about the same time. One of the baby boys died, devastating his mother. Desperate, she claimed that the other new mother had taken her living son from her while she was asleep and placed the dead baby in her bed. These women quarreled bitterly until they went to the wise king Solomon to settle the dispute.

After Solomon heard all about the situation, he asked for a sword and told the mothers that the fairest thing to do was to cut the boy in half and divide him between the two mothers. One mother begged the king to spare the boy and not harm him. "Let the other mother have him," she pleaded. The other mother said, "Yes, kill him and divide him so that neither of us can have him!"

The king instantly knew who the real mother was. She was willing to totally deny herself and give up her rights to ensure the safety of her only child. In the same way, God willingly gave up his only Son so you and I could be safe and saved.

Sometimes our hearts are cut in half with our own deceit and indecision. But surrendering our hearts to God the way the loving mother was willing to surrender her child will ensure for us the tender, wise care of a Father whose passionate love for us outweighs the matchless love of a mother for her child. We can trust that kind of love with our lives!

Father, thank you for your unselfish love toward me,
that while I quarreled in sin, you spared my life. Amen.

Thelma Wells

Weathering the Weather

Indeed, in our hearts we felt the sentence of death. But this happened
that we might not rely on ourselves but on God, who raises the dead.
–2 CORINTHIANS 1:9

I just observed a deep theological truth on the Nickelodeon cartoon series *Little Bear*. One of the characters on the show said:

Whether the weather be cold
Or whether the weather be hot
We'll weather the weather whatever the weather
Whether we like it or not.

The theological implication being that in spite of whatever is happening to us, in spite of not even liking what is happening to us, we will get through it.

Paul expressed the same thought in language containing far less alliteration:

I know how to get along with humble means and I also know how to live in prosperity; in any and every circumstance I have learned the secret of being filled and going hungry, both of having abundance and suffering need (Philippians 4:12 NASB).

What is the secret to weathering the weather or thriving in both feast and famine? Paul says the secret is found in trusting the God who supplies "all [our] needs according to His riches in glory in Christ Jesus" (Philippians 4:19 NASB).

That's the bottom line, isn't it? Trusting in the God of glorious abundance. When I trust myself, sooner or later I'll realize I'm bankrupt. When I trust God, I'm saved from ever running out of resources.

Trusting in you, dear God, means I can rest in your ample provision.
Thank you! Amen.

M a r i l y n   M e b e r g

The Dance Goes On

A time to dance.
—*ECCLESIASTES 3:4*

When I first spotted the print hanging in a local store, I was smitten with the image. It now hangs in my home.

The illustration depicts a young couple in formal attire, dancing at the ocean's edge. Intimidating storm clouds hover above them, but they seem unaware. Behind the gentleman stands a butler holding an umbrella high over the pair's heads. Behind the woman is a maid sheltered from the strong wind under another umbrella. The beach is wet, and the waves are pounding, but the dance goes on.

I've made up all sorts of stories as to what's happening in this picture. Maybe the couple danced all night until the break of day to celebrate their newfound love, which made them oblivious to their threatening circumstances. Ah, sweet love.

Or maybe he's a prince who found his princess (his maid's daughter), and he proposed marriage at the seaside.

My favorite interpretation, though, is that the picture demonstrates God's encircling love, represented by the gentleman as he guides the lady gently yet securely through the storm. And while the Lord calls us to be servants, he assures us of his ongoing shelter during the winds of adversity until we reach the shoreline of eternity.

Call me a hopeless romantic, but I appreciate knowing I am loved by a Prince who takes the lead. And that the dance goes on forever.

*Lord, I notice the woman is allowing the gentle pressure
of the man's hand to guide her next step. May I be equally
supple in following your lead. Amen.*

Patsy Clairmont

No Way!

Blessed is he ... whose hope is in the LORD.
—PSALM 146:5

It is very hard for me to go to Costco and not buy stuff I don't need. Everything comes in such enticing bulk packaging, it is almost unavoidable. Just in case I get convicted about bulk-buying I always save my receipt so I can take back six of the eight boxes of Shredded Wheat I don't eat. Some of my receipts date back to the early '90s. You get the picture.

I remember shopping in Costco shortly after I bought my house. My bill was $223.84, a hefty sum for one who lives alone. Driving home I was kind of down on myself for not being more careful in spending. I was confessing this to the Lord when I stopped to pick up the mail. There was an envelope from an escrow company with whom I had done business, and in it was a nice letter. It read, in part, "We've been reviewing files and realized you have made an overpayment. Please find an enclosed check in the amount of $223.84 with our apology for not handling this matter sooner."

No way! I was stunned. I didn't cash that check for a week; I just set it on my dresser and looked at it every day, beaming.

The likelihood of an exact reimbursement is very rare, I know. But this was far more than money to me. It was a gracious message from God reminding me that he is completely in charge of my life. And I mean every single detail ... right down to the last penny.

Father, in you alone I put my trust. You are ingenious,
creative, and full of surprises. Help me to remember you can
bring money out of nowhere. Amen.

Luci Swindoll

Numerically Challenged

He performs ... miracles that cannot be counted.
—JOB 5:9

I don't do numbers—at least not well. Which makes my existence tricky since we're expected to know our zip code, social security number, license plate, ATM PIN number, telephone number, fax, cell, pager, clothing sizes, combination locks, date, and time.

My husband loves numbers. In fact, he's always doodling along the edge of his newspaper in long columns of equations. Just between you and me, I think that under Les's sombrero is a calculator. He's always adding, subtracting, and multiplying.

I still remember as a kid the endless flash card drills I endured as I tried to learn my multiplication tables. *Ugh.* It wasn't a successful era of my life. I did excel in spelling bees, or I would have packed up my pencil case and headed to Oz. The scarecrow and I could have traded in our straw craniums for some serious gray matter ... with numbers in it. Then we would show folks. Why, I'd even balance my checkbook, memorize my PIN number, and arrive at church on time.

Alas, Oz Land isn't an option, so I've learned to surround myself with pals who are number-friendly. One of my friend's love of numbers determined his livelihood as an accountant. Honestly, I'd be depressed if I had to wake each day and face endless lists of figures. It's all I can do to deal with my figure, which is always several pounds from where it should be. Eek! More numbers.

Here's the good news for those of us who are numerically challenged: There is One who counts the very hairs on our heads and numbers our days. His mathematics are impeccable, and his books balance. In fact, he has our number!

Lord, I count on you!
Amen.

Patsy Clairmont

I've Been Conned

Watch out that no one deceives you.
—MATTHEW 24:4

Furs, diamonds, nice cars, beautiful homes—all are common signs of people in high-dollar professions. Charming, intelligent, and sophisticated often are other characteristics. Writing hot checks doesn't quite jive with those distinctives.

A woman matching this description met me when I was a bank officer. She told me that an administrator at a hospital, where she was a psychologist, referred her to me. When I opened her account, everything checked out fine. I had no reason to think anything was wrong.

Our families enjoyed personal visits. One Friday they did not show up at our home for dinner. I called her house from Friday evening until Sunday afternoon when I finally got an answer. A strange voice said he did not know where she was, and she had left with his furniture. This was my first clue that something was amiss. (Oh yes, my husband had said something was fishy. But I blew him off.)

Large checks came in to the bank from department stores totaling over $33,000. I returned them for nonsufficient funds. Monday morning my "friend" called to tell me she was wiring money into her account and that she'd had to leave suddenly because her mother was critically ill. I was not buying it!

The authorities got involved. When police found her, she was driving a custom-designed luxury car and had a trunkful of fake identification cards. The officers didn't know her real identity. Even her family was a hoax.

Don't be impressed with a person's possessions or personality. Scrutinize her character and integrity before you trust her. Our reputation is what people think about us; our character is who we really are.

Lord, please grant me discernment and wisdom.
Amen.

Thelma Wells

Who Can I Trust?

Some trust in chariots and some in horses,
but we trust in the name of the LORD our God. –PSALM 20:7

Many of us trust "in spite of." Quite foolishly, sometimes. For example, I trust you to drive my car in spite of the fact you're nearsighted and lost your glasses yesterday. I trust you to feed my cat in spite of your severe allergic responses to cat dander. I trust you to gather eggs from my prize hens, Betty and Melba, in spite of your alektorophobia (phobic reactions to chickens).

Many persons have married, "trusting" that their atheist spouse would ultimately become a believer in spite of all evidence to the contrary. Parents trust that their undisciplined children will grow up to be courteous, thoughtful adults in spite of little modeling of these characteristics in the home. Politicians run for office on a platform of "you can trust me" in spite of . . . blah, blah, blah.

Is there anywhere we can place our trust that requires no "in spite of" clause? Jesus said, "Do not let your hearts be troubled. Trust in God; trust also in me" (John 14:1). Does that mean no one but God should receive our trust? No, but he is the only One who is *100 percent* trustworthy. The rest of us bring our humanity into the equation; none of us is worthy of anyone's complete trust.

In spite of that reality, God sees us as perfect and trustworthy—not because we have earned such favor, deserve it, or reflect his faith in us through our behavior. His "in spite of" favor was bestowed upon us at Calvary. Now, that's a mind-bending fact I can trust.

Thank you, Jesus, that I can trust you in all things.
Amen.

Marilyn Meberg

Full Redemption

With the LORD is unfailing love and with him is full redemption.
–PSALM 130:7

I read a little booklet about helping to save the earth. One suggestion was to recycle bottles and aluminum cans. Wanting to do my part, I stood in front of the grocery store with eighty-two containers for redemption.

The recycling machine had lots of instructions:

- Face bar code at 11:00.
- Can cannot be flat.
- Bottom first.
- Unable to read bar code on unacceptable containers.

The list went on.

As I was feeding this hungry monster, a distinguished-looking man approached with a box of evenly stacked cans and bottles. Surely he'd been here before. Every bar code was facing 11:00, and the machine efficiently devoured his loot in no time.

"You come here often?" I asked.

"Yeah, all the time. Gotta follow these instructions, though, or there's no redemption."

"You're tellin' me!"

"Funny thing...," he said, "the kids drink the drinks and want the money, but I do the redeeming. Everybody wants something for nothing, don't they?"

"For sure. Especially those who don't do the work."

That little exchange took place ten years ago, but I've never forgotten it. We all want something for nothing. Even spiritual redemption. But rarely do we remember the tremendous cost: Christ's death in our place. He paid the price; we get the benefits.

If you have never put your faith in Jesus Christ, I invite you to do so today. A personal relationship with God becomes yours when you trust in the redemptive work of his Son. Jesus said, "I am the way and the truth and the life. No one comes to the Father except through me" (John 14:6).

Jesus, thank you for paying the astronomical price
of my eternal redemption. Amen.

Luci Swindoll

October 27
Such a Blockhead

But God demonstrates his own love for us in this:
While we were still sinners, Christ died for us. —ROMANS 5:8

I've experienced people who were such blockheads that were you to hit them with a board they'd never feel it. These are the people who push in ahead of others in the bathroom line at the tennis matches, cut you off in traffic making it impossible to exit onto Washington, or talk loudly and endlessly on their cell phones during lunch at Palermos. I mutter, "What is wrong with these people?" But the sobering truth is, I too am a blockhead. My blockheadedness is possibly more subtle than the examples I've given, but I recognize the same insensitive instincts in me as well.

Fortunately, Jesus is a pro at working with blockheads. He was born into the home of a carpenter. He learned from his earthly carpenter father how to take a block of wood and, by cutting, chiseling, and shaping it, create a work of perfection, free of rough and splintered edges. And yet, when I'm the block, I resist the chiseling. It requires an awful lot of trust in the intent and skill of the carpenter.

But Jesus' intent and trustworthiness was demonstrated for me when he voluntarily took my splintered, rough-hewn, sin-stained soul to a wooden cross and died there for my redemption. That cross represents the final carpenter's touch of God. At Calvary the perfecting work was accomplished. And for whom was it accomplished? For all of us blockheads in the world!

Thank you, Jesus, for that old wooden cross.
Amen.

Marilyn Meberg

trust

Draped in Mystery

God will wipe away every tear.
—REVELATION 7:17

God makes no sense ... this side of glory. Try as we might, we can't reason through his ways. Scripture warns us that his ways are not our ways (Isaiah 55:8). Yet it still jars us when tragedy is part of the plan.

Word arrived over the weekend that a friend's daughter had been killed in a car accident. She was a young woman who planned to join a ministry but instead stepped into eternity. She had so much to live for and so many who loved her. Her family will never be the same.

How do we file this kind of loss? She wasn't a drug addict out of her mind on cocaine. She wasn't a convict trying to outrun the police. Her greatest desire was to serve the Lord with her gifts and her life.

When I was younger, I could explain away countless mysteries. Not anymore. Where once my answers hung as thick as draperies, today they are as wispy as sheers. Perhaps that is as it should be. For a sheer is much like a veil, and we're told that one day the veil will be lifted between eternity and us, and we will understand. That which once caused us heartbreak will finally make sense.

Until then, we are left to grieve and trust. Grieve our loss, grieve our dreams, and grieve our "rights," while we trust his sovereignty, trust his plan, and trust his heart.

Lord, keep us from adding to people's agony with pat verses, quick answers, and trite slogans. May we not be eager to spout answers, but instead may we be your arms and your ears. In the midst of others' frailty, may we tiptoe carefully while you mend them. Amen.

Patsy Clairmont

Follow the Map

The proverbs of Solomon son of David, king of Israel: for attaining wisdom
and discipline; for understanding words of insight. —PROVERBS 1:1–2

At a rental car counter in the Atlanta airport, a young lady gave me instructions to Helen, Georgia. "Just go 285 and follow the signs," she said. *Simple enough,* I thought.

I drove for miles following her directions. After an hour I discovered I was right back at the airport.

Something's wrong, I surmised. *How could I have missed those signs?* I went back to see the rental car agent. When I told her that I'd gotten on 285 as she had said, she clarified with some chagrin: "No, I told you to go TO 85 and follow the signs. The 285 is the airport loop."

Once I got on the right freeway, the signs were evident, and after an additional hour and a half I made it to my destination. Perhaps if I'd been given a map I wouldn't have gone the wrong way, wasting time, effort, and energy on the wrong journey.

There is a map available to each of us that will give us only correct information. It is called the Holy Bible. Every journey we take is mapped out in that road map of life. If we misunderstand it in one passage, it will become clear for us in another.

I've learned not to rely solely on people to tell me how to get to my destinations in life. I depend on the Map.

*Dear Master Mapmaker, thank you for directions
that will never lead me down the wrong road. Help me
to listen carefully to your instructions. Amen.*

Thelma Wells

October 30
Trying to Get It

What he trusts in is fragile; what he relies on is a spider's web.
—Job 8:14

I can be free of guilt, inadequacy, self-doubt, insecurity, and any other malady of the soul that clamors for attention and keeps me mired in uncertainty. You have the same potential for soul rest. What is it? Trust ... simply trust! Trust in what? God's boundless, unconditional, you-need-it-you-got-it love.

How simple. So why do I still struggle with my soul's maladies? Because my trust is often as fragile as a spider's web. It is easier to trust that God loves me unconditionally when I'm behaving myself. But when my humanity rises up, my carnal nature takes over, and my propensity to do the wrong thing instead of the right thing is obvious not only to me but perhaps to the world, I slink back into the corner. There I feel and nurse my guilt, inadequacy, etc., etc., and the cycle starts all over again.

Now, of course, my problem with not trusting in God's perfect love and grace-saturated forgiveness lies within me, not with God. But what human being has ever experienced complete and consistent unconditional love? None of us has here on earth. So how on earth can I really ever get it ... really trust ... really rid myself of the maladies of the soul?

The first answer that rises up from within is, *You'll never get it, Marilyn. Forget it!* But when God says his ways are not my ways (and therefore he loves differently than anyone on earth) I choose to trust that ... at least for this moment. And right now that's enough.

Lord Jesus, thank you for giving me many, many reasons
to trust you. Strengthen my faith when it is fragile. Amen.

Marilyn Meberg

Risky? I Think Not

Trust in the LORD with all your heart.
—PROVERBS 3:5

I had better trust Jesus because I sure can't trust myself. Oh, I'm trustworthy about some things. For instance, you can trust me to make my bed (okay, almost always). You can trust me to arrive on time (unless I'm running late). You can trust me to keep my word (of course, extenuating circumstances do occur). For sure you can trust me to tell the truth, although I wouldn't consider hurting your feelings. I wouldn't out-and-out lie—I just wouldn't "elaborate."

Poor Old-Testament Joseph understood out-and-out lies. In fact, he ran into some folks who taught him lasting lessons on lies and trust. Joseph trusted his brothers, who sold him into slavery and then told their dad he was dead. He trusted his boss, who threw Joseph into prison for a crime he didn't commit. He trusted a fellow prisoner to speak a word on his behalf to the king, but instead the ungrateful liberated prisoner forgot Joseph for years.

This trust-thing is risky—unless, like Joseph, we learn to trust the Lord. Listen to Joseph's words when he was reunited with his scoundrel brothers and divulged his identity. "And now, do not be distressed and do not be angry with yourselves for selling me here, because it was to save lives that God sent me ahead of you" (Genesis 45:5).

Imagine Joseph's releasing his brothers from their sin against him! He trusted God to take their treacherous behavior and to redeem it for good. His trust in God's ultimate plan enabled Joseph to become a wise leader and a forgiving brother.

I want to be like Joseph and rely on God alone.

Lord, you alone are absolutely trustworthy.
Amen.

Patsy Clairmont

NOVEMBER

Gratitude

*I will praise God's name in song and glorify him with thanksgiving. . . .
you who seek God, may your hearts live!* —PSALM 69:30, 32

Gratitude is a mighty force. It can change the whole landscape of our lives. It can take a situation that seems dead or hopeless and infuse it with light and life. Mostly, practicing giving thanks in all things changes us. It is a worthy habit to pursue.

Time after time in the Word of God we are called to give thanks. Not only is God more than worthy of our grateful hearts, but the very act of thanksgiving also reminds us of who we are and who he is. Every breath we take comes from him. Every good thought we have is a gift from him. When we lie down at night and sleep in peace, it is because of him. When we rise up and we are still with him, it is a gift. Gratitude is like laughter: It is internal medicine.

As we turn our hearts toward God in thanks, we turn our hearts toward each other too. We begin to notice simple kindnesses and receive them. The attitude of gratitude is a welcoming invitation to a party that never ends.

I love November. As nature begins its winter slumber, our hearts are invited to awaken to a season specially set apart for thanksgiving and jubilation. As we reflect on all we have to be grateful for in the month ahead, we prepare our hearts for the most beautiful birthday season of all time. Let's celebrate!

Sheila Walsh

In God I Trust

When I am afraid, I will trust in you. In God, whose word I praise, in God
I trust; I will not be afraid. What can mortal man do to me? —PSALM 56:3–4

In the year 835, Pope Gregory IV instituted a church-wide observance of
November 1 as All Saints' Day. During the Reformation of the sixteenth century, the Protestant churches understood the term "saint" in its New Testament context to include all believers in Christ and reinterpreted the feast of
All Saints' as a celebration of the unity of the entire church.

In medieval England the festival was known as All Hallows ("hallow"
meaning saint), and so October 31 became All Hallows Eve, from which we
get the term Halloween. There were also Celtic practices associated with
November 1 that predate Christianity. Pagans considered the first day of
November the beginning of winter and the Celtic new year, when all sorts
of evil was believed to roam the earth playing tricks on human beings to mark
the season of diminishing sunlight. The custom of children going from door
to door in scary costumes demanding "trick or treat" is a throwback to those
ancient rituals.

Halloween is controversial in the church. Some Christian parents see no
harm in letting their little ones dress up in silly costumes like their school
friends, while others are horrified that believers would allow their children
to ape such a pagan rite. The best scenario seems to be when Christians hold
their own God-honoring festival to celebrate the fact that even as winter
approaches and nights get longer, there is no need to fear. God is in control,
today and every day.

Dear Father, thank you that I need fear no evil when I trust in you.
Amen.

Sheila Walsh

November 2
The School of Faith

Knowledge will be pleasant to your soul.
–PROVERBS 2:10

I love autumn. The season's crisp-edged breezes affect me two ways: I root out warmer garb, and I want to skip. Maybe the colors cause me to twirl like a leaf or maybe the childhood memories of starting back to school put me into a spin.

Remember the feelings that came with the new school year? I always experienced a mix of dread and delight with a hefty dash of expectations. Every fall I could hardly wait to meet up with friends I hadn't seen all summer. And I could strut around in my new school clothes and meet my new teachers. I always wondered if this would be the year I'd meet some cool guy or receive my best grades ever.

Unfortunately, all my interest in school would wane by winter, when both my enthusiasm and the landscape were cold and blah. You'll note in my list of reasons to be excited about school starting I didn't mention the thrill of learning. I wanted good grades, but I didn't want to study. So I didn't excel; in fact, I barely made it through one grade and into the next. Then, when I was sixteen, I quit. That mistake left an indelible ache in my soul.

But I'm grateful we serve a Redeemer. After I gave my life to Christ, I found myself enrolled in the school of faith. I love my Teacher, and he's ever so patient when I don't get it. I often have homework and sometimes even detention, but now I love to learn. I understand that diligence yields great rewards, whether it's in the vibrant autumn of new beginnings or the long hard winter of discipline.

Lord, teach me!
Amen.

Patsy Clairmont

gratitude

November 3
A Good Life

I have come that they may have life, and have it to the full.
–JOHN 10:10

"Grammy, I have a good life!"

"Why'd you say that, Vanessa?"

"Because I'm so happy. I love my mommy, my daddy, my sister, and you, Grammy. It's just a good life."

How my heart pounded with joy when my six-year-old granddaughter said those words. Wouldn't it be great always to have the happy mind of an innocent child? Vanessa sees the good things in life and cherishes them.

It is pitiful that when we get to be adults, so many of us focus on the negatives instead of the good things. Sometime we need a reminder that there are more good things and good people in the world than bad. Let's see, there are:

Family and friends
The celestial heavens and galaxies
The beautiful earth with myriad plants and flowers
The miraculous ways in which our bodies function
The air we breathe but cannot see
Various means of transportation
Constant advances in medical science
Sanitation and clean water
Protectors of law and order
Emergency assistance
Instant telecommunication
Parties and celebrations
Safe places to worship
Gravity that holds us on the ground
Paved streets and highways with signs and signals
Safe foods and refrigeration
The privilege of property ownership
Great books and libraries
Masterful paintings, music, and sculptures
People to love us and for us to love...

You can finish this list with your own reminders of what a good life you have!

Jesus, thank you for giving me so much to be grateful for.
Help me to cherish every precious moment of my life. Amen.

Thelma Wells

The Lamb's Book of Life

I am going there to prepare a place for you.
—JOHN 14:2

Hobbes is one grateful dog. My little fur-faced friend is a miniature dachshund Pat Wenger got from the pound nine years ago. The only thing known of Hobbes's history is that he was found in the middle of a busy street in Laguna Beach, California. Cowering and terrified, he was grateful to be rescued from the threatening traffic. When he was placed in the security of a wire-mesh cage reserved for dogs, his gratitude knew no bounds. He licked the hands and faces of whoever stopped to chat.

Pat, who makes regular forays to the pound, discovered him a few days later. She was taken by his show-dog good looks and thought, *This little fellow is an aristocrat; he deserves a residence upgrade.* After a little paperwork Hobbes found himself in Pat's loving home.

Hobbes looks at Pat now with the most poignantly grateful expression one could imagine. If he had words, his little doggie heart would most surely say, "I nearly died . . . and there you were. You saved me and brought me home with you. Thank you, thank you, thank you!"

Hobbes inspires me to be grateful and to express my gratitude to God. I too was saved from a chaotic world, and without him I would have been homeless; I would have died. He's gone to prepare a permanent residence upgrade for me because I'm an aristocrat—a daughter of the King! The reason I know where I'm spending eternity is because the paperwork has already been done. My name has been "written in the book of life belonging to the Lamb that was slain from the creation of the world" (Revelation 13:8).

Lord Jesus . . . thank you, thank you, thank you!
Amen.

Marilyn Meberg

Daybreak

In the morning, O LORD, you hear my voice.
–PSALM 5:3

The morn is up again, the dewy morn, with breath as incense," wrote Lord Byron.

I love a new day with its clean slate and sun-drenched possibilities. In Michigan not all days are dazzled in dew; instead, some are knee-deep in crystal snow blankets. So whether I'm peeking out from under down covers at a frosty windowpane or peering out an open window full of bluebirds' songs, I know this day is a gift.

I confess, I've dreaded some days: days when I was waiting for test results, when I had a pressing deadline, or when a long day of travel lay ahead of me. Interestingly, many of those days weren't as difficult as I'd imagined. As a matter of fact, some of my best memories happened on days I wasn't even looking forward to. Other times I've had high expectations that turned out flat and disappointing. Clearly, I don't have a clue what a day will hold.

Scripture instructs us, "Do not boast about tomorrow, for you do not know what a day may bring forth" (Proverbs 27:1). The word *boast* means to make a show, to be clamorously foolish, to rave. Oh, dear, I've done all those at one time or another, which is why today I'm committing to change. Want to join me?

Here's what I plan to do. . . . When my eyes open, and I'm aware the morn is up again, when I see the dew (or the snowflakes) and smell the incense breath of the newborn day, my first words will be a prayer of gratitude: "Thank you, Lord, thank you."

Whatever this day holds, dear Lord, you are in it with me.
Thank you. Amen.

Patsy Clairmont

Give Thanks

We give thanks to you, O God, we give thanks, for your Name is near;
men tell of your wonderful deeds. —PSALM 75:1

Thankfulness has become a life theme for me, especially on bad days. Like everyone else, I sometimes feel God has passed me by, put me on a shelf, or left me in a basement to languish. But even if I can't be thankful for what I've received on those days, I'm thankful for what I've escaped.

I once heard of a little girl who was overjoyed one evening because broccoli wasn't on the dinner table! Whenever God puts broccoli on your plate or allows tears to flow from your eyes, remember it is only because he has a greater good in mind. He wants to grow a rainbow in your heart.

I don't know about you, but I don't want to live my life in the *past* lane. I want to find a zillion things to be thankful for *today*. What are you thankful for right this moment? Aim your mind in a thankful direction by being grateful for the tiniest things: water to drink, a moment to rest, the color of a flower or a sunset or a bird, a piece of bread, a familiar song on the radio. Keep looking for sights, smells, sounds, that make you feel pleasure, and write them down. One woman told me, "I've been writing at least five things I'm grateful for each night. It's been wonderful. I certainly see a change. I was such a negative person."

Decide to be thankful, and encourage one another to cultivate grateful hearts. And also remember that God is thankful for *you*.

Dear Lord, thank you for all the ways you are blessing me!
Amen.

Barbara Johnson

Write It Down

At the LORD's command Moses recorded the stages in their journey.
–NUMBERS 33:2

I come from a long line of note-takers. When Mother and Daddy were living they kept records of everything they thought important. Both my brothers chronicle memorable events. And I? Well... I'm the *queen* of journaling. Within my line of sight right now I count twenty-eight books chock-full of my scribbling through the years.

And isn't this cool?—The Quakers have a tradition of keeping "Gratitude Journals." They focus on life's often-unnoticed gifts rather than on their problems. This is a great way to bear witness of God's goodness. Some folks regularly write down meaningful quotations, which encourage them when they're going through trials.

Books and journals like this are our thank-you notes to God. They give us a place to "sing" praises, applaud blessings, and transfer appreciation from our minds and hearts onto a page. And we get an incredible benefit as well. I can't tell you the countless times I've gone back and re-read something I wrote ten or fifteen years before. These jottings validate the fact that God gives victory when I hang in there.

So start a little gratitude journal. It will provide invaluable reminders of your own human resilience and God's absolute faithfulness. The records of gratitude you keep today will be a consolation to someone else after you've gone on to sing endless praises to God in heaven.

Journaling enriches creativity, deepens insight, and helps you see in black and white—or any color!—your own life's story. And that story is God's gift to you.

Thank you, Lord, for making your presence known
in the daily unfolding of my life. Give me discernment to see
and record your goodness toward me. Amen.

Luci Swindoll

We've Got Options

I bring you good news of great joy that will be for all the people.
—LUKE 2:10

Visiting India was heart-wrenching for me. I saw the results of Christians being beaten and flogged for their beliefs. One young man showed me his scars from the torture he received when his family converted to Christianity. His parents were killed. He escaped, leaving behind everything they owned.

A doctor in an AIDS/HIV facility told me that the only medicine she had for the patients most of the time was the Word of God, because there was no money to buy medicine. Victims are ostracized from their communities and families without any assistance.

The worst was seeing the beautiful little girls whose parents had sold them into prostitution. Lives of females are often considered worthless.

These are just a few of the conditions in some Third World countries. Often the very worst conditions in America are the best conditions in many parts of the world. I wonder if we Americans realize how fortunate we really are. We've got options for dealing with almost any situation.

In America, Christians can acknowledge their faith and worship without fear of physical persecution. Since the tragedy of September 11, 2001, Christians have become more outspoken and more and more people are listening and accepting Jesus Christ as Savior.

Federal grants, celebrity fundraisers, individual donations, and corporate contributions are going into coffers to make sure AIDS and HIV patients have the medicine and medical care they need.

It is unthinkable that parents would sell their little girls into immorality in most American families, no matter how poor they are.

So why do we complain so much? Maybe it would be a good thing if God sent all of us to a Third World country for a weekend. I think we'd come home with an attitude of gratitude.

Master, I'm thankful to be an American.
After seeing conditions in other lands, make me aware of what
I can do to help them enjoy some of the options we enjoy.
Amen.

Thelma Wells

Press On

I know what it is to be in need, and I know what it is to have plenty. I have
learned the secret of being content in any and every situation, whether well
fed or hungry, whether living in plenty or in want. −PHILIPPIANS 4:12

C. S. Lewis added his own twist to this verse in Philippians when he said,
"We ought to give thanks for all fortune: if it is 'good,' because it is good, if
'bad' because it works in us patience, humility, and the contempt of this world
and the hope of our eternal country."

For me, the key phrase in Lewis's quote is "works in us." Doesn't that have
a soul-wrenching ring to it? It reminds me of when my mom would run water-
soaked clothes through the wringer to extract the liquid; they would come out
flat as a crepe. After they'd hung in the sunlight to dry, she would press them
on her Ironrite (electric ironer). Fat heated rollers pressed the wrinkles into
oblivion. The clothes looked and smelled better, but what an excruciating
process.

Grateful people are so winsome one can't help but be drawn to them. I've
noted that these folks are those who have been wrung out with grief and
pressed to the limits with hardships yet have come forth with grateful hearts.
Of course, some emerge from suffering bitter, caustic, and volatile. The suffering process doesn't guarantee a sweet spirit. But if we're willing to believe
that the Lord is at work in us for good in *every* situation, then we might begin
to relate to Madame Guyon who, after many years of imprisonment, penned,
"My Lord, how full of sweet content; I pass my years of banishment."

Lord, work in me gratitude.
Amen.

Patsy Clairmont

Signal Fires

There the angel of the LORD appeared to him in flames of fire from within
a bush. Moses saw that though the bush was on fire it did not burn up.
–EXODUS 3:2

God didn't plop down the burning bush at Moses' feet that day on Mount
Horeb. We get the feeling Moses first saw it out of the corner of his eye. The
Bible tells us he had to "go over and see" the strange sight that piqued his
curiosity.

And God didn't exactly choose the most convenient time to order Moses
to lead his people out of Egypt. After all, Moses had grown up right there in
Pharaoh's court. If God had wanted it to be convenient for him, he might have
directed Moses to begin organizing the Jews undercover while he was living
in Egypt. But no, that's not God's style. Or maybe it is just that he has a flair
for drama, a supernatural way of weaving into the fabric of our lives one little thread that becomes the amazing lifeline connecting us to glory. Perhaps
while Moses was surrounded by all the glitter of Pharaoh's court, he might not
have noticed a simple little bush burning on the sidelines. But then something
went wrong and he fled for his life, and it was then that God spoke to him.

I've been there, haven't you? On the far side of the desert, up against a
mountain. There have been days when a vast wilderness of pain and heartache
stretched endlessly before me. And then God caught my eye, burned himself
anew into my heart, and sent me back across that desert to carry his loving
help to others.

God, keep me ever watchful for the signal fires
you light along my way. Amen.

B a r b a r a   J o h n s o n

Forever Grateful

*Therefore, I tell you, her many sins have been forgiven—for she loved
much. But he who has been forgiven little loves little. –LUKE 7:47*

The lion is an animal associated with gratitude in both sacred and secular literature. Once a Roman slave named Androclus was condemned to confront a lion in the amphitheater. The lion was released into the circle, but when it reached Androclus, it knelt at his feet and began to lick them. The slave was brought before the Roman consul to see if he could offer any explanation for the lion's unprecedented behavior.

"I was compelled by cruel treatment to run away from your service while in Africa," Androclus explained, "and one day I took refuge in a cave from the heat of the sun. While I was in the cave a lion entered, limping, and evidently in great pain. Seeing me, he held up his paw, from which I extracted a large thorn. We lived together in the cave for some time, the lion catering for both of us."

A lifelong allegiance is born out of gratitude for deliverance. Mary spilled everything she had at Jesus' feet because she knew the depths of sin from which she had been delivered.

"Do you see this woman?" Jesus said to Simon the Pharisee. "I came into your house. You did not give me any water for my feet, but she wet my feet with her tears and wiped them with her hair. You did not give me a kiss, but this woman, from the time I entered, has not stopped kissing my feet" (Luke 7:44–45).

*Lord Jesus, you have delivered me from death to life.
I will be forever grateful. Amen.*

Sheila Walsh

Just a Tiny Sin

For from within, out of men's hearts, come evil thoughts,
sexual immorality, theft, murder, adultery, greed, malice, deceit,
lewdness, envy, slander, arrogance and folly. All these evils come
from inside and make a man "unclean." –MARK 7:21–23

It has been said that overeating is the most worthy of sins because it does not break up marriages or cause traffic accidents. Though I find that statement mildly amusing, it insinuates a serious thought. It seems to be typical of most of us to evaluate sin as either big or small; hurtful to others or not at all; bad for the body or not at all; destructive to the marriage or . . . But according to Jesus, all sin is big!

If you reread that passage from Mark 7 again, you will note that Jesus puts arrogance and envy in the same lineup as murder and adultery. The whole list spells e-v-i-l. Now, that seems a bit offensive. Most of us don't murder or steal. Shouldn't Jesus have let us off the hook for the "small stuff" we all do like gossip and lie, and given us credit for not doing the "big stuff"? When I don't do the big stuff, I have a sense of pride . . . *oops*.

Jesus wanted to make it unmistakably clear that our sinful nature, the big stuff *and* the small stuff, is totally abhorrent to God; *all* sin is unacceptable and nonnegotiable. Where does that leave us? Kneeling at the cross in gratitude for his gracious redemption.

Lord, forgive my pride when I set myself apart from those who are guilty of the "big sins." I humbly confess my sinful, self-righteous superiority and thank you for your abundant mercy. Amen.

Marilyn Meberg

Ol' Eagle Eye

The lamp of the LORD searches the spirit of a man;
it searches out his inmost being. –PROVERBS 20:27

Yikes, what a convicting verse!

When I was young and my mom found out company was en route, she turned her family into the Clean Team. Every nook and cranny was cleansed and then inspected by ol' eagle eye herself. I spent years of my youth on my knees buffing baseboards. (My mom would tell you I was on my knees trying to crawl away from my responsibilities. Come to think of it...)

I brought that panic-button approach to cleaning my home after I married. When the phone rang announcing unexpected guests, everyone within earshot was put on house alert. The difference in Mom's approach and mine was obvious. Instead of having the family spittin' and polishin', I had 'em hiding our "debris" in high cupboards, remote closets, and basement corners. While Les raced out the garbage, Marty, our oldest, vacuumed; Jason, our youngest, grabbed up old newspapers; and I galloped through the house wiping down counters, shaking rugs, and spot-cleaning mirrors. By the time guests arrived, the house looked fine, but we were a wired mess, thanks to my Gestapo approach.

I'm afraid I often treat my interior issues like my household clutter—waiting till the last minute and then stuffing unsightly items into dark corners. Then I hear a knock and open the door. Jesus is standing there with his lamp. Uh-oh.

But wait; it's okay. He isn't offended by my debris. He even offers to carry it out! Then I realize he didn't come to judge my housekeeping but to provide me with a clean heart. And when he's done, even ol' eagle eye is impressed.

Oh, Lord, thank you for loving me.
Amen.

Patsy Clairmont

No Ugly People

How attractive and beautiful they will be!
—*ZECHARIAH 9:17*

We saw no ugly people while traveling with the relief organization World Vision in India. I looked. Even those less attractive than others were prettier than a lot of us Americans. In my group, I was about the ugliest.

It's the hair. I cannot get my hair wet! It kinks up, stands on end, and reminds everyone of a prizefight promoter.

One day while we were traveling by boat we were all hot and sweaty. I pulled my cap off and everyone practically fell over laughing. One of my "friends" *had* to take my picture. I looked so ugly when I saw it, I scared myself.

To make matters worse, I scheduled a shampoo and set in the beauty salon at the hotel. I should have known better, but when you're desperate from having a series of bad hair days, you look anywhere for a solution! Of course, the Indian hairstylists had never put their hands on African hair (as they called it) in their lives. They didn't know how to blow-dry it to get it straight, and they had never held, let alone used, a curling iron. When they were done with me, I was a mess. Yes, I was ugly! Thank goodness I knew that when I got back to the States, my daughter Lesa could make me pretty again.

Maybe your life feels like a continual bad hair day. Take heart. Jesus is waiting to give you a permanent shampoo in his cleansing, straightening power. Your hair may still look ugly, but your heart will be beautiful!

> *Lord, thank you for making me beautiful in your sight.*
> *I want to be pretty for you—both inside and out. Amen.*

Thelma Wells

The Marvelous Mumleys

This service that you perform is not only supplying the needs of God's
people but is also overflowing in many expressions of thanks to God.
—2 CORINTHIANS 9:12

Bill and Julie Mumley live in Kenya, East Africa, and work for Campus Crusade for Christ. They have five adorable children: JP, Geoff, Jared, Jordan, and Joelle. I met them in 1996 when Mary Graham and I went to their home in Nairobi. It was love at first sight with the whole family.

Because Mary had worked for Crusade, she knew the Mumleys and suggested we take them a "goodie-bag" of surprises. I wholeheartedly agreed. We loaded everything in there: clothes, videos, games, books, cassettes, candy, popcorn, school supplies. You name it, we packed it! Eighty-seven pounds of fun stuff.

Never in my life have I witnessed such gratitude for the simplest of gifts. As each item was taken from the bag, everybody went crazy with continuous yells of glee and copious "thank yous." I was so moved by the sincerity of their appreciation, I cried. From ballpoint pens to Tootsie Pops, everything was a hit.

Isn't it regrettable how we forget to be grateful for small things? We take so much for granted. What's the big deal about a pencil or a bar of soap or a little box of raisins? Maybe because the Mumleys live outside the USA, they appreciate things more. I don't know. But I do know the Lord loves a thankful heart. I also know that when I notice small things with gratitude, those around me do too. Everything becomes a gift, not an entitlement.

You be the one today to start the ball of appreciation rolling.

May I see your kindness around me, Lord,
even in the smallest things. Amen.

Luci Swindoll

Aww . . .

A man's heart reflects the man.
–*PROVERBS* 27:19

When my husband, Les, turned the corner onto our street he noticed several young entrepreneurs stationed in their front yard selling decorated paper airplanes for fifty cents each. Wanting to do his part to encourage future executive efforts, he stopped, rolled down his window, and inquired about their goods. He then reached into his wallet and discovered he had only a twenty-dollar bill.

He said to the little boy, "I only have a twenty, so you'll need to give me a second airplane to make it worth my while." Then, leaving three children mystified over their windfall, Les came home and showed me his purchase.

"You gave them how much?" I spouted. "What if they don't realize how much that is? What if they lose it? What if they get into trouble with their parents for taking so much? You know you've ruined them for any reasonable purchase by other customers." My huffing and puffing about his good-hearted act managed to take the wind out of his sails.

The following day I heard a tapping on our front door. Three darling children with a red wagon stood on our porch. The oldest began, "Mr. Clairmont was very generous to us, and we would like to give him these thank-you pictures." They held out their artistic renderings, and my heart softened toward my husband's extravagance.

Then the girl said, "We brought our wagon and wondered if we could pick up the sticks in your yard as a way of saying thank you." *Aww. . .*

Les didn't ruin them at all; in fact, his generosity gave them an opportunity to exercise some of their own. What heart!

Lord, as you have blessed me, may I bless others.
Amen.

Patsy Clairmont

King George

The LORD reigns, he is robed in majesty.
—PSALM 93:1

Finding a way to say "I love and appreciate you" to my husband in a tangible way was not easy. But I remembered when we were younger he called himself King George. How regal! *That's what I'll do at our gala celebrating my twenty years in ministry,* I decided. *I'll crown him king!* Off I went to secure his royal robe, jeweled crown, and grand scepter.

When the exciting night arrived, our grandson promenaded into the ballroom carrying a purple-and-gold robe, a golden crown, and a bejeweled scepter. When I finished reading a love poem to my husband, I placed the robe around his shoulders, the crown on his head, and the scepter in his hands. He was grinning from ear to ear.

That was the most wonderful surprise I could have given George for his decades of support, encouragement, kindness, and friendship as God has called me to speak and travel around the globe. People in the audience were crying and applauding. Sweet emotions surged throughout the room.

But feelings far greater than those flow throughout the universe when we show appreciation to our heavenly Bridegroom, the King of Kings and the Lord of Lords. "The LORD reigns, let the earth be glad; let the distant shores rejoice" (Psalm 97:1). Blessed be the name of the Lord! How can you crown him King in your heart today?

O mighty King, teach me to appreciate all the things
you do for me. Help me to understand that you alone deserve
all honor and glory every day, forever. Amen.

Thelma Wells

Thanks, in Great Part, to You

Be thankful.
—COLOSSIANS 3:15

My dad and I loved writing letters to each other. While I was away at college, we corresponded twice a week. He was the most gregarious, warm man—funny as could be—and so thoughtful. My hero!

When Daddy died in 1980, I wrote in my journal a letter of thanks for all he poured into my life. I remember thinking then, *I'm so glad this isn't the only letter I ever wrote to Daddy.* Shortly thereafter I mentioned this to a friend and she confessed she'd never written her dad once nor gotten a letter from him. How very sad! I found myself wondering how many people go through life that way.

On Daddy's birthday twelve years after he died, I again wrote in my journal:

Happy birthday, Daddy. I love you and miss you. How I would enjoy having a chat with you today to thank you for all you taught me. Next week I'll be sixty, you know. You were forty the day I was born, and sixty years later you're 100. (See how my math has improved. I now *add*.) I wish I could see your face. (I always loved your face.) Think I'll be around when I'm 100, Daddy? If not, I'll be with you! ALL RIGHT! Until then, I'm having a wonderful life . . . thanks, in great part, to you.

Gratitude is one of the sweetest feelings in the world. It is an appreciation for the favors and benefits we've received. Show your gratitude today to someone who means a lot to you. Do something for them—anything—to let them know you're thinking of them, with love.

Give me a spirit of thankfulness, Father.
Then remind me to pour it out onto others. Amen.

Luci Swindoll

A Dream Come True

*Honor your father and your mother, so that you may live long in the land
the LORD your God is giving you. —EXODUS 20:12*

Back in May I told you about the trip to Paris my husband and I enjoyed
and the gracious way we were treated by the locals. Well, what I didn't tell
you was how the whole trip was born in the gracious and thankful heart of one
of our children.

On Christmas day 2000, all of our children and grandchildren gathered
together at our house. One of the last gifts to be opened was an envelope
labeled "A Dream Come True." It was addressed to George and me. It felt so
light. What could it be?

When I opened it I could not believe my eyes. There were two airline tickets with the word "Paris" written on them. Paris? As in Paris, France?!

Yes! Our daughter Vikki had gotten them in July and kept them a secret
until Christmas. She'd remembered me saying many times that the only place
I really wanted to visit someday was Paris. This gift was definitely a dream
come true. Vikki thanked us for being deserving parents who tried to give all
their children the best of everything.

For George and me, it is a dream come true to have three wonderful children who love the Lord and who do everything they can to honor their parents. If your parents are alive today, consider what you can do to express your
gratitude to them. No matter what kind of relationship you have, even if it's
far from ideal, God wants you to honor them. How can you do that during this
season of gratitude?

*Father, thank you for being a parent worthy
of all my honor and reverence. Amen.*

Thelma Wells

Mine!

Freely you have received, freely give.
—MATTHEW 10:8

Since one of the first words most children say is "mine," I suppose selfishness is a deep-seated issue of the heart. Actually, I don't have to suppose. I'm intimately acquainted with this disturbing attribute, one that we battle or indulge as long as breath is in our bodies. As adults we might disguise selfishness, dressing it up in other clothes, but it remains a constant intruder on our maturity regardless of what garb it dons.

Some things are easier to give up than others. For instance, I can relinquish the last helping of food in the bottom of a dish, the selection of which restaurant to eat in, and even my dessert to a salivating friend. But don't edge in front of me in the grocery store line, call someone's name before mine at the doctor's office when I've been waiting longer, or look off at other people when you and I are talking.

To overcome these self-centered irritations, I'm learning (yep, still learning) to practice gratitude. So when someone cuts in front of me on the highway, I can say, "Lord, thank you that I can extend a sacrificial courtesy lest I remain self-absorbed." And when someone is divided in her interests when we're talking, I can pray, "Lord, thank you for showing me that either the person or the time isn't the right choice."

Expressing gratitude helps us to step out of ourselves long enough to consider others. And most important, it pleases our heavenly Father. Jean Ingelow puts it this way: "It is a comely fashion to be glad—Joy is the grace we say to God."

*Lord, thank you for continuing to teach me how
to be gracious and grateful. Amen.*

Patsy Clairmont

Benevolent Mail

Give, and it will be given to you. A good measure, pressed down, shaken together and running over, will be poured into your lap. –LUKE 6:38

It seems like every charity in the country solicits my husband's goodwill. He keeps their requests on his desk until they pile up. Then, about once a quarter, he writes a check to all of them.

The funny thing about this is that George accuses me of giving away all our money. He is known for his statement: "If it was left up to her, we wouldn't have a dime 'cause she would give it away." But the joke in my office is that he gives away more by accident than I do on purpose!

I don't argue about what he gives. It is truly better to give than to receive. When we give, we ought to be prudent and wise. The Bible is very clear about how to give and to whom. So don't ask me for money unless you want to be thoroughly investigated! As a good steward of God's wealth, that's my responsibility.

I get some of the same benevolent mail my husband does, but I try to remember to ask God whom he wants me to give to. Sometimes his Spirit prompts to give generously. Sometimes I'm prompted to trash the request. Through it all, I learn again and again that God always gives more back to me than I give to others. That's his promise! As we give to big causes, let's remember needy people in our own neighborhood.

> *Father, thank you that you are a God of addition and multiplication. You always pour more back into my life than I give away. Benevolent is your name. Amen.*

Thelma Wells

Earthly Pleasures

Therefore, since we are receiving a kingdom that cannot be shaken,
let us be thankful, and so worship God acceptably with reverence and awe.
–HEBREWS 12:28

I'd like to go on record with this definition of a glutton: It is a person who takes the piece of pizza I wanted. I experienced that kind of gluttony last night as I sat across the table from my grandson Alec. There was one piece of pizza left. I'd been eyeballing it for several minutes but didn't want to simply snatch it off the plate. When my daughter Beth asked, "Anybody want this last slice of pizza?" I held my tongue but was poised to pounce. With a mouth still full of pepperoni and a face smeared with sauce Alec shouted, "I do!" I smiled disingenuously and commended Alec on his healthy appetite. I also determined the next time I bring a pizza to that household, I'll bring an extra large.

In spite of my mild hunger, I drove away from the evening filled with gratitude: gratitude for my renewed health that allows me to fully participate in life—including an animated pizza square-off with my beloved little glutton. I'm grateful for earthly possessions like my golf cart, my little condo on a gorgeous golf course, my leather-bound books, and, most recently, my new fondue pot with long forks.

Some of life's earthly pleasures are large, like health; many are small, like a fondue pot. All are tinged with God's touch of provision and sanction of love.

*Lord, may I be filled with gratitude today for the
earthly evidences of your love. Amen.*

Marilyn Meberg

Double the Pleasure

I praise you because I am fearfully and wonderfully made;
your works are wonderful, I know that full well. –PSALM *139:14*

Knowing "The Twins" has doubled my pleasure and doubled my fun. They look alike, talk alike, laugh alike, walk alike, and think alike. *Exactly* alike. They respond on cue with the same vocal inflection. Two peas in a pod . . . indistinguishable in every way. It's uncanny.

Deb Godt and Jan Sturges are identical twins. One lives in Sacramento, California, and the other in Coeur d'Alene, Idaho. I loved them right off the bat. In fact, we bonded so quickly we could have been triplets had I been younger, thinner, and cuter. Even after seven years of friendship, when one of them calls me, I'm never quite sure which twin it is. I have to listen carefully to every nuance; then I know. They've told me they can actually feel each other's pain or joy, even when they're miles apart.

Interestingly enough, God doesn't see Deb and Jan the same at all. In his eyes they are totally separate individuals, each created with his unique design. To him they are incomparable, original, singular, and special. We all are. He doesn't compare us to each other or confuse us with anybody else. He cares for each one of us as if we were his only child.

There are no "twins" in God's universe. Only individuals who are fearfully and wonderfully made. We praise him because we know this "full well."

It is such a comfort, Lord, to know that you love me because I am
myself and for no other reason. Thank you so much! Amen.

Luci Swindoll

Nothing's Wasted

Always give yourselves fully to the work of the Lord, because you know that
your labor in the Lord is not in vain. –1 CORINTHIANS 15:58

One of my friends can name every one of her family's camping trips that ended in disaster. Once they pitched their tent on the side of a mountain and were nearly swept away when a sudden thunderstorm sent torrents of rainwater rushing down the hill. Another time they locked their keys—and all their camping gear—in the family van when they checked in at the ranger's office. And then there was the time they went river camping in canoes in a remote area and remembered everything they needed—except matches and a can opener.

My friend laughs as she recalls these family fiascoes. "I can't believe what all we survived," she says, amazed. What's even more amazing is that she can hardly remember the many times when everything went smoothly. They went camping as a family to create memories. And even when things went wrong, their efforts were not in vain. Now, looking back, she sees that the calamities they experienced became the catalysts for family bonding as they pulled together to survive the latest setback.

The same thing happens, said the apostle Paul, when we give ourselves fully to serving God, even when things don't go as we planned. Maybe the home Bible study we start draws few participants. Maybe someone we've led to the Lord seems to stray. But we can know without a doubt that, in God's economy, our efforts on his behalf are never wasted. Someday, looking back, we'll see that bonds were formed. Understanding was created. Lives were changed.

Lord, thank you that you have a different economy than I do!
Amen.

Barbara Johnson

A Rose by Any Other Name

A good name is more desirable than great riches.
—PROVERBS 22:1

The meanings of names fascinate me. Sometimes I think a name's definition gives a clear insight into the person; other times I think an individual's handle must be what that person is called to become.

My name, for instance, means "gracious one." Uh, I don't think so. But I admit graciousness has always been a garment I've admired in others' wardrobes, and I would like it to fit me one day.

My husband's name is Leslie, which means "camp." Long before we knew what his name meant, Les became involved professionally in camping. He was with the Boy Scouts of America, Youth for Christ, and a church camp. His name was a prophecy of his lifework. Hmm . . . our names may play a larger role in our destinies than we realize.

Deborah means "honeybee" and is an apt description of Deborah from the book of Judges. Her life was busy, and her wisdom was sweet. Deborah was a wife, a judge, a songwriter, a singer, and—get this—a warrior. She led her people to a victory that was miraculous since they were weaponless when they swooped down on their well-armed opponents. Deborah's name is a honey-like reminder of what God can do with a life fully focused on him.

So whether your name is one that gives an insight into who you are, whom you would like to become, or even who you hope never to be, the truly important name to have defined in your life is Jesus. His name is above every name in heaven and on earth. And one day every knee will bow to him.

Jesus, Rose of Sharon, thank you for your perfect victory to come.
Amen.

Patsy Clairmont

The Narrow Path

*But small is the gate and narrow the road that leads to life,
and only a few find it.* —MATTHEW 7:14

The street is about three feet wide and a half-mile long, sandwiched between many two-story buildings. Only a motorbike, bicycle, or a pair of people walking shoulder to shoulder can get down the street at the same time.

As I admired the bright, golden glow of lights that illuminated the narrowest street in Paris, France, I was reminded that the walk of the righteous is a narrow path too, well lit with the light of God's Word. It is not so narrow that it restricts us from enjoying the wonderful aspects of life, for Jesus came that we would live more abundantly. But it is narrow in that the path of righteousness does not allow room for things that burden us on our journey—like strife, envy, malice, resentment, and shame.

When we walk on the narrow street of righteousness, we may find ourselves walking virtually alone at times. Sometimes we must go as fast as a motorbike from one situation to another because time is of the essence. But thank goodness that much of our ride through life is at the steadier pace of a bicycle. It is fast enough to get us where we are going without incident and slow enough to allow us to stop and consider the best strategies for reaching our destinations. The most effective strategies are always found in God's Word.

When you're riding down life's narrow streets, don't forget to take your map: the Bible.

*Lord, when I need to know how to travel down
the narrow path of righteousness, I appreciate the clear
direction you give me in your Word. Amen.*

Thelma Wells

Grateful Hearts

Let the word of Christ dwell in you richly as you teach and admonish one
another with all wisdom, and as you sing psalms, hymns and spiritual songs
with gratitude in your hearts to God. And whatever you do, whether in
word or deed, do it all in the name of the Lord Jesus, giving thanks to God
the Father through him. –COLOSSIANS 3:16–17

The apparent reason for the writing of Paul's letter to the Colossians was the
arrival of Epaphras in Rome. He brought disturbing news to Paul about the
presence of heretical teaching at Colosse that was threatening the well-being
of this fledgling congregation. What Paul provided in the short paragraph
above is a way to keep our hearts and minds centered and secure in God and
in his Word.

Paul clarifies our need for one another. We need each other's wisdom when
we can't see clearly. I am so grateful to have godly friends who love me enough
to head me off at the curve if they see me walking toward the edge of a cliff.

The music of worship is a gift that calls for the involvement of our whole
being. When we lift our voices to the Lord in grateful praise, we see life in perspective once again; we are reminded that God is still on his throne.

And whatever we do, whether in word or deed, when we do it in the name
of Jesus, we experience the dignity of our identity in him. There are no menial
tasks or unimportant words. All are a means to gratefully serve our Father in
heaven.

*Heavenly Father, I offer all I do and say in the name of my
Lord Jesus Christ, as an act of grateful worship. Amen.*

Sheila Walsh

Lord, Make Us Mindful

It is good to praise the LORD and make music to your name,
O Most High, to proclaim your love in the morning and your
faithfulness at night. —PSALM 92:1–2

Life is a great gift!

As you sit around a Thanksgiving table today, acknowledge your appreciation to your heavenly Father. Thank him for the fact that he created you, he loves you unconditionally, and he provides for your deepest needs. Be grateful for the abundant grace that has brought you this far in your journey.

Sing songs of praise to the Lord—for health, family, friends, bounty, safety, and forgiveness. Thank him for the clothes on your back and the food on your table. Consider the fact that he gives you work and rest, laughter and tears, struggles and victories, because every one of these is designed by his almighty hand to help you grow and mature.

Thank God for his Word—a source of comfort and encouragement, a lamp to guide you, a sword with which to conquer the enemies of your soul. Recognize that God's Word is constant, unchanging, inerrant, and able to discern the thoughts and intentions of your heart. It gives peace. It gives hope. It helps you remember that God will never make a mistake with your life. And, most important, it introduces you to Jesus Christ, who is life abundant and life eternal.

While you're thinking on all these things today, I will be too.

Lord God, help me appreciate everything I have—to be content with my life and eager to share it with others. Make me mindful that your gifts are without parallel and that the best gift of all is your Son, Jesus Christ, who died for me. Amen.

Luci Swindoll

Shortcut to a Feast

LORD my God, I will give you thanks forever.
—PSALM 30:12

What fun to remember Thanksgiving Days past! As a child, I marveled at all the hustle-bustle in the kitchen and loved the delicious aroma of the turkey roasting in the oven. My sister Janet and I helped our mother by setting the table and washing the vegetables. And when everything was ready, we bowed our heads at the table as our pastor father asked God's blessings upon the special meal.

Later, when Bill and I were rearing our four boys, I was directing the hustle-bustle in the kitchen, still loving the wonderful sounds and smells and tastes of Thanksgiving Day. How I love to remember those holidays when all of us gathered around the table for the meal and then, for dessert, shared not only pumpkin pie and ice cream but also delicious gales of laughter and fun.

I love these memories, but I'm glad I don't have to put on the Thanksgiving "show" any longer. These days, I'm grateful for the shortcuts to the feast. I pop a turkey breast in the Crock-Pot to fill the house with the wonderfully familiar Thanksgiving smell all day. When the turkey's done, I microwave some vegetables, pour the milk, and call Bill to dinner! It's a different setting, a different meal. But the smell of the roasting turkey brings back the memories, and we share our tiny banquet and enjoy again the merry gatherings of hustle-bustle holidays gone by.

Dear Father, just as I am thankful for the bounty you provide,
I am grateful too for the memories you have helped me create. Thank you,
Lord, for bringing through my life loved ones who
sat at my table and gave happy thanks with me. Amen.

Barbara Johnson

Praise the Lord

The heavens declare the glory of God; the skies proclaim
the work of his hands. —PSALM 19:1

Velvet nights showcase stars spilling out the dippers while other stars ride twinkling on the bear's back. "Giddyup," you can almost hear them say as they scurry to their places for a dazzling festival of lights.

And is that music I hear? Lean in and listen. That's the echo of praise as a billion-plus stars proclaim their Maker.

This scenario isn't so far-fetched when you read that all creation groans, waiting to acknowledge the Lord. We are told that even the stones would cry out his name, if he didn't silence them. Now, folks, if hunks of rock with the brains of granite long to speak his name, how much more should we?

Have you lingered in a towering forest and felt God's presence in the powerful silence? Or have you bathed your mind in a sunset only to have a spontaneous song of celebration spring up inside you? Perhaps you have heard a waterfall's thunderous praise, a sparrow's aria of adoration, or the pounding waves' applause.

Nature resounds with responsiveness to the Lord. Cattails sway to the music in the breeze; willows weep for joy; raindrops dance across the water; and daffodils lift their faces to the sun. Creation is full of praise. Come, let us join in.

Creator God, I am awed by your willingness to listen to my
offerings. May you find my praise and my prayers pleasing.
Thank you for your clear signature throughout this stunning world you
have designed. Blessed be the name of the Lord. Amen.

Patsy Clairmont

DECEMBER

Peace

It is I who made the earth and created mankind upon it. My own hands stretched out the heavens; I marshaled their starry hosts. —ISAIAH 45:12

My sense of peace is firmly rooted in my belief that God is sovereign. That belief enables me to relax in the midst of uncertainty simply because he "works out everything in conformity with the purpose of his will" (Ephesians 1:11). That knowledge enables me to rest, trust, and regain my peace. He is in charge and his perfect will shall be accomplished.

Although the word *sovereign* is not used specifically in Scripture, the definition of the word is reflected in all God is. The word *sovereign* means "supreme rank and power." God is called "Almighty" (all-powerful); he is described as "the blessed and only Ruler, the King of kings and Lord of lords" (1Timothy 6:15). The psalmist declares, "Our God is in heaven; he does whatever pleases him" (Psalm 115:3).

And yet coupled with this awe-inducing sovereign power is God's tender and matchless love. The oft-recurring theme "His love endures forever" means that love will never drain away, run out, or become exhausted. "I the Lord do not change" means he'll love me forever because his love-nature won't change.

So then, when I present my needs to a sovereign God who is both absolutely powerful and infinitely loving, my peace rests in his person and not on my efforts. He says to me about my circumstances (which may be threatening my peace): "What I have said, that will I bring about; what I have planned, that will I do" (Isaiah 46:11).

As you enter the season that celebrates the incarnation of the Prince of Peace on this earth, perhaps the blessed fact of his sovereignty will speak to you in a fresh way.

Marilyn Meberg

December 1
Surely Not ...

Now in the sixth month the angel Gabriel was sent from God to a city in Galilee, called Nazareth, to a virgin engaged to a man whose name was Joseph, of the descendants of David; and the virgin's name was Mary. *—LUKE 1:26–27*

Every year Advent begins the celebration of an out-of-wedlock pregnancy. Those are words that jar me; put me off. But at the same time they inspire me ... inspire me with the recognition that God is not bound by convention. He, the almighty God of the universe, chose to supernaturally impregnate a virgin girl from a dusty little town called Nazareth, with the life-giving hope that would be Jesus.

Such an unconventional and mildly offensive plan startles me. But how refreshing that God's ways are not my ways. His ways display for me potentialities that cannot be anticipated or explained. They happen because he is God and he does as he wishes. He is not bound by any restraint except his own perfect character. I can only stand by in wonder, in awe, and fight the human inclination of thinking, *Surely not* this *way. . . .*

I pray that in this month of marking the time in anticipation of Jesus' most peculiar and inauspicious birth, God will expand our minds and hearts so we won't miss the star in the East simply because it doesn't "make sense." May we recognize with the startled shepherds that a Savior who is Christ the Lord was born to give us life.

Lord God Almighty, I worship you and reflect in humble awe
at your creative, outlandish plan to save the world. Amen.

Marilyn Meberg

Hustle-Bustle

For to us a child is born, to us a son is given.
—ISAIAH 9:6

Larry King has said if he ever got to do the interview of a lifetime he would interview God and ask him two questions: "Are you God, and do you have a son?"

The answers would be, "Yes, and yes." Great questions and wonderful answers that promise peace to each one of us if we will but pull away from all the hustle and bustle for a while.

This is the season of stress for most people. Something about the approach of Christmas heightens the hunger inside each of us for something more than what we are living with. We long for peace but stay overcommitted. We long for truth but are afraid to face it. We hunger for a Father but hide our faces from him.

The gift of this season is that everything we could ever want or imagine has already been given to us in the gift of the Christ child. The hustle of the season is nothing new, and neither is the solution. "Then, because so many people were coming and going that they did not even have a chance to eat, he said to them, 'Come with me by yourselves to a quiet place and get some rest'" (Mark 6:31).

Oh come let us adore him: Christ the Lord.

Jesus, remind me to "come away" with you every day during this glorious season. It's all about you, after all! Amen.

S h e i l a   W a l s h

December 3
Peaceful Gestures

Why are you downcast, O my soul? Why so disturbed within me?
Put your hope in God. —PSALM 42:5

For busy families, December is often a hurry-up, hubbub month full of joyful holiday activities. But for families mired in grief, the holidays can be a very difficult time. It is common for them to want to flee all the happy commotion and hide out in a quiet, peaceful place where no one knows them.

That's what one family did after their twenty-year-old son was killed the week before Thanksgiving. Instead of accepting their friends' Thanksgiving dinner invitation, Chattanooga writer Nell Mohney recalled how she and her family opted to eat their holiday meal in a restaurant they'd never visited before. During the meal Nell noticed that they didn't know anyone else in the restaurant. "Yet when we tried to pay our bill, the cashier said it had been paid," she said.

The family never knew whether the kindhearted person who bought their dinner "read the pain on our faces or whether he was missing his own family" or whether he or she was simply extending a holiday gesture of kindness. Nell called it "one of God's gracious serendipities."

Her story reminded me that one of the kindest gifts we can give to those who grieve during the holidays is a quiet refuge of peace and a thoughtful, unobtrusive act of kindness.

Dear Jesus, as I celebrate your birth with festive rejoicing,
help me remember those whose hearts are broken. Help them
hide in you, Lord, and grant them your peace so that soon
they can join again in the blessed hallelujahs. Amen.

Barbara Johnson

Palm Branches

Turn from evil and do good; seek peace and pursue it.
—PSALM 34:14

In the 1800s George William Curtis wrote, "I think that to have known one good old man—one man who, through the chances and rubs of a long life, has carried his heart in his hand, like a palm branch, waving all discords into peace, helps our faith in God, in ourselves, and in each other, more than many sermons."

I love the picture of a person's heart outstretched like a palm branch, erasing discord. Peace is a wonderful gift to wave over our unsettled world. I often wish it took only the swish of a frond to bring about a spirit of goodwill between quarreling factions, whether that is nation against nation or my hubby and me in our latest squabble.

Les and I aren't into brouhahas, but we do occasionally get on each other's nerves. We usually have tiffs over little stuff like wanting our own way. Or like who left the garage door open.

"I did not."

"You must have because I sure didn't."

"Well, it wasn't me."

Actually, my husband often is the first to seek peace. Les's fuse may sometimes be a quick wick, but his heart longs for an amiable resolve. He becomes uneasy in the discomfort of our tension and will extend a palm branch.

I've heard some wonderful preaching over the years, but I'd have to agree with George that a person who lives his life as a peacemaker is his own kind of sermon. Peace is an indelible message written in the Spirit of Christ.

Instead of wrapping up a necktie for Christmas, I think I'll extend a palm branch to my dear husband.

Lord, wave your Spirit of peace over our fractious world.
Amen.

Patsy Clairmont

Soul Shape-Up

This is what the LORD says: Put your house in order.
−2 KINGS 20:1

I'm a "neat-nick" and I know it. Fortunately, I don't care how other people live or keep house, but for me everything has a place and when it's out of place . . . well, I tend to lose my mind.

A few years back I decided my soul needed the same shaping up. Several things felt "out of whack" inside . . . no order! So after spending time soul-searching, I noted there were five areas that could use some work. I wrote down what I thought I wanted most:

A *meaningful relationship with God*: This is primary. I want it every day.
A *sense of homeostasis*: Wherever I am in the world, I want to be "at home."
Contentment in all circumstances: I want to feel at peace. No more striving.
An *abiding knowledge that my life has purpose*: I want a reason to get up every
    morning.
Enough money to meet my needs: I don't want to be rich, just comfortable.

Once I outlined those rules of thumb, I relaxed inside. Other things may be desirable like good health or solitude or a great vacation, but these remain my top five. And guess what? They're mine more often than not.

Scripture says, "You do not have, because you do not ask God" (James 4:2). I wonder if we don't ask because we don't have a clue what we want! Look inside yourself today and determine what will give you peace. Write it down. Ask God for it. Then wait. Expectantly!

> *Help me get my house in order, Lord. Reveal the areas*
> *where I need to be more at peace. Then infuse me with*
> *your peace-producing presence. Amen.*

Luci Swindoll

No Hiding Place

If I settle on the far side of the sea, even there your hand will guide me,
your right hand will hold me fast. —PSALM 139:9–10

Vanessa, my five-year-old granddaughter, walked past me with a somber, closed-mouth expression on her face. It was a look that announced, *I'm thinking about something really serious. Do not disturb.*

After about an hour of quietness, she eased up to me looking like she had a deep, dark secret she wanted to share but was afraid to. When I asked what was on her mind, she said, "Grammy, you know when we were in the dress store where you got our Christmas clothes, and I asked you to buy me some lotion? You told me I couldn't have it. Remember?"

"Yes."

"Well, did you mean I couldn't have it then? Because I think I saw it in my room. It's in a blue, see-through purse. It has three bottles in it. One for me, one for Alyssa, and one for Alaya." She grinned sheepishly.

"Okay, Vanessa, you found Grammy's hiding place. Go get your present."

So Vanessa got the lotion, Alyssa got the bath gel, and Alaya got the bath crystals. And I learned something: Find a better hiding place for the gifts you bought for your granddaughters.

Just like that three-bottle surprise was not well hidden from my grandchildren, there is absolutely no hiding place from God. Psalm 139:7–12 confirms that no matter where we go, God is always there. But that's good news! Because he's always there to comfort and cheer, just when we need him most.

Lord, thank you for the consolation that I am never out
of your sight. Your hand holds me safe and secure. Amen.

T h e l m a   W e l l s

We Can't Lose

Many are the plans in a man's heart, but it is the
LORD's purpose that prevails. –PROVERBS 19:21

I hate the notion that my own will or goals in life might deter me from God's will or purpose for my life. The idea that in my human foolishness I can miss the voice of God creates tremendous insecurity. But the wise proverb states that it is "the LORD's purpose that prevails," regardless of my plans. *Ahhh...* That consolation puts my soul at ease.

Ephesians 1:11 states so reassuringly: "In him we were also chosen, having been predestined according to the plan of him who works out everything in conformity with the purpose of his will." Many experiences in life do not produce peace, so the nagging accusation that my willfulness set it all in motion is devastating. But the reminder that he "works out everything" causes me to settle down and regain my peace.

I hear some "yeah, buts" out there. You're saying, "Yeah, but I've made stupid choices and I will always live with the consequences." So have I and so do I. But here's the peace-producing point: His purpose for you and for me prevails in spite of us! His working everything out includes our seemingly poor choices, which he graciously uses for our development and highest good.

In essence, we can't lose! That gives me peace. How about you?

Thank you, God, that my will can never prevail over yours.
Amen.

Marilyn Meberg

"It's Already Inside You"

God has called us to live in peace.
—1 CORINTHIANS 7:15

I have a close friend who is the CEO of a large firm. She is a devout Christian with a lot of professional savvy. Occasionally, she asks my opinion or advice on a difficult matter she's facing. I listen attentively, knowing full well it is not counsel she wants but a listening ear and a sense of peace about her dilemma.

After hearing her out, I always say, "Trust your gut. The answer you need is already inside you. Search it out, then do that. You won't go wrong."

We really can't tell anyone else what to do. We can offer opinions or impart lessons learned from our own experience, but each of us makes the final decision within ourselves. It helps to remember a few key truths:

Peace is a *choice*. Isaiah 26:3 says, "You will keep in perfect peace him whose mind is steadfast, because he trusts in you." We must keep our focus on Christ.

Peace is a *balance* between desire and possibility. We may not get exactly what we want, but with negotiation and modification within ourselves, we find a place where we're okay with the outcome.

Peace is *freedom*. It keeps us from sweating the little things, or trying to right the whole world. We can chill out!

And finally, peace is *profound*. Although we may not understand the workings of God in our dilemma, we can experience a deeply felt sense of well-being that "passes understanding."

I've never met a person who didn't want peace—harmony, order, serenity. The good news is, we can have it. Today. Right in the middle of the storm.

I choose peace today, Lord, by keeping my mind on you.
Amen.

Luci Swindoll

December 9
Home Alone

*Now may the Lord of peace himself give you peace at all times
and in every way.* –2 THESSALONIANS 3:16

What a fun day. I've had the house to myself. Usually my home teems with folks.

In fact, last week when a salesperson stopped by, he was wide-eyed as person after person poured out of various parts of the house. My husband, Les; my son Jason; my daughter-in-law, Danya; my grandson, Justin; my office assistant, Amy; and two friends Debbie and Jessica streamed into the room the salesperson had settled into, leaving him pretty, uh, unsettled. They didn't all come out at once, nor did they use the same door. They seemed to seep out of every crevice.

But not today. My husband was out of town; my office was closed; and I loved the peace and quiet.

But now it's evening, and I've grown weary of the quiet. I miss my people. Quiet, while a nice change of pace, isn't how I want to live. Oh, I know many folks do, and my day may come, but for now, bring on my noisy crew.

What a good reminder that peace isn't about our outer circumstances but our inner environment. I sometimes think that if I had less activity around me, I'd experience less commotion within me. Yet here I sit at midnight, restless in the silence.

Is your life full of commotion? Do you depend on your surroundings for peace? Can you be alone comfortably? Perhaps my "home alone" day was just what the Doctor ordered so I could make peace with the quiet.

*Prince of Peace, may I enter both noise and silence
with your quietness in my heart. Amen.*

Patsy Clairmont

December 10
Eyes Wide Open

He who watches over Israel will neither slumber nor sleep.
—PSALM 121:4

Are you grateful for sleep? Does your heart well up with gratitude that at the end of a fatigue-producing day you can crawl into your cozy bed with the anticipation of drifting off into restful sleep? For me, the answer to both questions is an emphatic no!

I don't like sleeping. And according to my mother's records, I fought sleep with every fiber of my being since infancy. I'm still fighting it!

Now of course I can't fight my need for sleep, and grudgingly I give in to it. It's just such a waste of fun time, productive time, reading time, or just plain old hanging out time. I resent giving up those options just so I can spend seven or eight hours not having a clue what's been going on in my environment.

What's even more offensive is the establishment of "National Workplace Napping Day." The first such day was in 2000. Because of its great success a second National Nap Day was "celebrated" just a few weeks ago and created even more national enthusiasm than the first day.

Again, I'm not arguing about the necessity for sleep; I'm just resentful that I need it. Scientists tell me a nap in the middle of the day can recharge my batteries for the next three to four hours. I'd rather be charging my batteries in New York (the city known never to sleep). I love the fact that there's twenty-four-hour cable TV, twenty-four-hour stock trading, and all-night Wal-Marts. But my very favorite round-the-clock, peace-producing reality is that God never sleeps. I'd like to be just like him!

Father, I'm grateful that if I must rest, I can rest in you.
Amen.

Marilyn Meberg

Storm Warnings

His appearance was like lightning.
–MATTHEW 28:3

The winds are howling tonight. I hear them whipping the tree branches against our gazebo. Storms have been forecast throughout the night.

Storms were one of my greatest fears during my agoraphobic years. I was certain if there was wind or thunder, my life was about to terminate. More times than I care to confess I would take refuge under a table or in a basement. If it stormed all night, I stayed up all night and kept my family up as well. Those were terrifying years.

Today I think storms are invigorating and even beautiful. I love to stand at the window and watch their concert. The lashing winds and crashing thunder are like great bass instruments filling the heavens with rich sounds. The lightning bolts skitter across the sky, their contrast of night and day colliding again and again like cymbals on an inky backdrop. And when the winds still and the rains dry, a delightful fragrance rises like an aria of thanks from the earth to the heavens.

Soon I'll turn in for the night. Predictably, as my head touches the pillow, I'll drift off to sleep. The thunderous winds will serve as my lullaby, and I'll lie down in quietness and confidence.

What a miracle that I have been delivered to such a degree! My recovery wasn't fast, but I slowly learned to take refuge in the God who disperses lightning (Job 38:24), who scatters the winds over the earth (38:24), and who makes a path for the thunderstorm (38:25). Yes, he is the God of—and most importantly, the God in—the storm.

I take refuge in you, Lord.
Amen.

Patsy Clairmont

What a Racket!

That we may lead peaceful and quiet lives in all godliness and holiness.
—1 TIMOTHY 2:2

Feeling dazed, overwhelmed, and mildly threatened, I stood amidst the high-tech hubbub of flashing lights, dinging bells, and shouting children, all of whom were madly feeding tokens into various machines that produced even greater noise and stimulation.

"More tokens, Maungya ... I need more tokens!" Alec was intensely engaged in whopping purple plastic gopher heads back into their holes with a huge black rubber mallet. The whopping seemed to be satisfying a primitive instinct in him; numbly I handed him more tokens from my plastic token container. Ian, with the same frantic focus, shouted for more tokens to feed the wildly rocking and pitching beast he was riding. I marveled at how he managed to keep his pizza down.

Two hours later, having lost all internal and external peace, I insisted we leave the racket behind. But of course not before we redeemed the wad of tickets my grandsons had accumulated from each participating machine. Those tickets earned little prizes ranging in value from a miniature mirror to red, purple, or black rubber wiggly worms designed to fit nicely in any child's pocket.

Driving away, the words of Edwina Pickthorne popped into my mind. (She was my all-time least favorite Sunday school teacher.) "Everything leads to something," she'd said forty-six times too many. As a child, I never responded to her mirthless legalistic approach to the faith, and I certainly never understood or cared to understand what on earth she meant by that statement. Now ... I think I know.

Lord, please prevent the din of this life from robbing me
of the peace found only in living for you. Amen.

Marilyn Meberg

A Piece of Quiet

Jesus often withdrew to lonely places and prayed.
–LUKE 5:16

A friend sent me a funny little note: "Barbara, I'm here for you. When the going gets really tough ... you can always come hide in the closet with me!"

We all have days like that, don't we? Especially during the holidays! Times when the only thing that distracts us from a throbbing headache is the piercing pain in our backs. Days when it seems that all we hear is bad news. Days when our kids give us fits, our bosses give us impossible assignments, and our spouses and kids give us long to-do lists.

On those days, it is so tempting to want to hide. We think that if we could just find a quiet, calm place where no one wants anything from us, we'd surely feel better. That must have been how Jesus felt when he fled from the crowds and sought a few moments of solitude. He must have needed what a little girl described as "a little piece of quiet!"

We all need to be alone sometimes, yet when we finally get to a quiet place, we often feel our spirits sinking instead of lifting. We can't quite settle down and soak in the peace. We hide in the closet and feel nothing but darkness.

If that happens to you, picture yourself seeking solace in the arms of the Comforter. Imagine yourself climbing onto the lap of your Father like a weary, troubled child. Burrow your face into his heart, cover yourself with his blanket of love ... and rest.

Father, I come to you, weary and tense. I lay my head
on your shoulder, and you envelop me in your restorative love.
Thank you. Amen.

Barbara Johnson

Lie Very Still

Be still before the LORD and wait patiently for him.
—PSALM 37:7

In my first attempt to get a job after graduation from college, I was turned down with no explanation. Hurt, sad, and disappointed, I was unable to understand God saying no to that which I had wanted so much. I lay in bed that night, confused and brokenhearted. I was trying to sleep, but it was awfully difficult in light of my disappointment.

I distinctly remember thinking over and over, *Lie very still, Luci. Be quiet in your spirit. Don't fret. Don't try to figure it out. Go to sleep. Lie very still.* It was a heartfelt meditation that eventually gave me peace. Those repeated words helped me rest and eventually drift to sleep.

Three weeks later I applied for a similar job at Mobil Oil Corporation and was hired on the spot. And thirty years later, I retired from that company. Had the Lord allowed me to have my first choice, I would have missed that wonderful career.

That long-ago night lying in bed, a pattern began that has remained with me for more than fifty years. When I'm fretting over something, not feeling well, or disturbed by noise or distractions outside my control, I whisper to myself, "Lie very still, Luci. Be quiet in your spirit." I repeat that over and over. I concentrate on relaxing, all the while whispering, "Go to sleep . . . lie very still."

I'm here to tell you, folks: this works. For some reason it turns my burdens (even those I didn't know I had) over to the Lord. In Proverbs 3:24 there's a promise: "When you lie down, your sleep will be sweet."

Remember that at bedtime tonight.

Thank you, God, for the stillness within that comes from you.
Amen.

Luci Swindoll

Chaos Attack

The eternal God is your refuge, and underneath are the everlasting arms.
He will drive out your enemy before you, saying, "Destroy him!"
—DEUTERONOMY 33:27

Chaos is defined as "total disorder and confusion." My daughter Beth has recently experienced a time of total chaos. A month ago, on a rainy morning, she was driving to work and was hit from behind at an intersection. Her car was mangled but still functional. A week later, however, she was broadsided by a car that veered into her lane. This time her little Honda had to be towed home and declared "unfit to drive."

She purchased a brand-new car last week. Yesterday the radiator exploded; the car is in the shop for repairs.

None of these events were the result of poor judgment or wrong choices. They simply happened. What do we do when we experience a major chaos attack?

To begin with, we recognize that everything about God is orderly. Satan is an enemy of the soul, and everything about him is disorderly. He is the author of confusion and disarray. It is his intent to rob us of our peace and serenity. When we experience chaos, the Enemy is ecstatic. But when we remember we rest securely in the arms of the Almighty, the Enemy is defeated. The chaos may rage around us, but when we know to whom we belong and in whom we are safe and protected, our soul cannot be touched.

Lord, I feel like a victim today. Everything is falling down around me.
I need to crawl into your lap and feel your everlasting arms encircling me,
sustaining me, and giving me peace. Amen.

M a r i l y n   M e b e r g

December 16
Tripping over Gnats

We all stumble in many ways.
—JAMES 3:2

The morning of my wedding I awoke way before I intended, with butterflies the size of flamingos dancing in my stomach. They seemed to be having their sunrise aerobic class.

I stumbled out of bed, made my way across the room, and glanced in the mirror as I passed my dresser. I stopped in my tracks and peered at my reflection. Puzzled by what I saw, I leaned in closer.

"Mom!" I yelled frantically.

My mom responded with lightning agility. "What's wrong?" she asked as she burst into my room.

"Look." I pointed to my face. "What is that?"

Mom moved closer and replied with relief, "Patsy, it's just a cold sore."

"Cold sore?" I responded. "Cold sore?" I repeated with confusion in my eyes. "I don't have a cold. Make it go away!"

"It's probably nerves," she suggested.

"What am I going to do? I look diseased! This ugly thing will ruin my wedding and my pictures!"

"No one will even notice."

"Not notice?! It looks like the blight! No, make that the Plague!" (I've never been known to underestimate a situation.)

Mom shook her head and assured me that this eruption was a small matter in the scheme of life. Harrumph. Easy for her to say.

Today, forty years later (and still married), I realize she was right. In fact, she was right about a lot of things that I blew out of proportion. I could have saved myself considerable frustration through the years had I listened to her experienced voice.

Are you sore over some small eruption in your life? Chill out. This too shall pass.

Lord Jesus, teach me what matters. Calm my anxious heart.
Amen.

Patsy Clairmont

Don't Panic!

When you pass through the waters, I will be with you; and when you pass through the rivers, they will not sweep over you. —ISAIAH 43:2

Why did he have to hold my head underwater until I panicked? All I wanted to do was to learn how to swim.

I thought I was in a safe class with a sane teacher. But that guy was nuts. I was struggling, trying to raise my head up, and he was telling me to stay put and I'd be fine. I was convinced I would surely die. Needless to say, I got out of the pool, told him off, got dressed, and went home. That was my first and last day of swimming lessons.

Yes, I've gotten in a pool again and attempted to float and teach myself to not fear the water. But during swim class I felt like a big submarine sinking to the bottom.

Do you ever feel like your head is underwater and you're going to die? You may be drowning in bills, sickness, poverty, fear, broken relationships, church upheaval, abuse, addiction, overwork, depression, or whatever. Don't panic! A lifeline has already been thrown out to you that will save your sinking life. The quick and strong hand of God is that lifeline, and he sees you sinking. He's in a hurry to get you into the lifeboat. He promises that although the water may be frightening, you will not drown. Just grasp the lifeline.

God, help me to reach up for the lifeline of your presence
and be certain that you will not let me drown. Amen.

Thelma Wells

Never Left Alone

The LORD watches over you—the LORD is your shade at your right hand; the sun will not harm you by day, nor the moon by night. —*PSALM 121:5–6*

Our four-year-old son asked me to sign him up for soccer camp, which motivated me to finally join the YMCA. I drove to our local Y to see what else they had to offer kids. The girl who showed me around told me that they had a gym just for Christian's age-group. That evening he and I went to check it out.

I didn't realize that all the other parents dropped their children off and went to work out in the adult gym. There was no way I was going to do that the first time. I wanted to see what happened. I asked the girl in charge if I could stay. She looked at me as if I was a little unbalanced but said that I could. He had a great time. There were giant building blocks to climb up on and slides and a bouncy castle. They played all sorts of games and sang songs. I noticed though that every now and then he would look around to see if I was still there. When he spotted me, he gave me a thumbs-up sign. He won't need me to be there all the time, but when he was trying something new it made him more secure to know I was there, watching out for him.

The Lord is always watching out for us. Perhaps you find yourself in a new situation at the moment and you feel unsure, remember that he is right here beside you, day and night. You are never left alone.

*Thank you, Lord, that you are
always watching over me.*

Sheila Walsh

The Great Sorter-Outer

Those who are wise will shine like the brightness of the heavens,
and those who lead many to righteousness, like the stars for ever and ever.
—*DANIEL 12:3*

I bought some wrapping paper with shiny stars on it, and as I was wrapping a Christmas gift with it, this verse from the book of Daniel popped into my mind. Immediately I thought how blessed I am to have wonderful friends who "lead many to righteousness" and who will shine like the stars forever in God's kingdom. One of the brightest stars will surely be my daughter-in-love, Shannon. She radiates God's love to everyone who crosses her path.

What's really amazing, though, is that I was dismayed when Barney first started dating Shannon and told me she wasn't a Christian! To me, that ranked right up there as a bona fide crisis! Finally, I persuaded her to attend a Saturday evening concert with me at Calvary Chapel in Costa Mesa—and the rest is history! She flew down the aisle during the invitation that night, and since then she has dedicated every moment of her life to the Lord.

You know how some people ridicule mothers-in-law. One quipster said, "Mixed emotions are having your mother-in-law drive over a cliff in your new Cadillac!" But my relationship with Shannon is truly one of love, respect, and devotion to God. The whole experience has taught me not to fly off the handle the moment I see something that seems all wrong. Instead, I've learned to cultivate a sense of peace, knowing that God is in control and his good purposes will always prevail.

Father, help me remember when everything seems all
mixed up that you are the great sorter-outer. Amen.

Barbara Johnson

Healings

By his wounds we are healed.
–*ISAIAH* 53:5

Does God heal everybody who asks him? We know he doesn't. God can and does heal physical maladies, of course, but only God knows who to heal and when. When he doesn't heal, he gives peace to those who ask for it. However, during the year 2000, I witnessed two miraculous healings.

Toxic poisoning coursed throughout Marilyn Meberg's body, and she was given the unsettling news that she would not be able to speak at the Women of Faith conferences that year. Marilyn and others prayed. At the fourth conference, Marilyn came, weak and unstable, but believing God was healing her. Each week she got stronger until she was back to her bubbly, giggly, healed self.

I had painful, debilitating fibromyalgia that year. I slept in a chair many nights, unable to lie down because I hurt so much. However, I followed the godly instructions of a praying friend, and God healed me.

Perhaps your faith is greater than ours is, yet you are still ill. *What's wrong with me?* you ask. *Nothing!* God knows, sees, hears, and is concerned about you. I believe God healed Marilyn and me because he knew that the assignment he gave us requires the physical ability to carry out his purpose. According to his sovereign will, he chose to heal us so we could carry out his plan in our lives, for his glory.

God has not forgotten you. And he certainly doesn't love you any less than he loves us! Our heavenly Father doesn't play favorites. He will meet you at your point of your need and grant you peace.

Great Physician, give me strength to accept your sovereign decisions regarding healing. Please speak peace to my soul in the process. Amen.

Thelma Wells

December 21
In Acceptance Lieth Peace

Who do you think you are?
–JOHN 8:53

Do you ever have those days where you wonder why you're here? Or who you really are? Or what you should be doing? I do. Maybe it's part of the human condition, but I've recorded such musings in my journal. Here's a paragraph from a few years ago:

Friday, June 24, 1994:

Isn't it strange... So often I have the *illusion* that if I strive hard enough or go far enough into a project or event, I will emerge younger or thinner or richer or more energetic. Maybe that's the mind not wanting to let go of what I really am—a fluffy woman in her sixties. Maybe it's part of the aging process to think like this. I want to wake up some morning different from who I am now, ready for whatever... a sprightly, thin, thirty-year-old. Am I nuts? Do I not want to accept who I am in the present? Do I not like me?

Occasionally I feel I'm the only person alive with these thoughts. But I know better. Everybody has them—wanting to be someone else, live somewhere else, do something else in life.

Amy Carmichael wrote, "In acceptance lieth peace." It's true. We can accept ourselves and be at peace, or spend the rest of our lives fighting a losing battle. Let's try very hard to go with the first option. The Bible says God loves us as we are, and we can trust him on that since he doesn't lie.

I'm not going to think about this anymore. I'm going for a Snickers.

Dear Lord, what a wonderful relief to know that you accept me.
When I start to disbelieve that, please remind me. Amen.

Luci Swindoll

A Prayer of Peace

Great peace have they who love your law, and nothing
can make them stumble. –PSALM 119:165

I slipped into my seat just in time to hear Janet Parshall speak. We were sharing the platform at a woman's conference in Louisiana. She spoke on the great faithfulness of God to his children. It was a wonderful message.

Then she told us about her own son, Sam. As she began to tell his story I knew that this was every mother's nightmare. She told us she was wrenched from sleep by a knock at the front door. She looked out the bedroom window and saw a police car in the driveway. She woke her husband and they went downstairs together.

"Do you have a teenage son named Sam?" the officer asked.

"We do," they answered.

"I'm sorry to tell you that he's been shot. I don't know if he is dead or alive."

As they drove to the hospital, Janet said she prayed this prayer: "Lord, if he is gone, I praise you that he knows you and he is safely home. If he is still here, I praise you that you have gone ahead of me and are already ministering to him."

Sam was alive.

"I've never seen anything like this," the doctor said as he showed Sam's parents his x-rays. "The bullet went in the back of his head, did a U-turn, and came back out."

I love Janet's prayer of faith. It exhibits the great peace that comes as a result of resting in the confidence that God is in control, no matter what.

Father, today I rest in you. I lift my family to you.
I give my life to you. Amen.

Sheila Walsh

The Only Map I Need

Do not be afraid, Abram. I am your shield, your very great reward.
—GENESIS 15:1

Abram was seventy-five years old and had already had a rich, fulfilling life when God told him, "Leave your country . . . and go to the land I will show you" (Genesis 12:1). And off Abram and his wife went, headed to Canaan. "God's voice was the only map he had," wrote Barbara Brown Taylor, "and he and Sarai learned to live by it, though it led them down to Egypt and back again."

I wasn't quite as old as Abram when God led me off on a new adventure—to Egypt and back again—but I was equally bewildered by the territory I found myself in. Suddenly I was jerked up out of everything familiar—traveling constantly on the Women of Faith tour, answering basketfuls of mail, producing a monthly newsletter, and spending hours on the telephone every day, encouraging hurting parents—and dropped into foreign territory: the land of cancer, brain surgery, chemo, and so many prescriptions that I carried my daily allotment of pills in a muffin tin. Sometimes I sat with the thirty other bald women in the chemo room and wondered, *What am I doing here?*

In those times, only one voice made sense. It was the same voice that had led me through all the other painful deserts of my life: God's voice. It reminded me that he was there, in the next chemo chair, in the hands of the nurses who administered the drugs, in the technicians who eased my body into the MRI tube, in the surgeons who looked inside my brain. His voice is always there, the only map I need.

Speak, Lord, and I will follow.
Amen.

Barbara Johnson

God Has Come to Us

"The virgin will be with child and will give birth to a son, and they will call him Immanuel"—which means, "God with us." –MATTHEW 1:23

One night in December
One light from a silver star
One child to remember
God has come to us
God has come to us

How tiny the baby
How perfect in every way
How can we deny that,
God has come to us
God has come to us

Come now and be near him
Come. Rest a while.
Kneel down and receive him
God has come to us

He was a perfect gift in such an imperfect place. The Son of God in a straw bassinet. The Lamb of God with the lambs of this world.

How could such a tiny, fragile child change human history? What if there had been problems with the delivery? What if the night had been too cold to sustain a newborn child?

All the what-ifs in the world could not stop the heart of God from reaching out in love to you and to me. So, draw near to that little One. Come rest your head on the straw. The world may be troubled tonight, but the peace that allows our hearts and minds to rest is incarnated in this truth: God has come to us!

Father, there are no words to begin to thank you for this perfect gift. I receive him with a grateful heart, singing, Hallelujah! And amen.

Sheila Walsh

The Gift He Keeps on Giving

He will be called Wonderful Counselor, Mighty God,
Everlasting Father, Prince of Peace. Of the increase of his government
and peace there will be no end. *–ISAIAH 9:6–7*

Merry Christmas! Are you up early to get the dinner preparations going? To make sure Santa's trip down the chimney came off as planned? (Don't forget to nibble the cookies the kids left out on the plate. One mom said she forgot that detail one year, and her youngsters were crushed that Santa didn't like what they'd left.)

For many women, Christmas is one of the most joyful, hectic, exciting, rewarding, *exhausting* days of the year. For others of us, it is a day tinged with sadness when we think of loved ones who aren't there to share the festivities. Still, so often we feel their presence.

Nell Mohney wrote about how the doorbell rang on Christmas Eve, and she opened the door to find an unknown woman holding a hand-painted wooden purse Nell had admired in a gift shop several weeks earlier. "This is a present from your son," the woman said. "He ordered it a month before his accident." Nell's son had been killed the week before Thanksgiving. She opened the purse to find a note: "Merry Christmas, Mother, from Rick."

Jesus' gift to us is similar. It was planned for us long before but arrived unexpectedly on a Christmas night two thousand years ago. It arrives again with each new day: this gift of love, peace, and hope—a purse filled with immeasurable goodness, unforgettable sacrifice . . . and unending life.

Happy Birthday, Jesus!
Amen.

Barbara Johnson

December 26
Like a River

The LORD will be our Mighty One . . . a place of broad rivers and streams.
—ISAIAH 33:21

Have you noticed how often great hymns of the faith use the image of a rushing river as a place of peace? Seems like an oxymoron.

> *Like a river glorious is God's perfect peace,*
> *Over all victorious in its bright increase;*
> *Perfect yet it floweth fuller every day;*
> *Perfect yet it groweth deeper all the way.*

Here's another:

> *When peace like a river attendeth my way,*
> *When sorrows like sea billows roll;*
> *Whatever my lot, thou hast taught me to say,*
> *"It is well, it is well with my soul."*

Rivers fascinate me. I learned to swim in a river, have fished and water-skied in rivers, and love great cities characterized by rivers: London on the Thames, Paris on the Seine, St. Petersburg on the Neva. So often rivers are tree-lined and serene, bringing unexpected beauty to an otherwise busy landscape.

But the image of *"peace* like a river" conjures up more than physical beauty. The river is a metaphor for life-giving nourishment. Psalm 1 sings of the spiritual health of one who delights in God's ways. "He is like a tree planted by streams of water, which yields its fruit in season and whose leaf does not wither. Whatever he does prospers" (v. 3). This is a wonderful promise of abundance, growth, and success.

So, when peace "attendeth" your way, count on being the shade tree under which others can find rest, peace, and nourishing fellowship in the middle of a hectic day.

> *Bless me, Lord, with your peaceful abundance . . . and use me*
> *to give solace to others who need your blessing. Amen.*

Luci Swindoll

Look Out—It Vomits

I am in the midst of lions; I lie among ravenous beasts—men whose teeth
are spears and arrows, whose tongues are sharp swords. –PSALM 57:4

I don't mean to sound irreverent, but sometimes I get a kick out of God. Actually I get a kick out of some of his creation. For example, did you know there's a little sea creature resembling a cucumber that prowls around the ocean floor sucking up whatever? Apparently its most obnoxious and socially unacceptable habit is relentless vomiting. When threatened by a predator, a sea cucumber will retch up its insides, practically turning itself inside out like an old glove, and spewing forth a poison that is frequently fatal to the attacker.

Interestingly enough, I've encountered a few sea cucumbers in my life, and they weren't prowling around the ocean floor. One was sitting in the pedicure chair next to me just a few days ago. This toxic cucumber was so furious at the operator for cutting her nails too short that she vomited out a barrage of poison so annihilating, we all thought we'd drown. I couldn't get out of there fast enough, and I'm sure the others would have fled with me if they hadn't had wads of cotton between their toes.

I've witnessed cucumber parents spewing out words at their misbehaving children; cucumber basketball players vomiting on referees; cucumber motorists honking, gesturing, and yelling; and the list goes on. Maybe a bunch of sea cucumbers crawled out of the sea, bought homes, and filled up our cities. I guess I don't get a kick out of them after all.

Lord, I don't want to have a tongue like a sword. May I bring
peace to my environment and not poison. Amen.

Marilyn Meberg

Turn Up the Heat

*If we are thrown into the blazing furnace, the God we serve is able
to save us from it, and he will rescue us from your hand, O king.
But even if he does not, we want you to know, O king, that we will
not serve your gods. –DANIEL 3:17–18*

When I was in Sunday school we sang a little song about Shadrach, Meshach, and Abednego. It was just a sweet song of faith that little children learn and parrot back to their Sunday school teachers. The reality of the men's situation, however, was horrifying.

Nebuchadnezzar was a powerful megalomaniac who demanded absolute obedience. When the three friends refused to bow to his demand that they worship a false god, they were sentenced to death. Their confidence in Jehovah God was so great, however, that they were able to say that whether God delivered them or not they would not bow to Nebuchadnezzar.

The king was furious and ordered the furnace to be seven times hotter than normal. He had the men bound and thrown into the blaze. The fire was so overwhelming that the soldiers who threw the three in all died. But when Nebuchadnezzar looked into the furnace he saw four men. They were walking around, untied, talking to one another. God had met them in the flames! When they were brought out, not a single hair on their heads was singed.

Perhaps you feel as if you are about to be thrown into an impossible situation where the heat will be turned up several degrees beyond what you can bear. Take strength from this story, for God himself will meet you in the furnace.

*Lord, my peace can be found in you alone.
Amen.*

Sheila Walsh

God's AAA

I am with you and will watch over you wherever you go.... I will not leave you until I have done what I have promised you. –GENESIS 28:15

Once when my daughter-in-love, Shannon, was driving home from the airport late at night with her two small daughters, her car suddenly started fuming and smoking. Of course it happened in the worst part of the city imaginable, and Barney was out of town. Shannon was rattled, but she pulled into a dark, lonely service station and sat for a moment, whispering a prayer. Then the greatest sense of peace came over her, she said, even when two homeless men approached the car. She thought at first they were coming to ask for money; instead, they wanted to help.

Within a few minutes the shabbily dressed men managed to diagnose the problem, put together a temporary fix, and send her and the girls on their way. Before driving off, Shannon bent down to find something in her purse to offer them—and when she looked up, the men were gone! She was convinced they were angels, sent from God's heavenly AAA service!

I remember Shannon's experience whenever crises threaten to wreck my life. I find a quiet place and call God's twenty-four-hour help line. In other words, I pray! Inevitably, whether or not the crisis abates, a sense of calm soon sweeps over me, and I'm ready to face what must be endured. I am at peace, trusting that God has put me exactly where he wants me to be.

Lord, thank you for always being there when I call to you. I trust you to calm my fears and give me peace, even in the midst of the storm. Amen.

Barbara Johnson

Rx for Peace

Do not be anxious about anything, but in everything, by prayer and petition, with thanksgiving, present your requests to God. And the peace of God, which transcends all understanding, will guard your hearts and your minds in Christ Jesus. —*PHILIPPIANS 4:6–7*

I find the coupling of prayer and petition interesting partners. Can I ask for and seek God's will and my own in the same breath? Can I both worship and request? Whatever his intent, Paul underscores his teaching with thanksgiving.

There will be many moments in our lives when mingling obedience, personal desire, and gratitude will be a tall order. Imagine that your child is seriously ill and you are begging God to move on her behalf. I can imagine being awash with thanksgiving if God answered the prayer, but we are called to offer thanksgiving *at the moment of petition* while a fever still glistens on her brow.

A wonderful, transforming principle is wrapped in this strange package. Thanksgiving in the midst of uncertainty or pain is a sacrifice of devotion to God. It says with Job as his life lay in waste around him, "Though he slay me, yet will I trust in him" (Job 13:15 KJV).

When by God's grace we are able to pray this way, there is a gift from God tucked in the folds of the sacrificial offering. "The peace of God, which transcends all understanding, will guard your hearts and your minds in Christ Jesus." When we acknowledge that God is sovereign and bow the knee to him alone, the peace of Christ washes over the fear and bathes the wounds of uncertainty.

Father God, thank you that even though my days are uncertain you are a sure and safe hiding place for me until the storm has passed. Thank you.
Amen.

Sheila Walsh

Reflections

> My times are in your hands.
> —PSALM 31:15

Who can think of New Year's Eve without hearing strains of "Auld Lang Syne" in her mind? Where does the time go? Do you remember as a kid when a week seemed eternal? Today, for me, a year is as transient as frost on a pumpkin.

For each of us, this past year has been filled with sweet remembrances, family connections, friendship revelries, laughter, and tears. Over these twelve months we've reflected together about hope, prayer, friendship, wonder, grace, joy, freedom, humor, vitality, trust, gratitude, and peace. Each of us on the Women of Faith team has shared her foibles and her fears; we've chuckled and commiserated with you; and now we celebrate with you God's goodness as we close out the year.

No one knows what a day will bring, so we surely haven't a clue how a year will unfold. When we shake them out, some years size up well while others seem hopelessly rumpled. Certain years we would like to relive for the sheer joy of them, while others we would relive to do them better. But we eventually learn that even the hard times, the losses, and the disappointments are so full of fodder that we can see—with hindsight, of course—some of their bittersweet value.

Luci, Sheila, Thelma, Barbara, Marilyn, and I invite you to join us as we acknowledge the Keeper of our days and the divine distributor of our tomorrows. Now toot your New Year's horn and call out with us, "Happy New Day!"

> *Help me, Lord, to embrace each moment you've allotted me,*
> *not in frenzy but in purposeful appreciation.*
> *Thank you for the precious gift of time. Amen.*

Patsy Clairmont

Author Index

For more information about Women of Faith:

www.womenoffaith.com

Resources for Women of Faith℠

BOOKS/AUDIO

WOMEN OF FAITH BIBLE STUDY SERIES

Share Your Thoughts

With the Author: Your comments will be forwarded to the author when you send them to *zauthor@zondervan.com*.

With Zondervan: Submit your review of this book by writing to *zreview@zondervan.com*.

Free Online Resources at
www.zondervan.com

Zondervan AuthorTracker: Be notified whenever your favorite authors publish new books, go on tour, or post an update about what's happening in their lives at www.zondervan.com/authortracker.

Daily Bible Verses and Devotions: Enrich your life with daily Bible verses or devotions that help you start every morning focused on God. Visit www.zondervan.com/newsletters.

Free Email Publications: Sign up for newsletters on Christian living, academic resources, church ministry, fiction, children's resources, and more. Visit www.zondervan.com/newsletters.

Zondervan Bible Search: Find and compare Bible passages in a variety of translations at www.zondervanbiblesearch.com.

Other Benefits: Register yourself to receive online benefits like coupons and special offers, or to participate in research.

ZONDERVAN®

ZONDERVAN.com/
AUTHORTRACKER
follow your favorite authors